The Repression of Crime

Patterson Smith Reprint Series in Criminology, Law Enforcement, and Social Problems

A listing of publications in the Series *will be found at rear of volume*

PUBLICATION NO. 56: PATTERSON SMITH REPRINT SERIES IN CRIMINOLOGY, LAW ENFORCEMENT, AND SOCIAL PROBLEMS

The Repression of Crime

Studies in Historical Penology

BY

HARRY ELMER BARNES, PH.D.

Professor of Historical Sociology, Smith College. Historian to the Prison Inquiry Commission of New Jersey, 1917; and to the Pennsylvania Commission to Investigate Penal Systems, 1918

Montclair, New Jersey

PATTERSON SMITH

1969

Patterson Smith Publishing Corporation
Montclair, New Jersey

SBN 87585-056-1

Library of Congress Catalog Card Number: 69-14911

TO

GEORGE WASHINGTON KIRCHWEY

Who has brought to the science and application of penology a distinguished equipment in jurisprudence, a broad interest in the social sciences and human affairs, courageous devotion to public service, and that rare and salutary orientation compounded of scientific discrimination and reformist zeal.

Preface

Several sensational recent crimes and a vast alleged increase in the amount of crime in the United States have of late aroused much public interest in the subject of the causes and prevention of delinquency. Our contemporary system of criminal justice and prison administration has been subjected to severe criticism by persons who desire a complete abolition of the present system of repressive justice and by others who wish to see the contemporary methods enormously increased in severity. The newer knowledge in the field of criminology is being assimilated and brought together in excellent textbooks and manuals. The all-important work of the psychiatrists in the field of criminology has been synthesized in the writings of Myerson, the Gluecks, Hoag and Williams. M. H. Smith and Healy. This revolutionary technique and mode of approach are being gradually introduced into court-procedure, particularly in connection with the juvenile courts. More progress has been made in regard to the scientific understanding of the causes and prevention of crime in the last quarter of a century than in the preceding two thousand years.

In spite of the fact that the vitally relevant knowledge in the fields of criminology and penology has been developed within the last generation, a history of past procedure is not without real value in aiding the cause of enlightenment and progress in criminal science and prison administration. The history of criminal procedure and penal practices is one of those few phases of historical study which are directly useful to the reformer. By indicating the nature of the methods which have been tried and have failed the historian can guard society against attempting to solve current problems through an application of devices and processes which have failed notably in the past. The present demand to attempt to lessen crime by an increase in the severity of the penalties imposed is an admirable example of the way in which the historian of criminal procedure in the past may warn of the futility of a proposal which has been repeatedly proved to be wholly lacking in efficacy, and productive of many incidental elements of viciousness. The historical approach can also aid the cause of criminological progress by lessening respect for present methods through indicating their remote and unscientific origin and nature, and revealing their anachronistic concepts and procedure. Scepticism of present methods is the first step toward future improvement.

Some thirty years ago, in his classic work on *Punishment and Reformation,* the late Frederick Howard Wines attempted with great effect to exploit the historical mode of approach in the interest of the advancement of criminal science and prison methods. The present work is an effort to do much the same thing on the basis of the achievements in these fields since 1895. The scope of the book is, however, somewhat different. The historical sections are confined more specifically to American data and achievements and are somewhat more detailed in nature. The range of subjects covered is slightly more comprehensive. The writer does not pretend, however, in the slightest degree to the achievement of any such pioneer or original work as was contained in Dr. Wines' book or to the long and intimate personal association with practical problems of prison administration and reform of which Dr. Wines could justly boast.

The present work is not intended as a general textbook on criminology and penology. There are already admirable manuals on this subject. Rather, the aim is here to present those historical facts which will constitute the only intelligent background against which to begin the systematic study of criminal science in its present stage of development. It is hoped that this genetic survey may serve better to indicate the defects of the present and to suggest lines of departure for an improvement of future methods.

The author here desires to thank the editors of the New York Times *Current History Magazine, The Friends' Historical Bulletin,* the *Journal of Criminal Law and Criminology,* the *Prison Journal,* the *Political Science Quarterly,* the *Open Court,* the *Prison Handbook,* the *World Tomorrow,* the *American Mercury,* the *New Republic* and the *Journal of Social Forces* for permission to reprint here material which originally appeared in these journals.

I am indebted to my friends and former students, Mr. John F. O'Brien and Mr. John F. Ratigan for reading the proof of the entire volume.

HARRY ELMER BARNES.

NORTHAMPTON, MASS.
May 1, 1926.

Contents

ANALYTICAL TABLE OF CONTENTS

The Repression of Crime

CHAPTER I

Crime in the Light of Modern Social Science

I. INTRODUCTORY CONSIDERATIONS

The recent trial and conviction in Chicago of the youthful delinquents, Loeb and Leopold, on the charge of murder have done more to focus public attention upon the causes and treatment of crime than has any public occurrence since the trial of Harry Thaw some twenty years ago. It apparently requires some sensational event, highly charged with publicity value, to arouse society's attention to the progress achieved in social thought and practice. In reality there was nothing unique or unusual about the Chicago murder trial. More than two years ago Clarence Darrow, counsel for the defense in this case, set forth in his illuminating book on criminology an even more progressive theory of crime and its treatment than that which he expounded in the courtroom. Crimes of this sort are in no way infrequent, and though an impression of mystery was spread abroad by the newspapers, the nature of the psychopathic condition of the youthful defendants was as readily discovered by the psychiatrists as a prominent carbuncle would have been diagnosed by a contemporary surgeon. Furthermore, Judge Caverly's attitude and rulings, which were so roundly denounced by orthodox clergymen and other highly trained experts in the field of criminology, were in reality not an advanced position taken by a sociological jurist, but rather the effort of a benign judge to go as far as possible in the way of adapting our anachronistic criminal jurisprudence to humanitarian considerations.

In many ways, however, the Chicago trial unquestionably possessed an educational value.[1] It notably increased general appreciation of the fact that our knowledge of crime and its causes constitutes a progressive body of information which has already completely outdistanced our static or very slowly progressing legal principles of criminal procedure. It showed that even within the restrictions imposed by our antiquated courtroom procedure the psychiatrist can actually be more important than the lawyer in the question of determining the responsibility of an accused criminal.

The fact that the public has thus been aroused to an interest in the matter of criminal responsibility makes this a highly appropriate time to review some of the outstanding phases in the progress of criminal science in the last century; a progress exemplified by the gap existing between the concepts expressed by Mr. Crowe, prosecutor in the Chicago case, and those set forth by Mr. Darrow for the defense. Without attempting to pass judgment upon the relative degree of personal rectitude and legal acumen of these two men, it is not unfair to state that the gulf which separated their respective positions measures the progress which criminology and criminal jurisprudence have made in the period between the days of Blackstone and our own time.

II. THE EVOLUTION OF CRIMINOLOGY

A brief survey of the modern attitude toward what is technically known as "the scientific determination of con-

[1] See the articles by Dr. George W. Kirchwey, in *The New York Sunday Times,* Sept. 7 and Sept. 28, 1924; the *Survey Graphic* for October, 1924; the articles by Dr. Leonard Blumgart, in the New York *Nation* for Sept. 10, 1924; and M. McKernan, *The Amazing Crime and Trial of Leopold and Loeb.*

duct" is an indispensable, and the only proper, background for any illuminating discussion of the progress of criminal science in recent times. The problems of ethics and conduct have hitherto been looked upon as a field which should be cultivated almost exclusively by the theologian and the metaphysician, while ethical control has, in practice, been referred to a varying group, extending all the way from ministers of the gospel to the housewife gossips of the small town and countryside, to members of the Ku Klux Klan and to other voluntary inquisitorial groups. The progress of science and philosophy in the last century, however, has almost completely disintegrated this entire position. We have given up the notion of man as a free moral agent and have come to the conclusion that human conduct is the resultant of a vast number of influences, alike hereditary and cultural, which make our action at any time as thoroughly determined as any other natural phenomenon. The human personality, in other words, has been revealed as a proper subject for the cooperative study of biologists, physiologists, psychologists, psychiatrists and sociologists, and it is to these men that we must in the future refer the problem of determining the nature of moral conduct and the degree of personal responsibility therefor.

The theories of crime and criminal responsibility which have held the field in various stages of human evolution have shown a close relation to the prevailing state of cultural development. The first theory which was advanced to explain criminal conduct was the theory of diabolical possession and instigation. When metaphysics developed to the point where it became the dominant type of intellectual orientation, and supplanted the theological interpretation of the universe among the Greeks, we find the rise of a new, but related, doctrine of the causation of crime. The individual was represented as a free moral agent who was at perfect liberty to choose between good and evil. The individual was free to decide whether he would grant the victory to God or the devil; and the criminal was obviously one who decided in favor of Satan. The free moral agent theory, then, was only a further metaphysical elaboration of the primitive interpretation of diabolical possession.

With the rise of modern biology it was natural that the more advanced thinkers should give up these theological and metaphysical interpretations of the causation of criminal action and consider the physical causes of crime. This led the distinguished Italian physician and anthropologist, Cesare Lombroso (1836-1909), to work out a theory of the criminal based entirely upon physical criteria. He held that the typical criminal was characterized by certain definite physical stigmata, such as, among many others, a low and slanting forehead, long ear lobes or none at all, a large jaw with no chin, heavy supraorbital ridges and either excessive hairiness of the body or an abnormal absence of hair. He was brought to these conclusions by an observation of the large number of abnormal physical types in the Italian prisons of his day. He explained the presence of these traits among the criminals on the basis of biological reversion, or atavism. These somatological characteristics of the criminal, Lombroso held, were also the physical traits of primitive man, and he looked upon the criminal as a biological "throwback" to a primitive type.

Though some advanced thinkers of today, such as Thomas Mott Osborne, deny almost in toto the accuracy of Lombroso's theory, it would seem that his explanation of the criminal is not without significance. No one who has had any extensive contact with criminals can doubt the unusual prevalence among them of these abnormal physical types which Lombroso so thoroughly described. The chief valid criticism of his theory is that it is not an adequate explanation for the entire criminal class. These physical stigmata which he alleged to be characteristic of the criminal are found with even greater frequency among the feeble-minded and other defectives than they are among convicted criminals. This means, in other words, that they are characteristic of degenerate human beings in general, and not of criminals alone. Moreover, Lombroso's theory does not account for the presence of a large number of relatively perfect physical specimens in our prison populations, or for the existence of his classic stigmata among law-abiding citizens.

The inadequacy of Lombroso's doctrine led to the proposal of a large number of specific explanations of criminal conduct, as, for example, the pressure of physical want, the contagion of crime waves, the morbid suggestions of an unfortunate social environment, insanity and feeble-mindedness. It was obvious that all these interpretations possessed some value, but it was equally apparent that no single explanation was adequate, when taken by itself, for we have many criminals who come from wealthy homes, others who commit crimes without any reference to a pattern or suggestion, and many who come from the best cultural groups in the community and who are neither feeble-minded nor legally insane.

What was needed was some mode of approach to the interpretation of the criminal combining all these various theories from Lombroso to the present. This was supplied by psychiatry or medical psychology. The advantage of the psychiatric approach is that it is possible for the psychiatrist to take into account *all* possible influences operating upon the criminal, inasmuch as they all come to a focus in his mental activities. All good psychiatrists are adequately trained in biology, psychology and sociology, as well as in their own specialty, and are thus men uniquely fitted to investigate and evaluate the various influences which, in any particular case, impel an individual to execute an anti-social act.

The net result of the application of psychiatry to the problem of criminology has been the entire repudiation and elimination, once and for all, of the theological and metaphysical interpretations of criminal conduct and responsibility. It has been shown that a criminal act is absolutely determined for the individual on the basis of his biological heredity, his past and present experiences, or both. There is not the slightest iota of freedom of choice allowed to either the criminal or the normal citizen in his daily conduct. Further, this modern scientific analysis of criminal conduct proves the absolute absurdity of the old notion that the degree of degradation of the criminal personality can in any fundamental way be measured by the nature of the crime. Modern criminology has shown that the most hideous crimes may be committed by individuals of high intellect, with only slight mental disorders readily amenable to treatment, while many feeble-minded potential murderers may commit nothing more serious than petty larceny. Again, psychiatry has tended to eliminate the element of mystery in regard to criminal activity. To the trained psychiatrist, as I have already intimated, the case of Leopold and Loeb was as clear and simple to solve as it would have been for the skillful surgeon to diagnose a case of hernia or a facial cancer. A large amount of time was taken up in the courtroom by the circuitous and dilatory procedure required by our archaic criminal jurisprudence, in order that the psychiatrists might expound with formal legal correctness the simple fact that Leopold was suffering from a compulsion neurosis on a homosexual basis which seemed headed toward a paranoid psychosis, while Loeb was in the initial stages of a dementia-præcox psychosis. Likewise, the famous Los Angeles Bluebeard, who had murdered his nine wives, was suffering from a compulsion neurosis created by overcompensation for his inferiority complex generated by a physical defect.[2]

III. THE HISTORY OF THE PUNISHMENT OF CRIME

The various doctrines which have prevailed with respect to the desirability and object of punishment have borne a very close and immediate relationship to the theories of crime and criminal responsibility. In primitive days, when the theory of diabolical possession dominated, the conventional notion of punishment was either to exorcise the devil or to exile or execute the criminal. In part, this doctrine was based upon the notion of protecting the community group against further outrages by the offending individual, but far more important was the notion of the necessity and the desirability of placating the gods.

The next stage in the evolution of the doctrine of punishment appeared when more stress was laid upon the element of social revenge. This attitude developed in conjunction with the notion of crime as the wilful act of a free moral agent. Society felt outraged at such an act of voluntary perversity and indignantly retaliated by a savage manifestation of group vengeance. Many forms of crime were identified with sin and were believed to offer a challenge to God and orthodox religion. It scarcely needs to be pointed out that this theory of punishment

[2] On this point see Blumgart, loc. cit.; H. H. Goddard, *The Criminal Imbecile;* W. Healey, *The Individual Delinquent;* B. Glueck, "Recent Progress in Determining the Nature of Crime and the Characteristics of the Criminal," in *Proceedings of the National Conference of Social Work,* 1917; "Psychiatric Aims in the Field of Criminology," in *Mental Hygiene, October,* 1918; W. A. Potts, "Crime and Delinquency," in *The Mind and What We Ought to Know About It,* London, Hodder & Stoughton, 1923, Chap. VII; S. S. Glueck, "State Legislation Providing for the Mental Examination of Persons Accused of Crime," in *Mental Hygiene,* January, 1924; and *Mental Disorder and the Criminal Law.* See also B. Glueck in White and Jelliffe, *The Modern Treatment of Nervous and Mental Diseases,* Vol. I., Chap. V.; F. H. Wines, *Punishment and Reformation,* new ed., Chaps. XII. and XIII.; L. N. Robinson, *Penology in the United States,* Chap. X.; B. Glueck, "Concerning Prisoners," in *Mental Hygiene,* April, 1918.

is the one which still dominates contemporary criminal jurisprudence, however much it may be modified and mitigated by certain incidental innovations.

With the development of the biological theory of the criminal, as set forth by Lombroso and others, and which was based upon the notion that the criminal represented a degenerate physical type incapable of reformation or notable improvement, the theory of the desirability of incarceration or segregation for life developed wide popularity. It may be said, indeed, that this theory has been definitely accepted by the most advanced criminologists of today, in so far as it is related to the type of criminal that Lombroso had in mind. This solution was based upon the fundamental objective which dominates contemporary criminal science, namely, the protection of society from anti-social individuals.

If social protection is to be the great object of the criminology and penology of the future, it becomes necessary to consider calmly and objectively in what manner this end is most likely to be realized. With the modern notion of determinism in conduct and the general acceptance of the view that the act of a criminal is as inevitable as that of a clergyman or a missionary, and that the criminal himself is in no way personally responsible for his acts, it readily appears as illogical and unscientific to *punish* a criminal as it would be to punish an individual because he suffers from some organic disease or mental aberration. From a careful study of the past results in the treatment of criminals, it is readily apparent that savage punishment, whether justifiable or unjustifiable, has never served to repress criminality. The old and respectable theory of the deterrent value of punishment has been shown to be of dubious significance. Most crimes are committed as a result of deep underlying subconscious compulsions or from impulse and anger, and neither severity nor certainty of punishment will do much to deter in such cases. The sane method of procedure is to give up the whole notion of punishment, on the ground that it is as anachronistic and indefensible as the ideas of witchcraft and magic, and to concentrate attention upon the various ways in which the criminal class can be handled in such a manner as to insure to the highest possible degree the reformation of the reformable element and the permanent segregation of those whose rehabilitation is quite unlikely or entirely out of the question.

One of the most fascinating and at the same time most gruesome phases of the study of criminology is the history of the methods which have been followed by society in treating criminals. In primitive days, as already indicated, the usual method of punishing the criminal was either by death or exile, the motive being in each case the desire to repudiate the crime and to placate the gods. For the less serious crimes there were provided various types of corporal punishment or penitential exercises. In the period of barbarism separating savagery from civilization, there developed that remarkable notion, technically known as the theory of the "lex talionis," or the concept of "an eye for an eye, a tooth for a tooth."

The principle of the lex talionis was gradually modified in the direction of a general scheme of corporal punishment. During the greater period of human history, corporal punishment, together with fines of various sorts, was the typical method by which society avenged itself upon the violator of its laws and social codes. The varieties of corporal punishment were as numerous as they were savage, including such practices as whipping; cutting off the hands, ears or nose; branding on the forehead, in the hand or on various other portions of the anatomy; pulling out the tongue; gouging out the eyes; or the use of the stocks, pillory or ducking-stool for the less serious types of criminal acts.[3] These types of punishment dominated in the repression of crime almost to the close of the eighteenth century, having been universally the basis of criminal jurisprudence and court procedure in the Colonial period in America.

The reaction against the brutality of corporal punishment seems to have been due almost entirely to the Quakers, or members of the Society of Friends. This group took its Christianity very literally. In the last quarter of the seventeenth century, in the two Quaker colonies of West Jersey and Pennsylvania, the savage European and Puritan criminal law was repudiated, corporal punishment abandoned, and imprisonment substituted as the normal method of treating the violator of the law. Difficulties encountered in the New Jersey colony in connection with organization and in Pennsylvania with respect to relations with the mother country led to the temporary abandonment of this advanced and humane Quaker position in the three-quarters of a century preceding the Declaration of Independence. But as soon as independence had been secured and the Quaker group was no longer hampered by English interference, the change which had been desired a century earlier was actually realized. The Pennsylvania Constitution of 1776 directed a reform of the criminal law, and this was practically achieved by revolutionary legislation passed between 1787 and 1795. This once more wiped out the various forms of corporal punishment, other than hanging for capital crimes, and directed the substitution of imprisonment. From the Pennsylvania innovation this reform in criminal procedure spread throughout the United States, and by 1825 imprisonment had, in nearly every American State, supplanted the older and more barbarous methods of corporal punishment. Paralleling this movement in Amer-

[3] See W. S. Davis, *Life on a Medieval Barony,* Chap. X; F. H. Wines, *Punishment and Reformation,* Chap. V.

ica and somewhat influenced by it, similar changes were taking place in Europe due to the activity of European Friends and to the agitation of the reformers in criminal jurisprudence, such as Beccaria, Bentham, Romilly and others.

IV. FAILURE OF PRISONS

In the nineteenth century imprisonment marked the great experiment in the treatment of the criminal classes. Though this form of punishment was unquestionably more humane in most ways than whipping and mutilation, its reformatory effect upon the criminal classes was quite as futile and unsatisfactory as corporal punishment had proved in the preceding centuries. The chief types of institutional administration which were experimented with in connection with imprisonment were the famous Pennsylvania and Auburn systems of prison discipline.

In the Pennsylvania system, so called from its original establishment in the Philadelphia prisons following the year 1790, the convict was put in individual isolation in cells from which he was never taken, unless dead or insane, until he had served out his sentence. At first he had practically no contact with any other human being except the prison officers and an occasional visiting clergyman; he was not even allowed to communicate with relatives, to say nothing of having them visit him in prison. This was the Quaker theory of imprisonment which gained wide vogue, not only in America, but also and more particularly in Europe. In spite of the fact that it was designed to supplant the horrors of the old-time corporal punishment, it is highly probable that in many cases it begot even more severe suffering than the older practices of flogging and lopping off ears. In the Auburn system, which was adopted at the close of the first quarter of the nineteenth century in the prison at Auburn, New York, the prisoners were isolated at night in their respective cells, but during the day were allowed to work by groups in prison shops where absolute silence and non-communication were maintained. In spite of the most optimistic arguments and anticipations by the advocates of each of these schemes, both proved almost complete failures with respect to securing the reformation of the convict. Though these institutions served fairly well the purpose of social revenge, they thus failed to a very large degree to achieve the aim of social protection.

The weaknesses of the Pennsylvania and Auburn systems suggested to leading reformers in Europe and America the desirability of working out a prison system which would offer definite incentives to improvement and reformation. This ultimately culminated in the famous Elmira system, drawn very largely from the Irish prison system established by Sir Walter Crofton in the period following 1850. The procedure embodied in the so-called Elmira system was based upon the notion of classifying the convicts according to behavior and efforts at improvement while incarcerated. Good behavior secured them rapid advancement, special privileges and speedy release upon parole, while bad behavior or incorrigibility necessitated the serving out of the entire term of the sentence with the minimum degree of freedom and privileges while in the institution. Forward-looking as the Elmira system was, it had very little effect upon the prison administration of our country. In the first place, it was rarely applied to the adult convicts, but was reserved almost wholly for young first offenders not guilty of the more heinous forms of criminal transgression. Even more serious was the defect caused by the failure to apply the resources of modern medicine and psychiatry to the problems of the rehabilitation of the convict. Knowing, as we now do, that the convict is for the most part the victim of biological, psychological or social defects, it is quite obvious that no system of classification and promotion by itself can serve as an effective agency of reformation. No scientifically minded person would hold that the inmates of a State hospital for the insane could be safely and adequately restored to mental health by a mere system of classification according to behavior, and it is equally true that the Elmira system, whatever its merits, was totally inadequate, when taken alone, to serve as an effective agency for reforming the convict and transforming him into a safe member of society.

V. SCIENCE AND THE CRIMINAL

As the criminal, in nearly every case, is defective in one way or another, it is necessary to take positive remedial action with the aim either of eliminating his defects or rendering these defects no longer a danger to society. Furthermore, as the nature of these defects is extremely varied, it is obvious that the modes of treatment must be equally flexible and widely differentiated. In the new system of treatment the scientific procedure will be to bring every person convicted of crime before a competent and permanent examining body made up of physicians, psychiatrists and psychologists, who will be able to study and differentiate the convicts and prescribe the desirable methods of treatment indicated by the specific defects of the individual convicts. A certain number of convicts will be revealed at once upon examination to be of a type that should never, under any circumstances, be again restored to a life of freedom, but should be permanently segregated or painlessly exterminated. Feeble-minded criminals, paretic criminals and other types of low-grade degenerates or incurables would make up the bulk of this class. It is now generally admitted that institutional treatment should be resorted to only as the last alternative, necessary as it may be to the majority of those convicted of crime. For the less serious types of offenders probation should be almost universally employed rather than commitment to an institution. Where probation results in failure, institutional commitment will probably then be necessary.

Having eliminated from the general body of those convicted the types which should be experimented with in a probation system and those for whom there is no possibility of reformation and who require perpetual institutional segregation, there remains the group which, on the one hand, needs institutional treatment and, on the other, offers some hope of reformation. It is to this class in particular that a scheme like that introduced by Mr. Osborne at Sing Sing and Portsmouth is most applicable and among which it is most likely to end successfully. The majority of this type of convicts have committed their crimes either because of minor personality defects or an unfortunate social environment, or both. It is obvious that they can be transformed into safe members of society only by various methods of treatment designed to remove these defects. Mr. Osborne's plan constitutes the best scheme yet devised for providing adequate social education for those who have never been adequately trained in matters pertaining to social conduct and responsibility. But it is quite evident that those who are suffering from personality defects will be handicapped as participants in any such scheme unless the self-government plan is supplemented by a personal treatment of their cases by competently trained physicians and psychiatrists. Hence the Osborne Mutual Welfare scheme should be accompanied by a greatly augmented medical department particularly strong in neurology, psychiatry and mental hygiene. As many convicts are not adequately trained in vocations or professions enabling them to earn an honest livelihood, thoroughgoing provision for industrial and vocational education would also be essential in the modern institution designed to effect the re-education and reformation of the convict. In such a system, as will be readily apparent, the whole objective of savage punishment is totally disregarded and every effort is made to secure the ultimate reformation of the criminal, with the end in view that he may be safely released to a life of freedom.

Though present evidence would indicate that in most cases of such a combination of social re-education, psychiatric treatment and vocational instruction, a high percentage of reformation might be hoped for, it is apparent that there will be many failures, just as there are many relapses in the case of patients discharged as cured from the hospitals for the insane. Hence, modern institutions for the reformation of the criminal will need to have as a supplementary aid an adequate parole system, which will make it possible, on the one hand, to assist those successfully treated to make their readjustments to society and, at the same time, will make it easy to bring back for further treatment or ultimate segregation those whose reformation has not yet been adequately achieved. Many will doubtless allege that this institution of which we have been speaking is not, in the ordinary sense of the term, a prison. This will be cheerfully admitted by the majority of contemporary criminologists. For, in the modern criminal science, the old prison as an institution designed to achieve punishment and social revenge, has no place whatever. In its stead will appear the institution for the examination, differentiation, treatment, segregation or extermination of the socially sick or criminal class.

VI. NECESSITY OF PROGRESS IN CRIMINAL JURISPRUDENCE

It needs to be pointed out, in conclusion, that no scientific system of criminology and penology can well be established and executed without far-reaching changes in our present criminal law and procedure. Hitherto the question of the guilt of the accused has been the chief problem which has concerned court procedure, and criminal law has been largely devoted to an effort to fit the penalty to the crime. Both these concepts and objectives are totally renounced by modern criminal science. The problem of the guilt of an accused individual is far less important than the matter of his potential danger to society. Indeed, the question of guilt is interesting and significant only in relation to this very issue of the menace to the community. If competent psychiatrists discover that an accused person is potentially a social menace, modern criminal science would insist that such an individual must be segregated and properly treated, irrespective of his guilt or innocence of a particular criminal act. There have been many criticisms of the jury from the standpoint of its inadequacy in the matter of scientifically ascertaining the guilt of an accused party, but the most serious indictment that can be presented is that the very purpose which the jury is supposed to achieve is no longer regarded as the major goal of criminal procedure. The scientific method of handling a person accused of crime is to turn him over to a body of legally authorized and responsible experts in their respective fields, who will, if desirable, prescribe the proper type of institutional segregation and treatment, irrespective of the matter of guilt.

Another very important point is to remember the loose nature of the term criminal as applied in conventional usage. We tend to employ it to describe anybody who has been convicted of crime. The conviction will almost invariably have been by a jury, and may have been unjust. There are few persons who do not wittingly or unwittingly commit some crime during each year, or at least during a decade of their life. Most of them are not convicted because they are not detected, have powerful friends, or are able to engage able lawyers. A small proportion through stupidity, ill-luck, or lack of funds and influence are convicted. One conviction, even for a petty crime, is sufficient to brand that person a criminal for life, though he may be a perfectly normal individual in every essential respect. It is obvious that there are many undetected and unconvicted persons who are more truly criminal than some who are convicted. These considerations will show that the popular usage of the word criminal has practically no technical significance. The criminal personality is one which must be revealed by careful individual psychological study rather than by court records taken alone.

The aim of conventional criminal procedure "to make the penalty fit the crime" is even more out of date and indefensible than the jury system and the emphasis upon guilt. If there is any permanent and definite contribution which modern criminal science has made, it is establishment of the fact to which I have already referred, that the nature of the crime is but the most imperfect criterion of the danger of an individual to society. The "bobbed-haired bandit," Celia Cooney—the incurable moron—is obviously a more dangerous person to society than Leopold, even though she never committed a murder. The whole problem of the menace of an individual to society and of the possibility of his reformation is one which must be founded upon a thorough study of the personality of the individual in question, and can in no way be determined by the nature of his crime, except in so far as the latter may throw some little light upon the quality of his personality. It is probable that the new criminal science will go even further than the present principle of the indeterminate sentence, in that the disposition of the criminal will not be left to the determination of the judge at all, but will rather be vested in a body of combined experts whose conduct and procedure will be properly safeguarded and authorized from a legal point of view.

Many conventional critics of the new criminology and penology assert dogmatically that the modern criminal science would lead to inadequate defense of society against the criminal classes, but this allegation is shown to have no foundation when subjected to critical analysis. That our present system of criminal jurisprudence and prison administration has proved a grotesque failure is evidenced from such facts as these: that there is only one execution to approximately every 150 murders in this country, and that our homicide rate is seventeen times that of England. Even more impressive as evidence of the failure of the contemporary system is the enormous amount of "recidivism" in our criminal population, the present prison system rarely, if ever, securing the actual reformation of the criminal. It would be difficult to find a better example of the inability of the "right-thinking" citizen to learn by experience or of the perennial human tendency to "pass the buck" than is to be observed in the contemporary hysteria concerning the increase of crime and the accompanying attack upon scientific criminology and penology. The business men and lawyers who are organizing this "crusade" against crime are demanding an increase in the severity of formal penalties, more cruel and rigorous punishment, and an "elimination" of criminal science from judicial procedure. They further allege that the crime wave is due primarily to the "coddling" of prisoners by "sentimentalists," *i.e.,* scientific students of crime.

If such persons possessed even a rudimentary knowledge of the history of crime and its treatment they would know that increased severity in punishment has been tried for thousands of years and has invariably ended by producing a far worse demoralization of society than previously existed. Punishment by itself alone has invariably failed to achieve either deterrence or reformation, but has made so many more criminals and polished off so many more accomplished crooks. To lay the present deplorable state of affairs to criminologists and prison reformers is comparable to assigning the drought of the past summer in the southern and central states of our country to the economic doctrines of the Bolsheviks. The present system of criminal jurisprudence and penal administration is still wholly in the hands of the judges, lawyers and right-thinking business men, and for its merits and defects they and they alone are responsible. The criminologists have as yet made only the most nebulous impression on our criminal law, criminal procedure or prison administration. And a perusal of any study of contemporary prison conditions, such as Tannenbaum's *Wall Shadows,* will show the ridiculous nature of any charge that we are "coddling" prisoners. Prison administration is everywhere in this country still of the old repressive type. The reformers have had control of only one prison, namely Sing Sing, and the record of achieved reformation during the short period of experiment there puts to shame the records of prison administration in the whole country during the previous century. The modern criminologist is even more alarmed at the increase of crime than the lawyer and business man, for he knows so much better than they how unnecessary it is and how far we are from having enough social intelligence to introduce an adequate method of dealing with the menace. Where the criminologist differs from the point of view of some members of the National Crime Commission and the Hon. Richard Washburn Child is in not attempting to solve a difficult problem by advocating a larger dose of the very procedure which is responsible for the situation that is being attacked, and in a willingness to get away from obsolete and simple-minded dogmas to an actual and unbiased study of the factors and circumstances involved. Indeed, the present writer agrees with the thesis of Mr. George Jean Nathan as expressed in the *American*

Mercury for February, 1926, to the effect that the so-called crime wave is due to no small extent to the anti-social ideals and low ethical standards prevailing among the members of the legal profession itself:

That the recent tremendous spread of crime in the United States is due to any one or all of the reasons assigned, I seriously doubt. The responsibility has been placed upon everything from the late war to the modern novel, from Bolshevism to bad booze, and from insufficient police protection to the automobile and the easy means of escape provided by the latter. That these have been the main-spring of the crime wave does not convince me. Unless I am uncommonly mistaken, the responsibility lies in a different quarter and that is the enormously increased number of shady, but shrewd and competent, shyster lawyers who have sprung up like mushrooms all over America. These fellows, out for notoriety and money and willing to do anything to get them, have opened offices in almost every other block of every American town of any size. And their trade consists in large part of taking on as clients gentlemen who have illegally gotten away with swag of one kind or another and in getting as much of it as possible for themselves. They have nothing to lose and everything to gain. If they can prove the innocence of their clients or even merely that their clients no longer have the swag in their possession (whatever may happen to the clients after that), they are down in their luck if at least half of the cabbaged boodle doesn't find its way into their pockets. If, on the other hand, their clients go to the hoosegow, they are out only a little gab and time.

The crooks have been trained to know these shysters and to put confidence in them. And that confidence has been well repaid. Twenty years ago a criminal had difficulty in getting a lawyer to handle his case for him. Today, a dozen are waiting for him when the patrol-wagon backs up to the police station. These shysters, as I have said, are not merely charlatans; many of them have legal minds devious, sharp and immensely cunning. Look at the newspapers any day and you will read a sufficiently illuminating record of their successes. Against the overcrowded and tired court mind, a mind that has utterly no time to do justice to the prosecution, their own alert mind has a comparatively easy job. Only in the case of murder do they experience any difficulty and even here the statistics show a remarkable record of good fortune for them.

This new genus shyster is a fellow far superior in trickery to his brother of the past. He has made a study of it and has mastered it. The old shyster was simply a snide lawyer with a couple of political friends upon whom he had something, who were hence in his power and whom he could use to his client's advantage, plus a shabby Prince Albert and a loud mouth; but the shyster of today is no such low fowl. He knows criminal law inside and out, chiefly inside, and he is privy to the means as how best to jockey it to his client's favor. The criminal classes read that he has succeeded in getting Abe Flopbaum off easily by proving that Abe was dropped on his head when three years old and was therefore not in his right senses when he forged the check for $30,000, that he has managed to free Luigi the wop by proving that the mulatto whose body was found in the sewer was the one actually responsible for the seduction of the little Swedish servant girl, and that he got Aloysius Mulcahey, Jr., out of Sing Sing by showing that one of the jurors who convicted him was a Ku Kluxer, and they thereupon hitch up their trousers, get out the old family six-shooter and go out and beat up another Columbus avenue jeweler and make off with another quart or so of diamonds.

In any city where there are as many lawyers as policemen, crime is in high feather. The towns that have few lawyers in them are invariably found to be happy, peaceful, law-abiding communities.

The new system would insist at the outset upon the permanent segregation of all those degenerate types whose reformation is obviously impossible or highly unlikely.

It would provide the most scientific treatment for those whose reformation appears possible, but would grant them permanent freedom only when a proper test through parole had demonstrated the thoroughness of the cure. It would further insist upon a vast improvement of our present detective and police systems along lines like those suggested by Chief Vollmer, in order that arrest and treatment may be made much more swift and certain. Even further, the new criminal science would probably insist upon the desirability of a general inquisition and investigation of the whole population in order to put in segregation or bring under treatment the feeble-minded, psycho-neurotic and other types likely to be guilty of criminal conduct. It would, in other words, add to the element of reformation that of prevention.

It should also be pointed out that the deterministic theory of conduct which is embodied in modern criminal and psychological science stands exactly at the opposite pole from fatalism, with which it is often confused, and is much more dynamic and satisfactory than the old free moral agent doctrine. Determinism, by showing how conduct is the result of biological heredity and of personal experiences coming from the social environment, also points the way to a definite method of solving the problem of delinquency through eliminating biological defect and improving the social environment. With the free moral agent hypothesis no such satisfactory program was possible, as heredity and experience were thought to have no vital relation to conduct, and a person of the finest heredity and most advantageous social position might freely will to become a professional criminal. Nothing that any person could do would anticipate or avert this wholly arbitrary action.

Hence, instead of lessening the degree of social protection, as compared with contemporary methods and results, the newer criminal science would actually insure a vastly greater degree of protection to society from the menace of the criminal classes.[4]

SELECTED REFERENCES

Child, R. W. *Battling the Criminal.*
Darrow, C. S. *Crime: Its Causes and Treatment.*
De Quiros, B. *Modern Theories of Criminality.*
Gillin, J. L. *Criminology and Penology.*
Glueck, B. *Forensic Psychiatry.*
Glueck, S. S. *Mental Disorder and the Criminal Law.*
Goddard, H. H. *The Criminal Imbecile.*
Gordon, M. *Prison Discipline.*
Hobhouse and Brockway. *English Prisons Today.*
Hoag and Williams. *Crime, Abnormal Minds and the Law.*
Healy, W. *The Individual Delinquent.*
McKernan, M. *The Amazing Crime and Trial of Leopold and Loeb.*
O'Hare, K. D. *In Prison.*
Osborne, T. M. *Society and Its Prisons.*
Osborne, T. M. *Prisons and Common Sense.*
Parmelee, M. *Criminology.*
Robinson, L. N. *Penology in the United States.*
Shaw, B. Preface to S. and B. Webb, *English Prisons Under Local Government.*
Smith, M. H. *The Psychology of the Criminal.*
Sutherland, E. H. *Criminology.*
Tannenbaum, F. *Wall Shadows.*
Wines, F. H. *Punishment and Reformation* (New Ed.).

[4] E. B. Hoag and E. W. Williams, *Crime, Abnormal Minds and the Law;* A. Vollmer, "Aims and Ideals of the Police," in *Journal of Criminal Law and Criminology,* August, 1922; M. Gordon, *Penal Discipline;* W. H. Burnham, *The Normal Mind;* I. J. Sands and P. M. Blanchard, *Abnormal Behavior,* Chap. XIII; S. S. Glueck, *Mental Disorder and the Criminal Law.*

CHAPTER II

Criminal Codes and Penal Institutions of Colonial Times

I. THE CRIMINAL CODES

1. *Introductory*

While we have accumulated and made available a vast body of information concerning the details of colonial political and military history, and the more dramatic or curious aspects of colonial cultural and religious history, there still remains an amazing ignorance of the criminal jurisprudence and penal institutions of the colonial age. Yet we cannot understand in any intelligent fashion the genesis of the contemporary prison system without a knowledge of the situation which lay behind the work of the reformers from 1780 to 1825 that produced the abolition of brutal forms of corporal punishment and substituted imprisonment. In this chapter the effort will be made to set forth the salient facts with respect to colonial conceptions and procedure in handling the problems of delinquency. The state of Pennsylvania is chosen to illustrate these developments as it represents a more varied and comprehensive set of practices and institutions than those of any other colony. It not only combined experiences with the Quaker and the Puritan codes, but also employed both corporal punishment and imprisonment and utilized both the workhouse and the jail.

In order to interpret intelligently the content and significance of the criminal codes of colonial Pennsylvania it is necessary to understand the general nature of criminal jurisprudence at the time, and the relation that the Pennsylvania codes bore to the prevailing trends in contemporary criminal law.[1] Judged by present-day standards, the criminal laws of colonial times were extremely severe in the penalties they prescribed. A much larger number of capital crimes existed than are listed on the statute books of today. From ten to eighteen crimes, for which the death penalty was prescribed, were usual in the colonial period. The situation in England was, of course, far worse. There, at the close of the eighteenth century, nearly three hundred capital crimes were specified. Even more striking is the difference in penalties prescribed for crimes not capital. Instead of imprisonment some form of corporal punishment or fines was imposed. Imprisonment, as a method of punishment, was first permanently applied in this country in the period following 1789 in Pennsylvania.

In general, it may be said that the criminal codes of colonial Pennsylvania passed through three major transformations. The English or Puritan system was first introduced in 1676. This was superseded by the mild and humane Quaker code of 1682, which was a new and revolutionary departure in criminal jurisprudence. On account of friction over the Quaker demand for affirmation rather than oath-taking in court procedure, the English government in 1718 compelled the re-establishment of the Puritan code, which remained in force until after the close of the Revolutionary War.

2. *The Original Criminal Code of 1676*

On September 25, 1676, Governor Edmund Andros promulgated the laws of the Duke of York by an executive ordinance and thereby made them applicable to Penn-

[1] I have discussed the general setting of colonial criminal jurisprudence in an article in the *Journal of Criminal Law and Criminology*, May, 1921. See below, Chap. IV.

sylvania.[2] These laws had been compiled under the Duke's authority to be applied in the government of the territory he had conquered from the Dutch. They were described as having been "collected out of the several laws now in force in his Majesty's American Colonies and Plantations and digested into one volume for the public use of the territories in America under the government of his Royal Highness, James, Duke of York and Albany." They were first promulgated on March 1, 1664, at Hempstead, Long Island, and the criminal code contained therein is usually referred to as the "Hempstead Code." [3] The propinquity of Long Island to the New Haven colony, the intercommunication between the two colonies, and the resemblance between the wording as well as the content of the two codes would incline one to the belief that the Hempstead code was taken more or less directly from the codes of 1642 and 1650 enacted for the New Haven colony.[4] The following portion of the laws embodied the list of capital crimes:

1. If any person within this Government shall by direct, express, impious or presumptuous ways, deny the true God and His attributes, he shall be put to death.

2. If any person shall commit any wilful and premeditated murder he shall be put to death.

3. If any person slayeth another with a sword or dagger who hath no weapon to defend himself; he shall be put to death.

4. If any man shall slay, or cause another to be slain by lying in wait privily for him or by poisoning or any other such wicked conspiracy; he shall be put to death. . . .

5. If any man or woman shall lie with any beast or brute creature by carnal copulation they shall be put to death, and the beast shall be burned.

[2] *Charter and Laws,* Historical Notes, pp. 455 f.
[3] Ibid.
[4] H. E. Barnes, *History of the Penal Reformatory and Correctional Institutions of New Jersey,* pp. 27-28, 341-2.

6. If any man lieth with mankind as he lieth with a woman, they shall be put to death, unless the one party were forced or be under fourteen years of age, in which case he shall be punished at the discretion of the Court of Assizes.

7. If any person forcibly stealeth or carrieth away any mankind; he shall be put to death.

8. If any man bear false witness maliciously and on purpose to take away a man's life, he shall be put to death.

9. If any man shall traitorously deny his Majesty's right and titles to his Crowns and Dominions, or shall raise armies to resist his authority, he shall be put to death.

10. If any man shall treacherously conspire or publickly attempt to invade or surprise any town or towns, fort or forts, within this Government, he shall be put to death.

11. If any child or children, above sixteen years of age, and of sufficient understanding, shall smite their natural father or mother, unless thereunto provoked and forced for their self-protection from death or maiming, at the complaint of said father and mother, and not otherwise, there being sufficient witnesses thereof, that child or those children so offending shall be put to death.[5]

Lesser punishments were provided for other crimes and misdemeanors. Fornication was punishable by fine, corporal punishment, or marriage, at the discretion of the court. Forgery was to be punished by the pillory, double damages to the injured persons, and disability for again giving evidence in court. The penalty imposed for arson was death or full satisfaction to the injured party, at the pleasure of the court. Excessive drinking was penalized by fine, the stocks, or both. Lying and spreading false news was to be punished by fine, whipping, and the stocks. As to burglary and robbery, it was provided that the penalty for the first offence was to be branding, for the second branding and whipping, and for the third death. Adultery was punishable by corporal punishment, fine, or imprisonment. Minor punishments were also provided for

[5] *Charter and Laws,* pp. 14-15.

such petty offences as disturbing church meetings, disobeying parents, and like.[6] There were also included sundry laws regulating the treatment of such civil offences as would be likely to arise in a primitive agricultural society. These were not widely different from those provided in the Levitical code or the Code of Hammurabi.[7] The code abounds in humorous enactments, of which the following section of the law regulating the conduct of the inns of the time is a fair sample. This provided that—

> Every person licensed to keep an Ordinary shall always be provided of strong and wholesome beer, of four bushels of malt, at the least to a hogshead, which he shall not sell at above two pence the quart under the penalty of twenty shillings, for the first offence, forty shillings for the second, and loss of his license. It is permitted to sell beer out of doors at a penny the ale quart or under.
>
> No licensed person shall suffer any to drink excessively or at unreasonable hours after nine of the clock at night in or about any of their houses upon penalty of two shillings six pence for every offence if complaint and proof be made thereof.[8]

Petty offences were dealt with in the town courts constituted by the constable and two or more of the overseers. The more serious offences, with the exception of capital crimes, came under the jurisdiction of the court of quarter sessions. Here trial was by a jury of not more than seven or less than six, and a majority verdict was binding in all cases. The capital crimes were tried by the court of assizes. Here a jury of twelve was usual and the verdict had to be unanimous.[9] Minor punishments were inflicted by the constables of the towns or by other specially appointed persons, but the execution of those convicted of capital offences was a duty of the sheriff.[10]

6 *Charter and Laws,* pp. 18, 27-8, 62-3.
7 Ibid., pp. 15-17.
8 Ibid., p. 30.
9 Ibid., pp. 11, 21-2, 33-4, 44, 50, 62.
10 Ibid., pp. 21, 50, 456.

3. *The Quaker Criminal Codes of 1682-1718*

The provisions of the Duke's laws were superseded by those adopted by Penn's first assembly, which was held at Chester on December 4-7, 1682. Here were adopted the sixty-one chapters of what was known as "The Great Law or Body of Laws" of the province of Pennsylvania.[11] This contained the original Quaker criminal code of Pennsylvania and marked out clearly the wide differences between Quaker practices and theories and those of the Anglicans and Puritans in the other colonies and the mother country. This code can scarcely be appreciated without a brief examination of the intellectual and sociological background of Quaker jurisprudence.

The ideas and customs of the Quakers furnish the best explanation of the nature and content of their criminal code.[12] Mr. Applegarth, in his interesting study, *The Quakers in Pennsylvania,* has summarized the more important of their customs and ideas which went far to shape their legislation. The Quakers evidenced an almost puritanical asceticism and austerity in their mode of life, though they were not as cruel and vindictive as were the Puritans in punishing deviations from group regulations. All forms of sensuality were particularly repugnant to the Quakers, and they were especially careful to provide a strict legal regulation of sexual morality. Next to sexual laxity, profanity received the greatest amount of condemnation by the Quakers, and their laws repressing "prophane swearing" and cursing are humorously explicit and thorough-going. Gambling was also regarded as a serious offence, and in this category were included many games and amusements now considered quite harmless. Drunkenness was considered a most deplorable vice which they tried to repress by strict regulations, and smoking was

[11] Ibid., pp. 107 ff., and Historical Notes, pp. 465-82.

[12] See Isaac Sharpless, *A Quaker Experiment in Government,* pp. 21-46; and *Quakerism and Politics,* pp. 202-20.

regarded as only one degree less serious than drinking. Duelling, with its shedding of blood, was, naturally, forbidden by the Quakers. Again, they were opposed to the theater and public amusements and made their introduction and patronage punishable offences.

The Quakers did not rely merely upon legal regulation to secure a high degree of public morality, but resorted to an almost Calvinistic type of inquisitorial supervision over the morality of private citizens. It is stated upon good authority that one of the more prominent of the early governors of the province was in the habit of going through the inns of Philadelphia each night before he retired in order to disperse by personal application of physical force, if necessary, the hangers-on who might have delayed their home-going after the "unseemly hour of nine o'clock of the night." [13] Finally, it should be noted that the aversion of the Quakers to unusual cruelty, suffering, and the shedding of blood led them to substitute imprisonment for the death penalty, in all crimes except murder, and for the other more barbarous types of corporal punishment.[14]

Though the "Great Law" of 1682 was submitted by the Proprietor to the assembly for its sanction, it was not seriously altered, and it may be regarded as representing Penn's ideal of a criminal code.[15] It opened with the declaration, very unusual for the time, which proclaimed that liberty of conscience and freedom of worship should be guaranteed to all who acknowledged the existence and attributes of the one true God.[16] This eliminated at the outset from the province of Pennsylvania the long category of religious offences which marred the criminal jurisprudence of most of the other colonies at the time, as well as that of all the European countries.

13 Albert C. Applegarth, *The Quakers in Pennsylvania*, pp. 5-49.
14 A. S. Bolles, *Pennsylvania, Province and State*, p. 256.
15 *Charter and Laws*, pp. 99-104, 477 ff.
16 Ibid., pp. 107-8.

In the main, crimes of violence against the person were punished by imprisonment at hard labor in the "house of correction." For assaulting a parent the child was to be confined in the house of correction during the pleasure of the parent.[17] Assaulting a magistrate was punished by fine and by one month's confinement in the house of correction.[18] If a servant assaulted a master he was to be punished at the discretion of two justices of the peace.[19] In view of the fact that a very large proportion of the population of provincial Pennsylvania was made up of indentured servants, this enactment was of very considerable significance. Assault and battery constituted a breach of the peace and was to be punished "according to the nature and circumstances of the act." [20] Duelling was penalized by a fine of five pounds or three months' imprisonment.[21] Rioting was accounted an act of violence and was punished accordingly.[22] Neither murder nor manslaughter was included in the crimes and penalties enumerated in the "Great Law," but their punishment was provided for in the supplement to the original code, which was enacted by the assembly in March, 1683. Here it declared that manslaughter should be punished according to the nature and circumstance of the act, and it was decreed with respect to murder that "if any person within this province or territories thereof shall wilfully or premeditately kill another person, or wilfully or premeditately, be the cause of, or accessory to, the death of any person, such person shall, according to the law of God, suffer death." [23] Murder, then, was the only capital crime in the Quaker criminal code of Pennsylvania.

In defining the crimes against property and prescribing

17 Ibid., p. 113.
18 Ibid.
19 Ibid.
20 Ibid., pp. 113-14.
21 Ibid., p. 114.
22 Ibid., p. 113.
23 Ibid., p. 144.

the punishments therefor, it was decreed that arson should be punished by rendering double satisfaction to the injured party, imprisonment for one year, and by receiving such corporal punishment as the court should see fit to impose.[24] Breaking, entering, and theft of goods was punishable by fourfold restitution and three months' imprisonment. If the offender was not able to make restitution he was to be imprisoned for seven years.[25] Forcible entry into the possessions of another was regarded as a breach of the peace and was punishable accordingly at the discretion of the court.[26] Lands and goods of "theeves and fellons" were liable to confiscation in order to render satisfaction to injured parties, and, if they possessed no property, such offenders were to be set at work in the workhouse until satisfaction was rendered.[27]

The longest list of crimes and penalties related to offences against public morality. Especially severe were the penalties imposed for the sexual "crimes." The punishment imposed for "defiling the marriage bed" was whipping and one year's imprisonment for the first offence and life imprisonment for the second.[28] Incest was punished by forfeiture of half one's estate and one year's imprisonment for the first offence and life imprisonment for the second.[29] Sodomy and bestiality were penalized by forfeiture of one third of the offender's estate and six months' imprisonment for the first offence and life imprisonment for the second.[30] Rape was punishable by forfeiture of one third of the offender's estate and one year's imprisonment for the first offence and life imprisonment for a repetition of the offence.[31] Even the first offence of bigamy was to be punished by life imprison-

24 *Charter and Laws,* p. 112.
25 Ibid.
26 Ibid., pp. 112-13.
27 Ibid., p. 112.
28 Ibid., pp. 109-10.
29 Ibid., p. 110.
30 Ibid.
31 Ibid.

ment.[32] The penalty for fornication was not provided in the code of 1682, but in the additions made in March, 1683, it was provided that fornication should be punished by "enjoining marriage, or fine, or corporal punishment, or all or any of these at the discretion of the county court." [33] The various types of profanity were all penalized by a fine of five shillings or five days' imprisonment at hard labor, on a bread and water diet.[34] The first offence of drunkenness was to be punished by a fine of five shillings or by five days' imprisonment at hard labor on bread and water. All subsequent offences were punishable by a doubling of the penalty for the previous offence.[35] Those inn-keepers or others who allowed drunkenness to go on at their houses were also to receive the same punishment as the drunkard.[36] It was also provided that "if any person shall drink healths, which may provoke people to unnecessary and excessive drinking," he should be punished by a fine of five shillings and the pledger of the health likewise.[37] In spite of these restrictions on excessive drinking, cheap beer was assured by the provision that "all strong beer and ale made of barley malt shall be sold for not above two pennies Sterling for a full Winchester quart." [38] It was further decreed that, whereas selling liquor to Indians tended "to make the poor natives worse, and not better for their coming among them, which is a heinous offence to God, and a reproach to the blessed name of Christ, and his holy religion," any one convicted of so doing was to be fined five pounds.[39] No law against smoking was enacted in 1682, but in 1696 it was provided that any one detected smoking in the streets by day or night was to be fined twelve pence, and fines were to

32 Ibid., pp. 110-11.
33 Ibid., p. 145.
34 Ibid., pp. 108-9.
35 Ibid., p. 111.
36 Ibid.
37 Ibid.
38 Ibid., pp. 115-16.
39 Ibid., pp. 111-12.

be used in buying apparatus for fire protection.[40] The Quaker prejudice against games and theaters appears in the decree that "whosoever shall introduce into this province, or frequent such rude and riotous sports and practices as prizes, stage-plays, masques, revels, bull-baitings, and such like" shall be regarded as peace breakers, to be fined at least twenty shillings or to suffer ten days' imprisonment at hard labor.[41] It was further provided that "If any person be convicted of playing at cards, dice, lotteries, or such like enticing, vain, and evil sports and games, such persons shall pay five shillings or suffer five days' imprisonment in the house of correction." [42] Suitable punishment, consisting of fine or imprisonment, was also provided for lying, sedition, speaking slightingly of magistrates, scandalous reporting and scolding, bribery, and extortion.[43]

The wide reliance upon imprisonment as a mode of punishment is evident throughout the separate enactments of this code, and it was an epoch-making departure in criminal procedure. Excepting only the closely related Quaker colony of West Jersey, this code of 1682 in Pennsylvania unquestionably marks the first instance in the history of criminal jurisprudence in which imprisonment at hard labor was prescribed as a punishment for a majority of the acts which were branded as crimes by the community.[44]

The legal regulations for the adjustment of civil actions and disputes were not extensively included in this first code of 1682, but were embraced in the act of March, 1683.[45]

In addition to the court system, the law of 1682 made the following provisions regarding procedure in criminal cases. The testimony of two witnesses was required to

40 *Charter and Laws,* p. 260.
41 Ibid., p. 114.
42 Ibid.
43 Ibid., pp. 114-17.
44 Barnes, op. cit., p. 351.
45 *Charter and Laws,* pp. 127 ff.

establish proof in any case. Perjury was punished by the penalty which the accused did receive or might have received, satisfaction to the wronged party, exposure as a false witness, and disability from further right to testify in the courts of the province. Trials were to be by jury. In criminal cases the grand jury was composed of twenty-four, of which twelve must declare the accused guilty. Forty-eight jurors were to be impaneled for the trial jury, from which twelve were to be selected for the trial, unless fewer than that number remained after "reasonable challenges had been admitted." In that case a new panel had to be enrolled.[46]

While there were many additions and some changes in details, yet, when looked at from the broad standpoint of sociology and jurisprudence, this Quaker code of 1682 may be said to have persisted as the basis of criminal procedure in the province until 1718.[47] Though Penn was suspended from power between 1692 and 1694, Governor Fletcher, who was appointed to take his place, permitted the re-enactment of an almost identical code in June, 1693.[48] It was again confirmed by the act of November 27, 1700.[49] Though this law was repealed by the Crown, it was re-enacted on January 12, 1706, and remained in force until 1718.[50] The general tendency, however, in these successive acts was to increase the severity of the penalties and to introduce the more barbarous types of corporal punishment, such as branding, which had not appeared in the codes of 1682 and 1683. Terms of im-

46 Ibid., pp. 116-17. What was probably the first, and perhaps the only, instance of a jury of women in the American colonies occurred in Delaware County in 1689. An unusual circumstance called it into existence. A young woman was on trial for "carnal intercourse" and a jury of women was called to discover whether or not she was pregnant. They reported "that they cannot find she is, neither be they sure she is not." Punishment was accordingly delayed. George Smith, *A History of Delaware County*, p. 174.

47 Bolles, op. cit., pp. 257-8.

48 *Charter and Laws*, pp. 192-220.

49 *The Statutes at Large of Pennsylvania*, compiled by Mitchell and Flanders, Vol. II, pp. 3 ff.

50 Ibid, pp. 171 ff.

prisonment became longer and, though the death penalty was not inflicted on white inhabitants for any crime except murder until 1718, it was applied to negroes after 1700 if they were found guilty of murder, rape, buggery, or burglary.[51] By thus widening the application of the death penalty to what was regarded by them as an inferior race the provincial authorities accustomed themselves to its extension to their own kind a few years later. After a careful investigation of the changes in the penalties inflicted and in the degree of punishment prescribed in the period between 1682 and 1718, one is less likely than before to accept the popular conception that there was a total break with precedents in criminal jurisprudence in the law of 1718.[52] While the Quaker theories did prevail down to that date in a majority of cases, there can be no doubt that the transition to the English and Puritan system was being prepared for in the two previous decades.

4. *The Re-establishment of the Anglican and Puritan Codes, 1718*

The act of May 31, 1718, which brought the English criminal code into operation in Pennsylvania, was the product of the peculiar Quaker aversion to taking an oath and was one phase of the struggle between the Anglicans and Quakers. Down to the beginning of the reign of George I, in 1714, the Quakers had normally enjoyed the right of affirmation, but in 1715 an act was passed by Parliament which forbade affirmation as a qualification in criminal procedure and this act was extended in its application to the colonies. Governor Gookin was determined to carry out the royal decree, the provincial officers rebelled against it, and the administration of justice in

51 *The Statutes at Large of Pennsylvania,* Vol. II, pp. 79, 235.
52 For a somewhat different view see Bolles, op. cit., p. 258.

Pennsylvania was disrupted.[53] Dr. Bolles thus summarizes the dispute:

> This construction, which was maintained by the governor, and shut out many from their offices, and even from the protection of the law, threw the Province into confusion. The governor refused to administer the affirmation as a qualification for office; the judges refused to sit in criminal cases; the administration of justice was suspended, and two atrocious murderers remained in jail three years without trial. The Assembly was alarmed; but it resolutely asserted the rights of the people, and at length Gookin was recalled.[54]

Governor Keith, who was appointed in 1716, advised the assembly that the best method of inducing the Crown to grant the right of affirmation would be to adopt the English criminal code. This advice was accepted, and David Lloyd, the chief justice of the supreme court, was delegated to draw up a bill which would embody the criminal laws of England. His work was accepted and the bill became law on May 31, 1718.[55] By a strange coincidence Penn died in the same year that his advanced criminal jurisprudence was being uprooted. Professor Shepherd has made the following pertinent comment on this point:

> Indeed, there seems a melancholy significance about the fact that, as the life of William Penn, whose legislation marked by justice tempered with mercy, has been the admiration of the civilized world, was slowly ebbing away, his cherished ideals of humanitarianism were being ruthlessly destroyed and replaced by the gloomy severity of the Middle Ages.[56]

53 William R. Shepherd, *A History of Proprietary Government in Pennsylvania,* pp. 361-7; W. T. Root, *The Relations of Pennsylvania with the British Government, 1696-1765,* pp. 248 ff.

54 Bolles, op. cit., p. 257.

55 Shepherd, op. cit., pp. 388-9; Bolles, op. cit., pp. 255-7; Root, op. cit., pp. 248-53; *Charter and Laws,* pp. 371-82; *Statutes at Large,* Vol. III, pp. 199-221.

56 Shepherd, op. cit., p. 389.

The intent and purpose of the new criminal code was stated in the following words:

Whereas it is a settled point, that the common law is the birthright of English subjects, so it ought to be their rule in British dominions; but acts of Parliament have been adjudged not to extend to these plantations, unless they are particularly named in such acts.

Now forasmuch as some persons have been encouraged to transgress certain statutes against capital crimes, and other enormities, because those statutes have not hitherto been fully extended to this province.

Therefore, lest there should be any further failure in that behalf, may it please the Governor that it be enacted. . . .[57]

Though the right of affirmation was guaranteed, this concession was much more than offset by the complete adoption of the barbarous severity of the criminal code of England and of the Puritans in other American colonies. The new code was even more rigorous than that contained in the Duke of York's laws promulgated in 1676. In the Duke's laws twelve offences had been designated as capital, while in the code of 1718 no less than thirteen crimes were declared to be capital. The list included the various degrees of treason, murder, manslaughter by stabbing, serious maiming, highway robbery, burglary, arson, sodomy, buggery, rape, concealing the death of a bastard child, advising the killing of such a child, and witchcraft. Larceny was the only felony which was not made a capital crime. This was made punishable by restitution, fine, whipping, and imprisonment.[58] Counterfeiting of paper money and gold and silver coin was made a capital crime by the laws of September 21, 1756, and February 21, 1767,[59] and, with this addition, the sanguinary criminal code remained in existence until after

57 *Charter and Laws,* p. 371.

58 Ibid., pp. 372-82.

59 *Statutes at Large,* Vol. V, pp. 247-8. Vol. VII, p. 91.

the close of the provincial period, when a reforming era was initiated by the act of September 15, 1786.[60] The practice of whipping, branding, and mutilation for the punishment of lesser crimes, which was already growing up by 1718, was continued with general uniformity throughout the period.

In addition to the greater severity of the punishment, which became the rule after 1718, it should be noted that the penalties imposed were such that there was little need for penal institutions adapted to the substitution of imprisonment for corporal punishment. There is, accordingly, no difficulty in understanding why the "common gaol" rather than the workhouse became the typical penal institution of provincial Pennsylvania in the eighteenth century.[61] Mr. J. F. Watson, in his interesting compilation of provincial customs, originally published in 1830, offers the following observations upon the barbarous modes of punishment which prevailed down to the Revolutionary period:

> These barbarous measures of punishment were not in accordance with the spirit and feelings of our forefathers, who early aimed at commuting work and confinement for crime; but the parent country, familiar with its sanguinary code, always revoked the laws formed upon our schemes of reformation. These punishments, therefore, generally prevailed till the time of our self-government, when measures were speedily taken, first by societies of citizens, and afterwards by the Legislature to introduce those reforms into prison discipline which have made our city and state to be celebrated for its early "Penitentiary System."[62]

60 Ibid., Vol. XII, pp. 280-90.

61 Futhey and Cope assert that after 1718 in Chester County, which may be taken as typical of the eastern part of the state, whipping was the conventional punishment for all crimes other than capital. *History of Chester County*, p. 406.

62 J. F. Watson, *Annals of Philadelphia*, revised and enlarged by W. P. Hazard, 1898, Vol. I, pp. 361-2. Cf. Bolles, op. cit., pp. 258-9.

II. THE PENAL INSTITUTIONS

1. *The Origins of the Colonial Penal Institutions*

In a manner very similar to the development of the criminal codes in the colonial period, the evolution of penal institutions in provincial Pennsylvania passed through three main stages of evolution. The typical detention jail of contemporary England was provided for in the Duke's laws of 1676. This institution was replaced by the Quaker workhouse, or house of correction, in 1682, and the workhouse remained for about thirty years the basis of the system of penal institutions. After 1718, however, when the criminal code was altered so as to substitute corporal punishment for imprisonment in most instances, the jail reappeared and became the conventional penal institution of the province until the close of the colonial era. Even the few workhouses which remained or were constructed later were not penal institutions, but a part of the system of social relief designed for the repression of vagrants, paupers and unruly servants. But the theory and practice of imprisonment and the workhouse were not lost and both were speedily revived after the Revolution.

The first legislation relative to penal institutions in Pennsylvania occurs in the laws of the Duke of York, promulgated on September 25, 1676. Here it was decreed that,

> Every town shall at their charge provide a pair of stocks for offenders, and a pound for the impounding of cattle; and prisons and pillories are likewise to be provided in these towns where the several courts of sessions are to be holden.[63]

There was thus introduced into the province the conventional English detention jail of the period. It was

[63] *Charter and Laws* p. 47.

simply an institution for the "safekeeping" of accused persons during the interval between meetings of the court. As has already been pointed out, the penalties imposed by the code of 1676 were almost exclusively fines or corporal punishment and there was no need for penal institutions adapted to the permanent imprisonment of criminals. If the provisions of the above clause were carried out, there must have been three of these detention jails or prisons in Pennsylvania from 1676 to 1682, as court was held at New Castle, Whorekill, and Upland.[64] From the very beginning of Penn's administration the detention jail was supplanted, in law, at least, by the workhouse or house of correction as the basic penal institution. Even in the laws which Penn and his fellow Quakers had "agreed upon in England" in May, 1682, it was declared that "all prisons shall be workhouses for felons, vagrants, and loose and idle persons; whereof one shall be in every county" and that "all prisons shall be free, as to fees, food, and lodging."[65] It should be noted that, under Penn's application and interpretation, the workhouse became a true penal institution no longer limited to the treatment of the destitute and vagrant classes.

The above provisions were enacted with some slight changes as a part of the "Great Law" of December, 1682. Here it was stipulated that,

> All prisons shall be workhouses for felons, thiefs, vagrants, and loose, abusive and idle persons, whereof one shall be in every county.
>
> Gaolers shall not oppress their prisoners, and all prisons shall be free as to room, and all prisoners shall have liberty

[64] G. E. Howard, *Local Constitutional History of the United States,* pp. 368-70.

[65] *Charter and Laws,* p. 100. It is generally asserted that Penn derived his convictions as to the value of imprisonment and the workhouse system from his early travels in Holland, where he had observed the use of the workhouses as agencies for the repression of pauperism and for the employment of prisoners detained for trial. Richard Vaux, *Brief Sketch of the Origin and History of the State Penitentiary for the Eastern District of Pennsylvania,* p. 28.

to provide themselves, bedding, food, and other necessaries, during their imprisonment, except such whose punishment by law, will not admit of that liberty.[66]

The detention jail was not eliminated by this enactment, to be sure, as it had to be retained for holding accused persons for trial.[67] With the single exception of the law of November, 1681, in the neighboring Quaker colony of West Jersey, this act of December 1682 in Pennsylvania may be regarded as the first instance of the fusion of the workhouse and the prison and the consequent creation of the basis of the modern prison system.[68] The nearest competitor for chronological priority was Pope Clement XI, who, in 1704, established a combination prison and workhouse at San Michele in Rome.[69]

In the supplement to the "Great Law," which was enacted by the assembly in March 1683, there was a more specific and compulsory clause relating to the construction of workhouses. It was provided,

That every county within this province of Pennsylvania and territories thereunto belonging, shall before the last day of the tenth month, next ensuing, at their own cost and charge, erect, build or cause to be built in the most convenient place in each county, respective, a sufficient house, at least twenty foot square, for restraint, correction, labour, and punishment of all such persons as shall be thereunto committed by law; and that every county failing herein shall forfeit and pay forty pounds, to be levied on the goods and chattels of the inhabitants of such county.[70]

The provisions of the laws of 1682 and 1683 with respect to workhouses were retained without change in the laws promulgated by Governor Fletcher in June 1693.[71]

66 *Charter and Laws,* p. 121.
67 Ibid., p. 120.
68 Barnes, op. cit., p. 34, 351 note.
69 Wines, *Punishment and Reformation,* pp. 121-2.
70 *Charter and Laws,* pp. 202, 208.
71 Ibid., pp. 139-40.

They were also confirmed and retained without alteration in the laws of November 27, 1700,[72] and January 12, 1706,[73] with the exception that in 1706 an allowance of two pence per day was made for the support of each prisoner. It was also stipulated in 1706 that the jails should serve as workhouses until the latter should be erected. From this provision and from many other sources of evidence it must be concluded that even before 1718 there had come about a differentiation between the workhouse and the jail, with the latter the more common institution of the two. When the criminal code was altered by the act of May 31, 1718, and fines and corporal punishment were substituted for imprisonment as the typical mode of punishment, the workhouse tended to disappear, and, where it was retained, became an institution for repressing vagrants, paupers and incorrigible servants rather than a true penal institution. It seems that it was in Philadelphia alone that the workhouse was retained throughout the greater part of the provincial period somewhat according to the original conception of Penn. As the jail or county prison was much the more usual institution and the real basis of the penal system of provincial Pennsylvania from 1718 to 1776, attention will next be directed to the mode of the legal organization of the county jail system.

2. *The Legal Foundations of Colonial Penal Institutions*

The first complete organizing law creating a county jail in Pennsylvania was that of March 20, 1725, which decreed that a courthouse and a jail should be erected in Newtown in Bucks County. As this act became the model for all subsequent acts authorizing the erection of county jails, it is worthy of an extended analysis. It was declared that,

72 *Statutes at Large,* II, pp. 99-100.
73 Ibid., p. 243.

It shall and may be lawful to and for the said Jeremiah Langhorne, William Biles, Joseph Kirkbride, Thomas Watson, and Abraham Chapman or any three of them to purchase and take assurance to them and their heirs a piece of land situated in some convenient place in the said township of Newtown, in trust and for the use of the said county, and thereon to erect and build or cause to be built, a courthouse and prison sufficient to accommodate the public service of the said county and for the ease and conveniency of the inhabitants.

For the defraying the charge of purchasing the land, building and erecting the courthouse and prison aforesaid, it shall and may be lawful to and for the commissioners and assessors of the said county or a majority of them, who are hereby required to assess and levy so much money as the said trustees or any three of them shall judge necessary for purchasing the land and finishing the said courthouse and prison: provided always, the sum of money so raised do not exceed three hundred pounds current money of the province.[74]

The method then of providing for the erection of a county jail consisted in the appointment of a board of five special commissioners or trustees who were authorized to purchase the required land and estimate the cost of the jail. The sum thus determined was raised in the same manner as any part of the county rate, namely by the county commissioners and assessors.

The eight remaining acts passed during the provincial period providing for the erection of new county jails were modelled directly after this act of 1725, retaining even the same phraseology. All the subsequent jails erected were those which had to be provided for newly created counties, and the act authorizing the building of the jail was uniformly embodied in the general act creating and organizing the administration of the new county.

[74] *Statutes at Large*, IV, pp. 9-10.

The following acts, passed between 1725 and 1773, provided for the erection of a new county jail in the newly created counties:—Lancaster county by the act of May 10, 1729; York county by an act of August 19, 1749; Cumberland county by an act of January 27, 1750; Berks county by an act of March 11, 1752; Northampton county also by an act of March 11, 1752; Bedford county by an act of March 9, 1771; Northumberland county by an act of March 21, 1772; Westmoreland county by an act of February 26, 1773.[75] The only variations in any of these acts were that in the case of Lancaster county only four trustees were provided for, and that Northampton county was allowed four hundred and fifty pounds instead of three hundred pounds with which to build its courthouse and jail.[76] Therefore, nine of the eleven counties of provincial Pennsylvania had county jails distinct from the workhouse or house of correction. In Philadelphia and Chester counties it appears that the jail and the workhouse were combined in a single plant.[77]

After the act of January 12, 1706, there was no more legislation concerning workhouses until the act of February 27, 1718, was passed.[78] This act bears much the same relation to the subsequent workhouse acts that the law of March 20, 1725, holds to the later jail legislation. There was a great and fundamental difference, however, between the nature of the workhouse described in the act of 1706 and the type of institution contemplated in that of 1718. The workhouse provided for in the act of 1718 was no longer the Quaker institution for the imprisonment of criminals at hard labor, but was the typical European workhouse for the repression of vagrants and

[75] For the above eight acts see *seriatim* the following: *Statutes at Large*, IV, pp. 133-4; V, pp. 73-76, 90-93, 136-9, 143-6; VIII, pp. 48-52, 146-9, 316-20.

[76] *Statutes at Large*, VI, pp. 276-7.

[77] Ibid., III, pp. 168-9; VIII, p. 300.

[78] Ibid., pp. 167-171.

paupers. It was enacted that the workhouses and houses of correction to be erected should be

> Used and employed for the keeping, correcting, and setting to work of all rogues, vagabonds, or sturdy beggars, and other idle and disorderly persons, who by the laws and usage of Great Britain, or by the laws of this province, are to be kept, corrected or set to work, in such houses and back-sides.[79]

While the Quaker sentiment and traditions were strong enough to retain in Philadelphia, and to some extent in Chester county, something of the older organization and function of the workhouse of the late seventeenth century, as established by Penn, there can be no doubt that by 1718 the Quaker system of penal institutions and penal administration had begun to disintegrate, much as their criminal jurisprudence was shattered by the code of March 31st of the same year. The year 1718, then, may be taken as the most convenient date for marking the submergence of Quaker jurisprudence and penology and the ascendancy of the Puritan and English system in the province of Pennsylvania.

The act of February 27, 1718, providing for the erection of workhouses in the provinces declared in its enacting clause,

> Whereas the proprietary and first adventurers in their principal model of this government proposed that for crimes inferior to murder, the punishment might be by way of restitution, fine, imprisonment, and such like; and where the offender proved not of ability to make such satisfaction then he should be kept in prison or a house of correction at hard labor; but no effectual care hath been yet taken to erect such houses, by reason whereof many evil doers escape unpunished, and servants, who, for their neglect and abuses should be kept at work in such houses, are become incorrigible, and

[79] *Statutes at Large*, p. 168.

therefore may it please the governor that it may be enacted. . . .[80]

To provide for the much needed workhouses, it was enacted that the justices, or a majority of them, meeting in the next quarter sessions after May 1, 1718, might "set down and make orders for building, erecting, or causing to be built and erected or provided, one or more houses of correction and workhouses, with convenient backsides or yards thereunto adjoining, in some convenient places within their several counties or towns corporate." The order of the justices to provide money for the building of the workhouses was to be honored by the county authorities and the sum needed was to be raised as a part of the county rate.[81] It was further specifically enacted that within three years after March 25, 1718, a house of correction or workhouse should be built at Philadelphia in Philadelphia county, at Chester in Chester county, and at Bristol in Bucks county.[82]

These prospective workhouses were to be put under the control of a "president, a treasurer, and assistants," to be appointed by a majority of the justices of the county assembled in a quarter session from "the most able and honest inhabitants and freeholders of the said counties." The said president, treasurer and assistants were to constitute a "body politic and corporate in law to all intents and purposes" with all the legal characteristics and power of a corporation.[83] The corporation was to be responsible to the justices of the county, who were to inspect the corporate accounts at each quarter session and punish and dismiss offenders. At least one member of the corporation was "to give punctual and constant attention at

80 Ibid., p. 167. In spite of the phraseology of this law the workhouses were not employed as penal institutions except in Philadelphia and Chester counties.

81 Ibid., p. 168.

82 Ibid., pp. 168-9.

83 Ibid., pp. 169-70.

the workhouse and house of correction to which they respectively belong." This member of the corporation was to have general charge of the administration of the workhouse and of the discipline of the inmates. He was to present a quarterly report to the justices. The corporation as a whole was to estimate the amount of money needed to operate the workhouse and to present the estimate to the justices, who reviewed it and passed it on to the commissioners and assessors to be raised as a part of the county rate.[84] The governing corporation was further empowered to employ such officers as they needed to assist them in operating and administering the workhouse, to determine and allow their pay, to remove them for cause and to appoint their successors.[85] The sheriff, constables and all other officers of justice were ordered to give all proper aid and assistance to the corporation. No specific information was contained in the act relative to the type of work on which the inmates were to be engaged, but provision was made for the purchasing of the original stock with which to begin work and for obtaining the future supplies of raw material which would be required.[86]

As has been pointed out above, this act of February 27, 1718, was the general organizing law governing the establishment of workhouses in provincial Pennsylvania until 1767. The next act based upon this precedent was that of March 7, 1746, which was rendered necessary by the failure of Bucks county to carry out the provisions of the act of 1718. It declared that no workhouse had been erected in Bristol, as had been directed in 1718, and authorized the burgesses of Bristol to proceed with the establishment of such an institution. Its government was

[84] *Statutes at Large,* pp. 169-70.

[85] Ibid., p. 171. Futhey and Cope, however, state that the first keeper of the Chester county workhouse was appointed by the court of quarter sessions with the consent of the county commissioners and assessors. *A History of Chester County,* p. 411.

[86] *Statutes at Large,* III, p. 170.

to be the same as that provided for the government of the workhouses created by the act of 1718.[87]

An act of March 4, 1763, declared that the county of Lancaster

> had suffered most grievously, as well by unruly disobedient servants, as by idle strolling vagrants from divers parts who have taken shelter in that county and borough; and drunkenness, profane swearing, breach of the Sabbath, tumults, and other vices so much prevail that it is not in the power of the magistrates to suppress them and preserve peace and good order, having no house of correction for the punishment of such offenders.

To correct these abuses the justices were authorized to provide for the erection of a workhouse and to appoint a corporation to administer it.[88]

The general procedure in erecting workhouses in Pennsylvania was systematized by an act of February 21, 1767, which remained the legal basis for the establishment of such institutions in the state until it was superseded by an act of June 26, 1895. It was provided that if a grand jury at any court of quarter sessions should decide that a new workhouse ought to be erected or an existing one repaired or extended, they should make such recommendation to the justices of the court of quarter sessions and the county commissioners and assessors. If the justices, commissioners and assessors agreed with the recommendation of the grand jury, the money required to erect, extend or repair the workhouse was to be raised as a part of the county rate. The justices of the court of quarter sessions were empowered to appoint "some capable, discreet, and prudent person to be keeper of such workhouse." It was the duty of the keeper to furnish materials for the employment of the inmates, to sell the products,

[87] Ibid., V, pp. 31-38.
[88] Ibid., VI, pp. 280-282.

and to turn over the proceeds to the county treasury. The salary of the keeper was to be determined by the justices of the court of quarter sessions. In the workhouse were to be confined all "idle and disorderly persons, rogues and vagabonds." [89]

The last workhouse act of the provincial period was that of February 26, 1773, to erect a "new gaol, workhouse, and house of correction in the city of Philadelphia." [90] It should be noted that this act of 1773 was both a workhouse and a jail act. This is to be accounted for by the fact that in Philadelphia, while the jail and the workhouse occupied separate buildings, they were enclosed by the same wall and constituted a part of the same penal institution. The act stated that

> It has been represented to the Assembly that the gaol and workhouse in the City of Philadelphia are insufficient for the safe custody of the criminals and others committed to the same, and that from the smallness of the lot of ground, the inconveniency of the buildings and inner apartments and the increased number of persons confined therein, the health not only of the said prisoners, but of the inhabitants of the said city is greatly endangered.

To remove these abuses it was enacted that the commissioners of the county of Philadelphia were authorized to raise funds to

> purchase a lot of ground in some convenient part of the city and erect thereon a commodious, strong and sufficient gaol, workhouse, and house of correction, with a good yard to each of them, inclosed by walls of proper height and strength for confining and detaining in safe custody all felons, criminals, and others who shall be committed to the said gaol and workhouse.[91]

89 *Statutes at Large,* VII, pp. 86-87.
90 Ibid., VIII, pp. 300-304.
91 Ibid., pp. 300-301.

This act is unusually important in the history of penology, as the new jail and workhouse, which was created as a result, was the famous Walnut street jail, in which the first American experiments were conducted with respect to the system of solitary confinement.

Therefore, while every county of provincial Pennsylvania was provided with a county jail, only Philadelphia, Chester, Bucks and Lancaster counties erected workhouses, and only in the case of those at Philadelphia and Chester is there any reliable evidence that they retained to the slightest degree their original character as penal institutions. The characteristic penal institution of eighteenth-century Pennsylvania was the county jail or prison.

3. *The Administrative System of the Provincial Penal Institutions*

The legal basis of the administrative system of the provincial penal institutions has already been presented in the survey of the organizing laws; a brief summary of this aspect of penal administration will suffice at this point.

With respect to the provincial jails, the general control of the physical property was placed in the hands of five trustees and their heirs and assignees. These trustees were named in the general act creating the county. The trustees were also vested with the responsibility of keeping up the property and authorizing the raising of the required funds for this purpose. The money was to be raised by the county commissioners and assessors as a part of the county rate.[92] The actual administrative control of the jail was vested in the sheriff, but he usually delegated this function to an undersheriff or a "gaol keeper."[93] The classes of persons received in the jails

[92] Ibid., IV, pp. 9-10, 133-4; V, pp. 73-6, 90-93, 136-9, 143-6; VIII, pp. 48-52, 146-9, 316-20.

[93] Ibid., IV, pp. 179 ff.

of provincial Pennsylvania were highly diverse. They included debtors, those accused of all types of crimes who were awaiting trial at the regular court session and "gaol delivery," those convicted of capital crimes awaiting execution, and the very few convicted criminals that had been sentenced to imprisonment instead of receiving the more usual penalty of some brutal type of corporal punishment. It is quite unnecessary to add that no differentiation was made in the treatment of prisoners on the basis of age, sex, degree of mental stability, or grade of criminality. Roberts Vaux, writing in 1826, thus describes this wholly deplorable and vicious situation which existed fifty years earlier:—

What a spectacle must this abode of guilt and wretchedness have presented, when in one common herd were kept by day and night prisoners of all ages, colors and sexes? No separation was made of the most flagrant offender and convict, from the prisoner who might, perhaps, be falsely suspected of some trifling misdemeanor; none of the old and hardened culprits from the youthful, trembling novice in crime; none even of the fraudulent swindler from the unfortunate and possibly the most estimable debtor; and when intermingled with all these, in one corrupt and corrupting assemblage were to be found the disgusting object of popular contempt, besmeared with filth from the pillory—the unhappy victim of the lash, streaming with blood from the whipping post—the half-naked vagrant—the loathsome drunkard—the sick, suffering from various bodily pains, and too often the unaneled malefactor, whose precious hours of probation had been numbered by his earthly judge.[94]

In view of the foregoing description nothing needs to be said about penal discipline in provincial days, for such a thing could not well exist. The same might be said of

[94] *Notices of the Original and Successive Attempts to Improve the Discipline of the Prison at Philadelphia, and to Reform the Criminal Code of Pennsylvania, with a few Observations on the Penitentiary System.* Philadelphia. 1826.

penal labor in the provincial jails. Demoralizing idleness was the vicious partner of the corrupting intermingling and herding of inmates in this unspeakable situation in the colonial jails. The following paragraph summarizes the condition as presented by some of the most eminent of early Pennsylvania jurists in 1828:—

> The alteration of the criminal code which took place in 1718, in consequence of the pertinacious attachment of the British government to capital punishments, seems in practice to have restored the dominion of idleness in the interior of our prisons; for although to some minor offences, the punishment of confinement a short period at hard labor was annexed, yet the concurrent testimony of all who remember its condition, represents the provincial prison of Philadelphia as a scene of profligacy and license, in which all sexes, ages and colors were confounded without classification, without labor, and without restraint.[95]

The customary extortion and other conventional abuses of the jail system were not absent from the jails of provincial Pennsylvania. The sheriffs exacted excessive fees from those confined, sometimes even compelling them to live in the sheriff's own house or in taverns, and to make such payment for their keep as the sheriff or innkeeper demanded. Within the jail itself the sheriff or "gaol keeper" frequently "oppressed" the inmates by exorbitant charges, by personal favoritism and other well-known means. He often tried to swell his income by establishing a well-equipped bar in the jail, over which he sold liquor to the prisoners, and assured himself of their trade by forbidding them to obtain drink from outside.[96] Wealthy prisoners might readily obtain immunity from the degradation of confinement in the "common gaol" by bribing the sheriff to allow them to live in a tavern or

[95] *Report of the Commissioners on the Penal Code, with the Accompanying Documents,* Harrisburg, 1828, p. 12.
[96] Watson, *Annals of Philadelphia,* III, p. 178.

private house under only the most general surveillance of the officers of the law.

To eliminate most of these abuses was the main purpose of the act of February 14, 1730. It was thereby enacted that the sheriff should not take a prisoner to "any tavern, alehouse, or other public victualing or drinking house or to the private house of any sheriff, undersheriff or gaolkeeper without the voluntary consent of the person so taken and arrested." The sheriff was further directed to allow any prisoner to "send for and have any beer, ale, victuals, or any other necessary food from what place they please; and also to have and use such bedding, linen, and other things as he or she shall think fit." [97] The sheriff was forbidden to sell strong drink in the jail or to allow it to be sold in the jail by others.[98] The sheriff or "gaoler" was forbidden to take any fees except those determined by the justices of the county. These legal fees were to be displayed in a public place in the jail where they could be easily read by the inmates and the citizens. Finally, it was stipulated that the sheriff should not hold office for more than three years in succession, and that after he had held office for three successive years, at least three years must elapse before he could again be qualified to serve.[99] It should be noted that this reform act did not prevent wealthy and prominent delinquents from buying the privilege of confinement outside of the jails. Nor was it successful in preventing the sheriff or "gaoler" from maintaining a bar in the jail. Even as late as 1788, it is stated on the best authority that a well-equipped bar was maintained in the Philadelphia jail.[100] There is no reason for thinking that the act was any more efficacious in entirely eliminating extortion from the administration of the county jail system.

[97] *Statutes at Large,* IV, pp. 179, 180.
[98] Ibid., p. 182.
[99] Ibid., pp. 180-181, 183.
[100] *Report of Commissioners on the Penal Code,* p. 13.

Some conception of the brutal treatment of prisoners may be derived from the fact that in 1770 there was one death from starvation in the Philadelphia jail, while in 1772 three prisoners died from the same cause.[101]

A fair idea of the fees paid to the sheriff or jailor for his services in caring for a prisoner in the colonial period may be obtained from the following bill presented by the jailor of Chester county in 1736:—

Chester County Dr.
To Nathan Worley.

For maintaining Joseph Bivan from the 13th day of October, 1736, to the 2nd day of July, 1737.

	£	s	d
To Turn Kee fees for every capital crime...	0	10	0
To King's allowance 260 days @ 2d. per day.	2	3	4
To fireing and cloathing for him all winter..	2	3	4
To taking four pairs of irons off him when he was to be executed....................	0	6	0
To a shirt and pair of trousers for him when he was executed—for he was naked......	0	10	0
	5	12	8

The standard fee at that time for executing a condemned criminal was five pounds. Incidental expenses at an execution, such as erecting gallows, making a coffin, digging a grave, and conducting the funeral, amounted to twenty pence.[102]

An act of February 24, 1770, ordered that the sheriff or jailor should be allowed three pence per day for the maintenance of all persons imprisoned after the conviction of any criminal offence. This was to be raised from the county rate and paid to the sheriff.[103]

101 Scharf and Westcott, *A History of Philadelphia*, III, p. 1826.
102 Futhey and Cope, *History of Chester County*, p. 410.
103 *Statutes at Large*, VII, pp. 346-7.

The authority to establish workhouses was vested in the justices of the court of quarter sessions in each county. They were to estimate the amount of money needed for this purpose and to order the county commissioners and assessors to raise it as a part of the county rate. The general control over each workhouse was vested in a corporation appointed by the justices from the more prominent freeholders of the county. This corporation was to estimate the necessary annual expenses of the operation of the workhouse and submit it to the critical revision of the justices, who were to transmit it to the county commissioners and assessors to be raised in the county rate. The immediate supervision of the institution was vested in one active member of the corporation who was required by law to be present and regulate its administration. The details of the administration were delegated to the officers appointed, paid and dismissed by the corporation.[104] It has been shown above that, at least after 1718, the workhouses were employed almost exclusively for the repression of the vagrants, paupers and disorderly servants and not in any considerable degree to receive and punish the criminal classes. In other words, from 1718 to 1790, the workhouses were scarcely a part of the system of penal institutions.[105]

There is no evidence that there was any systematic differentiation in the treatment of the "rogues, vagabonds, sturdy beggars and other idle and disorderly persons" who were admitted to the workhouses. Nor is there any specific information available as to the type of work performed by those confined in the workhouses. One can only reconstruct the possible types of labor from a consideration of the method of employing inmates of the European workhouses of the time and the employment later used in the state penitentiaries. From these "com-

104 *Statutes at Large,* III, pp. 167-71; V, pp. 31-8; VI, p. 280.
105 Ibid., p. 168.

parative" sources of information it may be supposed that the work varied from the more rough types of manual labor, such as grinding grain, pounding stone, the coarser weaving and spinning, and "cordwaining" or cobbling, to labor which was in no sense productive but was adopted purely for its supposed deterrent value, such as running a tread-mill, turning a friction crank, and carrying heavy weights back and forth across the yard of the work-house.[106]

4. *Descriptive Details Concerning the Provincial Penal Institutions*

As the significance of Pennsylvania in the history of penology lies almost entirely in the experiments and advances made in the various institutions located in the city of Philadelphia, it is particularly gratifying that the most complete and specific knowledge is possessed of the successive penal institutions there erected, from the first "cage" of 1682 to the Eastern Penitentiary at Cherry Hill. This information enables the student to reconstruct the record of the entire evolution of modern penal institutions, and of those ideas and practices which constitute the body of modern penal philosophy.

The first record of a penal institution in Pennsylvania is the order of the council, on November 16, 1682, that "William Clayton, one of the Provincial Council, should build a cage against the next council-day, of seven feet long by five feet broad."[107] This was but a temporary expedient, and some time in the interval between 1682 and 1685 Lassy Cock was authorized to build a county jail in Philadelphia at an expense of sixty pounds. That this building was deemed insufficient by the time of its

[106] Cf. Wines, op. cit., pp. 115-18. G. Ives, *History of Penal Methods*, pp. 188 ff.

[107] Watson, *Annals of Philadelphia*, I, p. 356.

completion is evident from the following action of the provincial authorities:

At the eighth court 2nd of 7th mo. 1685.—The Grand Jury agree, that in lieu of sixty pounds to be paid Lassy Cock, for building of a log house in Second street intended for a county gaol, he shall have the said log house with the ground it stands on, with the spot of ground adjacent, and a legal title thereto to be procured from the governor with a proportionable lot in Second street, for which the said county shall satisfy the governor, and shall pay to said Lassy Cock sixty pounds out of the first collected public levy, on consideration, that it doth appear that the said log house cannot be sufficient for the purpose aforesaid intended.[108]

Instead of this structure erected by Mr. Cock, the authorities rented one side of the residence of Patrick Robinson on the corner of Second and High streets to serve as the county jail or prison. In 1685 the "High Sheriff" announced:

that the hired house of Patrick Robinson used by him as a prison, was refitting, and that, with the fetters and chains &c., and his own attendance and deputies, he hath a sufficient gaol; and if any escapes occurred he would not blame the county, for want of a gaol, nor the insufficiency of said house.

It appears that the Robinson family lived on one side of a common entry to the house and that the jail occupied the other half of the house.[109]

This rented frame building was not regarded as satisfying the requirements of a good jail or workhouse, and in the same year, 1685, the authorities agreed upon the following specifications for the construction of a new brick "prison":

The house twenty feet long and fourteen feet wide in the clear, two stories high,—the upper seven feet, and the under

108 *Watson, Annals of Philadelphia,* I, pp. 300-1.
109 Ibid., pp. 356-357.

six and a half feet, of which four feet under ground, with all convenient lights and doors, and casements,—strong and substantial, with good brick, lime, sand and stone, as also floors and roofs very substantial; a partition of brick in the middle through the house, so that there will be four rooms, four chimneys, and the cock-loft, which will serve for a prison; and the gaoler may well live in any part of it, if need be—the whole to cost 140 pounds.[110]

The prison, thus described, was not completed, however, until 1695, and in less than a decade it became antiquated. In 1702 the county grand jury presented "the prison house and prison yard, as it now stands in the High street, as a common nuisance." In the following year the court of quarter sessions appointed a committee of four to make inquiry and "to report the cost of a new prison and court house." In spite of annual complaints about the High Street Prison no practical steps were taken to remedy the situation until 1717. By that time the need of a new prison had become so pressing that "sundry persons offered large subscriptions for erecting a new prison at the present site." [111] In the next year the act of February 27, 1718, provided for the erection of a new jail and workhouse.[112] In 1723 the new stone prison at the corner of Third and High streets was completed and the old brick prison on High street was sold to "the highest bidder." Mr. Watson thus describes the new prison, which served as the jail and workhouse of Philadelphia until 1780:

When finished, about the year 1723, the pile consisted of a two-story stone building, fronting on High street, for the debtor's jail, and another two story similar building, fronting on Third street, for the criminals, called the workhouse—the latter some distance from the former, but joined to it

[110] Ibid., p. 358.
[111] Ibid., pp. 358, 359.
[112] *Statutes at Large,* III, pp. 167 ff.

by a high wall forming a part of the yard enclosure. The buildings were of hewn stone; half of the cellar story was above ground; the roofs were sharply pitched, and the garrets furnished rooms for prisoners.[113]

After exactly a half century of service this prison at the corner of Third and High streets was deemed no longer adequate for the needs of the county and city, and the act of February 26, 1773, authorized the construction of a new jail and workhouse in Philadelphia.[114] The new prison, erected according to the provisions of this act, was the historic Walnut Street Jail located at the corner of Walnut and Sixth streets.[115] It had been completed in part by 1776, when it was turned over to the government as a military prison. Later it was occupied by the British for the same purpose. It was finally completed and occupied as a prison in 1780, and an act of February 28, 1780, ordered the old jail at High and Third streets sold.[116]

There is no reason for believing that there was anything in the other counties so pretentious in prison architecture as the stone prison of provincial Philadelphia.[117] All the evidence available indicates that the jails and workhouses were generally rough frame buildings, at the best only satisfactory from the standpoint of a moderately safe and sure place of detention of the prisoners in custody. Particularly was this the case with the jails erected in the newer counties. It is stated that the jail erected in Westmoreland county in 1773 "was made of round, unhewn logs, one story high, having but one small room, where men and women, whites, blacks, and Indians were confined together." [118]

113 Watson, *Annals of Philadelphia*, pp. 359-361.
114 *Statutes at Large*, VIII, pp. 300-304.
115 Watson, *Annals of Philadelphia*, I, p. 361; III, pp. 177 ff.
116 *Statutes at Large*, IX, pp. 255-7; X, pp. 48-52.
117 Delaware erected a stone court-house and jail at Chester in 1724. See Smith, *History of Delaware County*, p. 234.
118 White, "The Judiciary of Allegheny County," in *Pennsylvania Magazine of History and Biography*, VII (1883), pp. 143-193.

5. *Summary of the Development of Provincial Penal Institutions*

The outstanding phases of the development of colonial penal institutions in Pennsylvania can be briefly characterized in the following summary: The first type of penal institution provided for by statute was the typical English detention jail of the period, which was employed solely for the detention of those accused of crime pending trial and was emptied at each quarterly "gaol delivery." The stocks, whipping-post, pillory and branding-iron were the only devices provided for the treatment of convicted criminals. Whether any of these detention jails provided for in the laws of 1676 were ever actually built cannot be determined, but, as the courts were in session at the period, it may be assumed that some provision was made for holding the accused in custody prior to trial.

The second type of penal institution created in the province was the Quaker workhouse, which for the first time brought into a combination the jail and the workhouse and made the latter a real penal institution. Apparently, outside of Philadelphia, this reform was primarily statutory rather than actually achieved, and few if any workhouses were built before 1718, after which the workhouse reverted from a penal institution to a resumption of its older European characteristics as an institution for the repression of vagrancy and pauperism. Therefore, the county jail was the characteristic penal institution of the colonial period, each of the eleven counties being provided with a jail and but four with workhouses. In the case of the workhouses not more than one or two were employed in any sense as penal institutions. The jails were utilized mainly for detaining those accused of crime and awaiting trial and for the confinement of debtors. Very few convicted criminals were confined in the jails, as the sentences assigned to them were mainly fines or corporal punishment.

The inmates of the jails suffered from the extortion of jailors, the demoralizing idleness and the corrupting intermingling of all classes, which were an inseparable accompaniment of the system. There was no differentiation in treatment or segregation in confinement provided for the inmates according to age, sex, color, degree of criminality, previous record or mental state, with the slight exception that in Philadelphia some attempt was made to segregate the debtors from the criminals. Finally, the absence of productive labor from the provincial jails made them a complete economic burden, in so far as they were not supported by the fees paid by the inmates. In short, the most conspicuous fact about the colonial period from this standpoint was the almost entire absence of true penal institutions and the hopeless failure of those which existed to act as reformatory and deterrent institutions.

III. GENERAL SUMMARY OF THE COLONIAL PERIOD IN ITS JURISTIC AND PENOLOGICAL ASPECTS

In colonial Pennsylvania, as elsewhere in the world at the time, there was no scientific conception of the nature of the criminal personality; the criminal was held to be a perverse "free moral agent" who should feel to the full the savage revenge of an outraged community. To carry this penal "philosophy" into application, there were provided barbarous penal codes with their extensive list of capital offences and their almost exclusive employment of brutal forms of corporal punishment as the penalty imposed for the lesser crimes. Little or no use was made of imprisonment as a corrective of the criminal, the only classes permanently confined being the debtors, who should not have been incarcerated at all.

The only ray of light which penetrated the almost uniform and dismal gloom of colonial penology consisted in the fact that in the brief period of the domination of Quaker theories and practices, from 1682 to 1718, a criminal code had been enacted and in part applied which abolished the ridiculously long category of capital crimes, substituted imprisonment at hard labor for the barbarous pillory, stocks, whipping-post and branding iron, and, for the first time, made the workhouse a vital part of the system of penal institutions. This constitutes the whole positive significance of colonial Pennsylvania in the history of penology. When the growing forces of enlightenment during the eighteenth century made it impossible any longer to endure with complacency the earlier crudities and barbarities, prison reform was made doubly easy in Pennsylvania because of this early Quaker precedent.

It is probable that the preëminence and priority of Philadelphia in prison reform in the late eighteenth and early nineteenth centuries was due more than anything else to the fact that reform was here not only desirable, but here alone was also *respectable*, since it had been a part of the social program of the "Fathers" of the colony. When the other states of the newly created nation were struggling to bring about reform they were burdened with the handicap of a colonial precedent of almost unrelieved barbarism, while Pennsylvania could look back to its early history and discover and accept a reform program which had been hallowed by association with the very name of Penn and the establishment of the province.

SELECTED REFERENCES

Applegarth, Albert C. *The Quakers in Pennsylvania,* in *Johns Hopkins University Studies in Historical and Political Science,* Vol. X, Numbers 8-9.

Barnes, H. E. *History of the Penal, Reformatory and*

Correctional Institutions of New Jersey (*Report of New Jersey Prison Inquiry Commission*, 1918, Vol. II).

Bolles, A. S. *Pennsylvania, Province and State.* 2 v. Phila. 1899.

Charter to William Penn and Laws of Pennsylvania, 1682-1700. Harrisburg. 1879.

Futhey and Cope. *History of Chester County.* Phila. 1881.

Howard, G. E. *Local Constitutional History of the United States.* Baltimore. 1889.

Report of the Commissioners on the Pennsylvania Penal Code, 1828.

Robinson, Louis N. *Penology in the United States.* Phila. 1921.

Root, W. T. *The Relations of Pennsylvania with the British Government, 1696-1765.* N. Y. 1912.

Scharf and Westcott. *A History of Philadelphia.* Phila. 1884.

Sharpless, Isaac. *A Quaker Experiment in Government.* Phila. 1900.

Sharpless, Isaac. *Quakerism and Politics.* Phila. 1905.

Shepherd, W. R. *A History of Proprietary Government in Pennsylvania.* N. Y. 1896.

Smith, George. *A History of Delaware County.* Phila. 1862.

Statutes at Large of Pennsylvania. Vols. II-XVIII (1700-1809). Harrisburg. 1896-1915.

Vaux, Richard. *Brief Sketch of the Origin and History of the State Penitentiary for the Eastern District of Pennsylvania.* Phila. 1872.

Vaux, Roberts. *Notices of the Original and Successive Attempts to Improve the Discipline of the Prison at Philadelphia, and to Reform the Criminal Code of Pennsylvania, with a few Observations on the Penitentiary System.* Phila. 1826.

Watson, J. F. *Annals of Philadelphia,* revised and enlarged by W. P. Hazard. 3 v. Phila. 1884.

White, J. W. F. "The Judiciary of Allegheny County," in *Pennsylvania Magazine of History and Biography.* Vol. VII. 1883.

CHAPTER III

The Historical Origin of the Prison System in America[1]

I. THE LATE ORIGINS OF PENAL INSTITUTIONS

There is an old and well-worn adage that "no prophet is without honor save in his own country," and it would seem fairly accurate to hold that the same sentiment may at times apply to prison systems and types of prison reform. While the writer was born within five miles of Auburn, New York, had passed by the Auburn prison hundreds of times, and had visited it in a score of instances, it was not until years afterward, as a result of a historical study of penology, that he received the slightest intimation that it had any historical significance other than that which might attach to any prison structure which could point to an existence of a century. Further, it may be doubted if there are a half dozen citizens of the city of Auburn who realize that the somber gray stone walls, surmounted by the stolid figure of "Copper John," enclose a structure that, with one possible exception,[2] is, historically considered, the most important penal institution in the western hemisphere, if not in the world—one which furnished the architectural and administrative pattern for an overwhelming majority of the prisons of the United States, and was visited and studied by the leading penologists and jurists of every important European country during the first half of the last century. It will be the purpose of this chapter briefly to indicate the historical background and origins of the Pennsylvania and Auburn

[1] Paper read before the annual meeting of the New York State Historical Society at Bear Mountain Park, October 7, 1920.

[2] The Eastern Penitentiary at Philadelphia.

systems of prison administration and their influence upon contemporary penology. In view of the limited space at my disposal it has seemed best to omit most details of local antiquarian interest and thereby make possible the treatment of the much more vital general historical circumstances which combined to produce these important types of prison discipline.

The prison, viewed as an institution for detaining men against their will, originated in the most remote antiquity. It probably goes back as far as the time of the general practice of cannibalism, when future victims were held in stockades to be fattened or to await their turn in contributing the chief course in the menu of their captors.[3] Throughout recorded history one frequently meets with references to prisons used for the confinement of political and religious offenders,[4] but the prison system of today, which is the agency through which imprisonment is made the mode of punishment for the majority of crimes, is an innovation of relatively recent origin.[5] It is quite impossible to fix the exact date of the general beginning of imprisonment as a punishment for crime, and it may, indeed, be seriously doubted if any such date exists, except in a metaphysical sense. All that can be stated with accuracy is that at the beginning of the eighteenth century imprisonment was unusual, except as applied to political and religious offenders and debtors, while before the middle of the nineteenth century it was the conventional method of punishing crime in both Europe and America. The eighteenth century was the century of transition from corporal punishment to imprisonment, and, though the process of change was most rapid after 1775, there can be no doubt that the general movement was in progress during the entire period.

[3] Cf. P. A. Parsons, *Responsibility for Crime,* pp. 95 ff.

[4] F. H. Wines, *Punishment and Reformation,* pp. 107 ff.; E. C. Wines, *State of Prisons and Child Saving Institutions,* pp. 1-67; A. C. Hall, *Crime In Its Relation to Social Progress.*

[5] Wines, *Punishment and Reformation,* pp. 117 ff.

During the colonial period there were two institutions in existence, the combination of which later produced the modern prison. They were the jails, or prisons of the time, and the workhouses. The jails or prisons were chiefly used for the detention of those accused of crime pending their trial and for the confinement of debtors and religious and political offenders. They were rarely used for the incarceration of what were regarded as the criminal classes. At each session of the court there occurred what was called a "gaol delivery," when the jail was practically emptied of its inmates, only to be filled again during the interval between the delivery and the next session of the court. Only political and religious offenders, debtors, and the few criminals who had received the rare penalty of imprisonment, remained in the jails or prisons longer than the period which elapsed between successive sessions of the courts. The workhouses, on the other hand, which began to appear about the middle of the sixteenth century, and reached their highest early development in Holland, were not for more than two centuries after their origin penal institutions in any strict sense of the word. They were utilized almost solely to repress vagrants and paupers and were not open for the reception of felons.[6]

It was the great contribution of the West Jersey and Pennsylvania Quakers to the development of modern penology to have produced the two-fold achievement of substituting imprisonment for corporal punishment in the treatment of criminals and of combining the prison and the workhouse. In other words, they originated both the idea of imprisonment as the typical mode of punishing crime, and the doctrine that this imprisonment should not be in idleness but at hard labor. Of the priority of their accomplishment in this regard there can be no doubt. A

[6] Wines, op. cit., Chap. VI. George Ives, *A History of Penal Methods*, Chap. I.

century later they added the principle that imprisonment at hard labor should be in cellular separation, and thus created a modern prison system in its entirety.[7]

II. THE NATURE OF THE CRIMINAL CODES AND TYPES OF PUNISHMENT IN THE COLONIAL PERIOD

1. *General Nature of European and American Criminal Jurisprudence in the Eighteenth Century*

In order to form a critical estimate of the nature and development of the criminal codes of colonial New York it is essential to review briefly the general status of European and colonial criminal jurisprudence down to the last quarter of the eighteenth century. Two tendencies stand out conspicuously—an extreme severity in the penalties prescribed and the almost exclusive employment of fines or some form of corporal punishment as the prevailing mode of executing the penalty imposed. A much larger number of crimes were then specified as capital offenses than is the case at the present time, though the situation was not as bad as it became in England a century later, when between two hundred and fifty and three hundred crimes were listed as capital. In the case of crimes not capital, some form of corporal punishment milder than death was usually inflicted. Whipping, branding, mutilating, confinement in the stocks or pillory, and "ducking" were among the most popular of these forms of punishment. At this same time the practice was beginning of banishing offenders to the colonial districts, a procedure which became so popular in the eighteenth century and in the first half of the nineteenth. Until the outbreak of the Revolutionary War the American colonies were the main destination of the banished criminals of England, but

[7] H. E. Barnes, *History of the Penal, Reformatory and Correctional Institutions of New Jersey*, pp. 32-5, 41-2, 86-93, 432-3.

after 1776 America was superseded by Australia. In view of these modes of inflicting punishment for crimes, it readily becomes apparent that there was little need for the modern prison system. At this time the jails were used chiefly for the detention of those accused of crime who were awaiting their trial, and the majority of those confined in the prisons of the time were debtors and political and religious offenders.[8]

At the close of the seventeenth century the barbarous English criminal code was in force in varying degrees in all of the English colonies in America, with the sole exception of the Quaker colonies of West Jersey and Pennsylvania. The American adaptation of the code of the mother country was never as extreme as the English code. The notorious "Blue Laws" of Connecticut, adopted in 1642 and 1650, provided for but fourteen capital crimes. The Hempstead Code promulgated at Hempstead, Long Island, on March 1, 1665, and introduced into New York as the Duke of York's laws, enumerated eleven capital offenses.[9] Though these American Puritan codes compare very favorably with the practice of the mother country, they present an unenviable contrast to the mild and humane Quaker codes of West Jersey and Pennsylvania. In the former only treason and murder were capital offenses and in the latter murder alone was punishable by death. Imprisonment at hard labor was prescribed in most cases for non-capital crimes.[10] While the Quaker codes did not long remain in force in either colony, it is

[8] F. H. Wines, *Punishment and Reformation*, Chaps. V-VI. George Ives, *A History of Penal Methods*, Chap. I. Maurice Parmelee, *Criminology*, pp. 357-72. J. F. Stephen, *A History of the Criminal Law of England*, especially Vol. I, Chap. XIII. J. E. Gillespie, "The Transportation of English Convicts After 1783," in *Journal of Criminal Law and Criminology*, November, 1922, pp. 359-81.

[9] *The Public Records of the Colony of Connecticut*, Vol. I, pp. 509 ff. *The Charter and Laws of Pennsylvania*, 1682-1700, pp. 14-15. *Colonial Laws of New York*, Albany. 1894, J. B. Lyon, Vol. I, pp. 6 ff.

[10] Leaming and Spicer, *The Grants, Concessions and Original Constitutions of the Province of New Jersey*, pp. 382-411. *Charter and Laws of Pennsylvania*, pp. 107 ff.

probable that the influence of these Quaker laws and theories did more than anything else to promote that movement for the liberalizing and humanizing of the criminal codes in this country, which began immediately after the Revolution and spread from Philadelphia throughout the states.[11] This Quaker influence, growing out of the revulsion of the Friends against the bloody juristic practices of the day, from the beginning operated mainly along two related lines of reform—the reduction of the number of capital crimes and the substitution of imprisonment at hard labor for corporal punishment as the most satisfactory penalty to be imposed for the commission of crimes other than capital.[12]

2. *The Criminal Code of Colonial New York*

The situation as respects crimes and punishments in the colony of New York did not differ materially from that which existed in the colonies at large before the Revolution. As late as the Act of 1788 for "punishing Treasons and Felonies, and for the better regulating of proceedings in cases of Felony," there were sixteen capital crimes enumerated on the statute books—treason, murder, rape, buggery, burglary, robbery of a church, breaking and entry, robbery of person, robbery and intimidation in dwelling houses, arson, malicious maiming, forgery, counterfeiting, theft of chose in action, second offense for other felonies, and aiding and abetting any of the above crimes.[13] During the earlier colonial period there had been a number of other crimes punishable by the death penalty, such as, for example, heresy, perjury, smiting of a parent, adultery of married persons, piracy and flight

[11] Wines, op. cit., pp. 142 f., 147, 344.
[12] Ibid. Barnes, op. cit., pp. 32-5, 38-42, 60, 87-8.
[13] *Laws of the Colony of New York,* 1788, Chap. 37, Sec. 1, Greenleaf Edition, 1792, Vol. II, pp. 78-79.

from servitude.[14] Where the death penalty was not inflicted corporal punishment of another and less severe type was employed. The stocks, pillory, whipping, branding and the ducking-stool were the normal methods used for imposing punishment. For the lesser offenses fines were prescribed, with an alternate sentence of corporal punishment if the fine was not paid. Imprisonment was rarely employed as a method of punishment. Nearly all who were imprisoned for any considerable period of time were debtors, imprisonment for debt not having been abolished in New York State until the laws of April 7, 1819, and April 26, 1831, were passed, the latter in part as a result of the campaign against imprisonment for debt carried on by Louis Dwight of the *Boston Prison Discipline Society.*[15] The great bulk of all others who were confined were those who were charged with the commission of a crime and were held pending trial at the next session of the court. Yet, even the expense of imprisonment while awaiting trial was deemed too great, the jails too frequently proved unequal to the task of safe confinement, and the families of the accused became public burdens. This led to the passage of the laws of October 14, 1732, November 10, 1736, and September 1, 1744, which authorized magistrates to prescribe corporal punishment for those charged with minor offenses if they could not furnish bail within forty-eight hours after arrest.[16] The use of imprisonment as a method of punishing crime made but very slow and partial progress in the colony of New York. It first appeared in relation to the offense of "barratry," made punishable by fine or imprisonment in the law of 1665.[17] The first step of any

14 *Laws of the Colony of New York,* 1665, 1699, 1745, 1756. For a good summary of the situation see Philip Klein, *Prison Methods in New York State,* Chap. I.

15 Cf. Frank Carleton, "The Abolition of Imprisonment for Debt in the United States," *Yale Review,* Vol. XVII, pp. 338-344.

16 *Colonial Laws of New York,* Albany, 1894, Vol. II, pp. 745-6, 920; Vol. III, pp. 377-9.

17 Ibid., Vol. I, p. 17.

significance came in Chapter 31 of the laws of 1788, which prescribed imprisonment for disorderly conduct, but the true beginning of the use of imprisonment as a method of punishing crime may be dated from the passage of the act of March 26, 1796, passed on the basis of the recommendations of Governor John Jay, General Philip Schuyler, Thomas Eddy, and Ambrose Spencer, and drawn from a study of the contemporary reforms in the adjoining state of Pennsylvania.[18]

III. THE ORIGINS OF THE PRISON SYSTEM IN NEW YORK STATE

1. *General Historical Background of Penal and Juristic Reform*

There are two sets of influences which constitute the chief phases of the historical background of prison reform in New York, namely, those general forces making for reform and progress of all kinds in the eighteenth century, and those specific attempts to reform criminal jurisprudence and penal administration during the same period, which center mainly about the writings and activities of Beccaria and Howard and the Pennsylvania reformers, such as Bradford, Rush, Vaux, Lownes, and others.

The ignorance, crudities, and barbarism of the "old régime" in Europe were effectively attacked in the writings of the French *Philosophes,* such as Montesquieu, Voltaire, Diderot, Turgot and Condorcet and of their English sympathizers and associates like David Hume, Adam Smith, Tom Paine and Jeremy Bentham. The assault on the old order in the work of these publicists was given concrete and objective form in the French Revolution, and its effect upon the other states of Europe.

[18] *Laws of the State of New York,* 1776-1797, Greenleaf Edition, 1792, Vol. II, pp. 52-54; Vol. III, pp. 291-99.

Probably the most important of the doctrines of these writers and of the Revolutionary period was the introduction of rationalism into social and political philosophy and the firm conviction that social progress and the resulting "greatest happiness for the greatest number" were possible of attainment through sweeping social reforms carried out according to the dictates of "pure reason." It is obvious that so barbarous and archaic a part of the old order as the current criminal jurisprudence and penal administration of the time could not long remain immune from the growing spirit of progress and enlightenment.[19]

America, in general, and Philadelphia, in particular, were well situated to feel the effect of these new forces. A large number of Frenchmen had been in America during the Revolutionary War, had brought with them many of the ideas of their publicists and had stimulated an American interest in French thought. In addition, many of the more important and influential Americans had been in Europe during the period of the American Revolution and the years immediately following. Philadelphia, as the real center of American civilization and political life during the last quarter of the eighteenth century, was particularly affected by these progressive European developments. Benjamin Franklin had long been a resident of France and was well acquainted with radical French thought. The political leaders who assembled in Philadelphia during the period were all more or less familiar with the advanced political thought of England and France. No other foreign philosopher so influenced the American Constitutional Convention of 1787 as did Montesquieu, and his exponents must have been nearly

19 See John Morley's biographies of Rousseau, Diderot and Voltaire and his essays on eighteenth-century thought in France in his *Critical Miscellanies;* A. Sorel's biography of Montesquieu; H. Higgs, *The Physiocrats;* J. M. Robertson, *A History of Free Thought;* Leslie Stephen, *History of English Thought in the Eighteenth Century;* and the excellent summary of the writings and thought of this period in Robinson and Beard, *Development of Modern Europe,* Vol. I, pp. 157-82, and the *Cambridge Modern History,* Vol. VIII, Chap. I.

as familiar with his doctrines on the reform of criminal jurisprudence as with his theory of the separation of governmental powers. As the capital of the country during much of the period, Philadelphia received many distinguished foreign visitors, bringing with them the doctrines of their countrymen. Brissot, the Girondist leader in the French Revolution, was among these. Finally, it was to Philadelphia that Jefferson came shortly after his return from France, where he had become most familiar with French revolutionary ideas and leaders. Then Philadelphia had the colonial precedents of Penn in prison reform to recur to as an inspiration and guide in juristic and penal reform. All of these conditions combined to make Philadelphia particularly well adapted to the carrying into execution of some of the more radical European and colonial programs of social reform.[20]

2. *The Attack on the Older Criminal Jurisprudence and Criminal Procedure*

Powerful and successful attacks were made upon the barbarous and irrational criminal jurisprudence and penal institutions by a group of able and influential European writers. The French publicist, Montesquieu (1689-1755), in his *Persian Letters* and his *The Spirit of the Laws,* condemned the barbarous injustice of the French penal code and advocated reforms which would make punishments less severe and more nearly adapted to the specific crimes for which they were imposed. His work attracted and stimulated a more influential writer in the history of the reform of criminal jurisprudence, the Italian, Beccaria (1735-94). His *Crimes and Punishments,* first published in 1764, was probably the most significant single contribution of the eighteenth century to the reform of

20 On the interrelation between early American and European thought see I. Woodbridge Riley, *American Philosophy, the Early Schools,* and Carl Becker, *The Declaration of Independence.*

criminal jurisprudence. He argued powerfully for the abolition of torture, the need of a more just and accurate method of trial, the necessity for a reduction in the severity of the penalties imposed, a larger use of imprisonment in the punishment of crime and an improvement in the administration of prisons. The greater portion of his work, however, was directed primarily toward securing a reformation of contemporary criminal law.[21] The English jurist, Blackstone (1723-1780), while not violent enough in his criticism of the old system to please Bentham, condemned the glaring injustices in the unspeakable English criminal code of his day. The multitudinous and diverse reforming interests of Jeremy Bentham (1748-1832) embraced voluminous writings on the reform of both criminal jurisprudence and penal administration.[22] Finally, many of the most important of the doctrines of the reformers were given concrete expression in the French Revolutionary penal code of September 25, 1791, which declared that "penalties should be proportioned to the crimes for which they were inflicted, and that they are intended not merely to punish, but to reform, the culprit." All of these developments towards securing a new and more rational and humane criminal jurisprudence were well known to intelligent citizens of Philadelphia before 1800.

3. *John Howard and the European Origins of Prison Reform*

The first clear anticipations of the modern prison system were the papal prison of San Michele, erected in Rome by Pope Clement X about 1704, and the prison at Ghent in Belgium, established by Hippolyte Vilain XIII

[21] M. Parmelee, *The Principles of Anthropology and Sociology in Their Relation to Criminal Procedure*, pp. 10-16, 202.

[22] On Bentham, see W. L. Davidson, *Political Thought in England, the Utilitarians*, pp. 107-113. On Beccaria, Bentham and Romilly, see C. Phillipson, *Three Criminal Law Reformers*.

in 1773. In both of these there was provided some sort of classification and cellular separation of inmates. Labor by the inmates was the rule and reformation was stated to be a chief aim of incarceration. Neither of these prisons, however, attracted much general attention in England or America until their virtues were discovered and reported by the distinguished English prison reformer, John Howard (1726-90). In his travels of inspection between 1773 and 1790 he visited these institutions several times and his writings contain vivid descriptions of their construction and administration. It was through his writings, well known to Philadelphians, that America gained a knowledge of these advanced institutions and caught the spirit of Howard's labors in behalf of prison reform. There is little or no evidence, however, that these institutions in Rome and Ghent directly influenced Pennsylvania penology to an appreciable degree. Their effect seems to have been indirect. Howard's recommendation of their system of administration, as a part of his penal philosophy, induced a number of enterprising and sympathetic English reformers to adopt these principles in English jails and prisons, and the latter became the models followed by the Philadelphia reformers. When, in 1790, the members of the *Philadelphia Society for Alleviating the Miseries of Public Prisons* desired to educate and inform the legislature of the state in order to secure the adoption of an advanced sytem of prison administration, their list of successful experiments in the new penology did not include any important reference to Rome or Ghent, but was confined almost entirely to the reforms in new English county prisons, particularly that at Wymondham in Norfolk, erected about 1784 by Sir Thomas Beevor, as a result of the enthusiasm generated by a reading of Howard's writings. In this prison there were provided a separation of sexes and of hardened criminals from first and petty offenders, separate cells for all prisoners at night and for incorrigible prisoners at all times, and a well-equipped workshop for the employment of the able-bodied prisoners.[23]

Beyond this indirect influence of Howard's work upon Philadelphia prison reform, ample evidence exists that the Philadelphia reformers were thoroughly conversant with the printed accounts of his travels in the inspection of prisons and with his recommendations of reform based upon these trips. The above-mentioned pamphlet of 1790 contains long extracts from Howards' works which were in accord with the changes urged upon the legislature. Two years earlier, in fact, the society had sent Howard the following letter:

Philadelphia, January 14, 1788.

To John Howard.

The Society for Alleviating the Miseries of Public Prisons, in the city of Philadelphia, beg leave to forward to you a copy of their constitution, and to request, at the same time, such communications from you upon the subject of their institution, as may favour their designs.

The Society heartily concur with the friends of humanity in Europe, in expressing their obligations to you for having rendered the miserable tenants of prisons the objects of more general attention and compassion, and for having pointed out some of the means of not only alleviating their miseries, but of preventing those crimes and misfortunes which are the causes of them.

With sincere wishes that your useful life may be prolonged, and that you may enjoy the pleasure of seeing the success of your labours in the cause of humanity, in every

[23] *Extracts and Remarks on the Subject of the Punishment and Reformation of Criminals.* Published by Order of the Society Established in Philadelphia for Alleviating the Miseries of Public Prisons, February 25, 1790.

part of the globe, we are, with great respect and esteem, your sincere friends and well wishers.

Signed by order of the Society,
William White, President.[24]

This letter, written less than a year after the formation of the society, would seem to indicate that even in its origin it was powerfully stimulated by Howard's work. Indeed, we know that at the fourth meeting of the society the members listened to a letter from Dr. Lettsom of London describing Howard's journeys on the continent in carrying on his investigation of prison conditions.[25] That Howard evinced a similar interest in progressive movements in this country is shown by the words of the following memorandum which he dictated:

Should the plan take place during my life of establishing a permanent charity under some such title as that at Philadelphia, viz.: "A Society for Alleviating the Miseries of Public Prisons," and annuities be engrafted thereupon, for the above-mentioned purpose, I would most readily stand at the bottom of a page for five hundred pounds; or if such society shall be instituted within three years after my death, this sum shall be paid out of my estate.[26]

Along with the influence of Howard's work, it is evident that Jeremy Bentham's *Panopticon* and its voluminous appendices, published following 1787, had some effect upon prison reform in Pennsylvania. The Western Penitentiary of Pennsylvania, authorized by the law of 1818, is one of the few institutions which were modelled to some degree after Bentham's ingenious plan for a perfect prison structure.[27] Finally, in concluding this

24 Robert Vaux, *Notices of the Original and Successive Attempts to Improve the Discipline of the Prison at Philadelphia and to Reform the Criminal Code of Pennsylvania,* Philadelphia, 1810, pp. 24-5.

25 Ibid., pp. 18-20.

26 Ibid., p. 25, note. *The London Society for the Improvement of Prison Discipline* was not established until 1815.

27 *Acts of the General Assembly of Pennsylvania,* 1820-21, p. 181. It is frequently asserted that both the original Western and Eastern Peni-

summary of the historical background of early prison reform in Philadelphia, the fact must not be forgotten that Pennsylvania, alone of all the states, was fortunate enough to have had its very origins linked up with the cause of judicial and penal reform. While the laws passed in Pennsylvania from 1718 to 1775 were usually about as far as possible from Penn's actual program, the memory of his purposes was kept alive in the enacting clauses. Therefore, when a reform of the criminal code and penal administration became necessary, the movement was rendered respectable and "safe" through its association with the venerable and esteemed name of the founder of the province.[28]

4. *The Pennsylvania System of Prison Discipline as the Model for Imitation by New York State*

Inasmuch as it is undeniable that the advances in criminal jurisprudence and penology in New York State between 1796 and 1830 were primarily the result of New York's imitation of the Pennsylvania precedent, it will be necessary to review briefly the progress made in this adjoining state during the same general period. The beginnings of prison reform in Pennsylvania are generally associated with the name of Richard Wistar, a member of the Society of Friends, who, just prior to the outbreak of the Revolutionary War, was attracted by the abject

tentiaries of Pennsylvania were built by John Haviland. This is not true. The original Western Penitentiary was built by William Strickland, a leading Philadelphia architect of the time. The Eastern Penitentiary was erected by John Haviland, who also built the state prison on the Pennsylvania plan in Trenton a few years later. See *Journal of the Twenty-eighth House* (Pennsylvania), 1817-18, pp. 385 f.; *Senate Journal*, 1818-19, pp. 51-52.

28 The most valuable summary of the rise of prison reform in Europe and the development of that movement in America is contained in the now rare monograph by J. B. Lindsley, *Prison Discipline and Penal Legislation*, Nashville, 1874. A copy exists in the New York Public Library. The most thorough history of the rise of the prison system in America and of the early American prisons is O. F. Lewis, *The Development of American Prisons and Prison Customs*, 1776-1845.

misery of the inmates of the provincial jail in Philadelphia, some of whom had in fact recently starved to death. Wistar had soup prepared at his own house and then taken and distributed among the inmates of the jail. Others became interested in the situation and, on February 7, 1776, there was formed *The Philadelphia Society for Assisting Distressed Prisoners.*[29] The reform of the criminal code and the introduction of the prison system might have begun at that date instead of a decade later had not the British occupation of the city put an end to the activities of the society.[30]

Immediately after the peace of 1783 a number of prominent citizens of Philadelphia, led by Benjamin Franklin, Benjamin Rush, William Bradford and Caleb Lownes, organized a movement for the reform of the barbarous criminal code of 1718, which was still in force. All were agreed that the number of capital crimes should be greatly reduced and Dr. Rush went as far as to advocate the total abolition of the death penalty. Their efforts resulted in the law of September 15, 1786, which substituted for the death penalty as a punishment for some of the lesser felonies "continuous hard labor, publicly and disgracefully imposed." [31] The results of the new law were not as satisfactory as had been anticipated, while the public exposure of the convicts in their labor brought their distressing condition before the attention of a larger number of persons than could have been the case when they were secluded in the gloomy jails of High and Walnut streets. The continued evils of the penal administration, together with the added publicity given to these deplorable conditions, promoted the formation of *The Philadelphia Society*

29 Roberts Vaux, *Notices,* pp. 8-9; *Sketch of the Principal Transactions of the Philadelphia Society for Alleviating the Miseries of Public Prisons,* Philadelphia, 1859, p. 3.

30 Roberts Vaux, *Notices,* p. 9; *Sketch of Principal Transactions,* p. 3.

31 *Statutes at Large of Pennsylvania,* Vol. XII, pp. 280-81. Caleb Lownes, *An Account of the Alteration and Present State of the Penal Laws of Pennsylvania,* Philadelphia, 1792, pp. 5-6.

for Alleviating the Miseries of Public Prisons, on the 8th of May, 1787, in the German School House on Cherry street.[32] This organization, the first of the great modern prison reform societies, set forth its fundamental impulses, conceptions and purposes in the preamble to the constitution of the society—

> "I was in prison and ye came unto me.
>
> ". . . and the King shall answer, and say unto them, verily I say unto you, inasmuch as ye have done it unto one of the least of these my brethren, ye have done it unto me" (Matthew, xxv: 36, 40).
>
> When we consider that the obligations of benevolence, which are founded on the precepts and example of the Author of Christianity, are not cancelled by the follies and crimes of our fellow-creatures; and when we reflect upon the miseries which penury, hunger, cold, unnecessary severity, unwholesome apartments, and guilt (the usual attendants of prisons), involve with them; it becomes us to extend our compassion to that part of mankind, who are subject to these miseries. By the aids of humanity, their undue and illegal sufferings may be prevented; the links which should bind the whole family of mankind together, under all circumstances, be preserved unbroken; and such degrees and modes of punishment may be discovered and suggested, as may, instead of continuing habits of vice, become the means of restoring our fellow-creatures to virtue and happiness. From a conviction of the truth and obligation of these principles, the Subscribers have associated themselves under the Title of *The Philadelphia Society for Alleviating the Miseries of Public Prisons.*[33]

While not more than one-half of the members of the Society can be identified as also belonging to the Society of Friends, it is well known that the most active element in the prison reform organization was made up of the

[32] Lownes, op. cit.; *Report of the Commissioners on the Penal Code,* 1828, p. 13.

[33] Roberts Vaux, *Notices,* pp. 10-11.

Friends, and the leading exponents of the Pennsylvania system of prison discipline during over a half century, Roberts Vaux and his son, Richard, were members of the Society of Friends. Of course, one must recognize the important part played in the reform activity by non-Quaker members of the society, such as Bishop White of the Episcopal Church, and the generous co-operation with the Prison Society on the part of those who were not members of the newly formed society, such as Benjamin Franklin and William Bradford. The work accomplished by the reform society fell into three related parts—the relief of the physical suffering of prisoners, the reform of the criminal code by reducing the number of capital crimes and by introducing imprisonment as the typical method of punishment in the place of corporal punishment, and the development of a great historic system of prison discipline—the Pennsylvania or *separate* system of confinement and discipline.

It has already been pointed out that the activities in Europe of Howard and Bentham were intimately related to the development of the reform of prison administration in Pennsylvania; it is equally certain that the reform of the criminal code of the state was based upon a sympathetic reception of the juristic principles of Beccaria and Montesquieu. Writing in 1793, William Bradford, the author of the improved Pennsylvania codes from 1790-1794, indicates the indebtedness of himself and his associates to these European reformers:

We perceive that the severity of our criminal law is an exotic plant, and not the native growth of Pennsylvania. It has endured, but, I believe, has never been a favorite. The religious opinions of many of our citizens were in opposition to it; and, as soon as the principles of Beccaria were disseminated, they found a soil that was prepared to receive them. During our connection with Great Britain no reform was attempted: but, as soon as we separated from her, the public sentiment disclosed itself and this benevolent undertaking was enjoined by the constitution. This was one of the first fruits of liberty and confirms the remark of Montesquieu, "That as freedom advances, the severity of the penal law decreases." [34]

The legal beginnings of the reform of the Pennsylvania criminal code date back to the state constitution of 1776, which directed a reform of the criminal law to the end that imprisonment at hard and productive labor might be substituted for the barbarous existing methods of corporal punishment.[35] The stress of the Revolutionary War postponed action for a decade, but the law of September 15, 1786, marked a notable step in advance by reducing the number of capital crimes, substituting imprisonment for corporal punishment in the case of a number of lesser felonies, and by abolishing for most purposes branding, mutilation, the pillory, whipping and the other conventional barbarities of the colonial period.[36] The progressive policy was sustained and somewhat extended in acts of 1788, 1789, 1790 and 1791, but the systematic revision of the criminal code appeared in the act of April 22, 1794, which abolished the death penalty for all crimes except murder in the first degree, and substituted imprisonment or fines for all other crimes in the place of corporal punishment of any type.[37] This code marked the first permanent American break with contemporary juristic savagery, was the forerunner of the reform codes of other American states, and was the essential basis of Pennsylvania criminal jurisprudence until the next systematic revision in 1860.

This reform of the criminal code making imprisonment

34 William Bradford, *An Inquiry How Far the Punishment of Death Is Necessary in Pennsylvania, With Notes and Illustrations,* Philadelphia, 1793, p. 20.

35 *Constitution of Pennsylvania,* 1776, Chapter II, Sections 38-39.

36 *The Statutes at Large of Pennsylvania,* Vol. XII, pp. 280 ff.

37 Ibid., Vol. XV, pp. 174-181.

the normal method of punishing crime necessitated the establishment of a prison system in the place of the crude arrangement of the colonial jails and workhouses. By acts of 1789, 1790 and 1794 the Walnut street jail was converted into a state prison, and an addition was constructed so as to allow the trial of what became the Pennsylvania system of prison discipline, namely, the confinement of the worst type of felons in separate cells.[38] Of these important laws the act of April 5, 1790, is conventionally regarded as the legal origin of the Pennsylvania system. In spite of promising beginnings in the years immediately following 1790, the attempt to apply the new penology in the Walnut street jail proved a well-nigh complete failure. The cells erected for the solitary confinement of the "more hardened and atrocious offenders," according to the act of 1790, were never numerous enough to accommodate all the convicts of this class, and the large congregate cells or rooms which housed the remainder became so overcrowded as to nullify completely all attempts to administer the institution in a scientific or effective manner.[39] The failure of the law of 1790 to secure the solitary confinement of those so sentenced and the general administrative and disciplinary demoralization of the Walnut street jail, due to overcrowding, were remedied from a legal point of view by the acts of March 3, 1818, and March 20, 1821, which provided for the erection of the Western and the Eastern State penitentiaries. It was here definitely stipulated that both penitentiaries should be constructed according to the principle of solitary confinement, but no provision was made for the employment of the convicts.[40] It was only after a series of controversies from 1826 to 1829 that the com-

[38] *The Statutes at Large of Pennsylvania,* Vol. XIII, pp. 246, 250-51; Ibid., pp. 523-5; Ibid., Vol. XV, pp. 178-9.

[39] *A Statistical View of the Operation of the Penal Code of Pennsylvania,* 1817, passim; Lownes, op. cit., pp. 12-13, 19 ff.

[40] *Acts of the General Assembly of Pennsylvania,* 1817-18, pp. 138-40; Ibid., 1820-21, pp. 94-7.

pleted Pennsylvania system was finally established. By taking advantage of conflicting recommendations made by public authorities, *The Philadelphia Society for Alleviating the Miseries of Public Prisons* was able to induce the legislature to enact into law its fundamental program in penal administration—solitary confinement at hard labor. This was finally and definitely prescribed in the law of April 23, 1829.[41]

The classical eulogy of the Pennsylvania system is to be found in the report of the inspectors of the Western Penitentiary for 1854. Here they worked themselves into an almost neo-Platonic ecstasy in their effort to set forth the many and numerous points of supreme excellence in the Pennsylvania system of prison discipline and administration. This is probably the most extreme and exaggerated praise that the system ever received from its advocates:

Pennsylvania, the precursor of all her sister states in the present system of prison discipline, has justified its wisdom before the world in the practical results of its successful administration in this institution. Anticipated evils, existing more in speculative humanity and morbid philanthropy than in substantive fact, have failed in their realization. Disease and mental imbecility so confidently predicted as necessarily incident to separate confinement, have resulted in health and intellectual improvement. Depraved tendencies, characteristic of the convict, have been restrained by the absence of vicious association, and in the mild teaching of Christianity, the unhappy criminal finds a solace for an involuntary exile from the comforts of social life. If hungry, he is fed; if naked, he is clothed; if destitute of the first rudiments of education, he is taught to read and write; and if he has never been blessed with a means of livelihood, he is schooled in a mechanical art, which in after life may be to him the source of profit and respectability. Employment is not toil nor labor weariness. He embraces them with

[41] Ibid., 1828-9, pp. 351-54.

alacrity, as contributing to his moral and mental elevation. They help to fill the zodiac of his time, which would otherwise be spent in unavailing complaint, and fruitless importunity for release. Shut out from a tumultuous world, and separated from those equally guilty with himself, he can indulge his remorse unseen, and find ample opportunity for reflection and reformation. His daily intercourse is with good men, who, in administering to his necessities, animate his crushed hopes, and pour into his ear the oil of joy and consolation. He has abundance of light, air, and warmth; he has good and wholesome food; he has seasonable and comfortable clothing; he has the best of medical attendance; he has books to read, and ink and paper to communicate with his friends at stated periods; and weekly he enjoys the privilege of hearing God's holy word expounded by a faithful and zealous Christian minister.

Thus provided, and anxiously cared for by the officers of the prison, he is in a better condition than many beyond its walls guiltless of crime. He labors, but it is for his subsistence, like any other member of the community, and by his industry he relieves that community of the burden of his support.

It is a fact worthy to be remembered by the Legislature, that for the last ten years, not one county sending convicts to the Western Penitentiary has been called upon to contribute a solitary dollar towards their subsistence. Such being the domestic economy of this institution, and such its happy results, we are not required to enter into an elaborate vindication of the principle upon which it is based. The system has disappointed the anticipations of its enemies and surpassed the confident expectations of its friends, and there, for the present, we leave it.[42]

[42] *Report of the Inspectors of the Western Penitentiary,* 1854, *Legislative Documents,* 1854, p. 271. For a vigorous criticism of the Pennsylvania system see George Ives, *History of Penal Methods.*

The historical origin of the Pennsylvania system is treated in detail in the writer's forthcoming work on the evolution of penology in Pennsylvania.

5. *The Beginnings of Prison Reform in New York State and the Origins of the Auburn System*

The situation after the Revolution in New York State with respect to criminal jurisprudence and penology was much the same as that which existed in Pennsylvania. The list of capital crimes was extensive and corporal punishment was the normal mode of inflicting the revenge of society upon the offender. Imprisonment as a method of punishing crime scarcely existed and no state prison had been provided. Yet progressive and enlightened individuals were not lacking who were gravely shocked by existing conditions and were keenly interested in all proposals for improving the situation. Among the leaders of enlightened sentiment in this respect in New York were Ambrose Spencer (1765-1848), legislator and jurist; Philip John Schuyler (1733-1804), soldier and statesman; Thomas Eddy (1758-1827), financier and philanthropist; DeWitt Clinton (1769-1828), political leader and social reformer; John Jay (1745-1829), statesman, jurist and diplomat; and John Griscom (1774-1852), scholar and philanthropist.

It was but natural that their attention would be attracted by previous and contemporary progress in Philadelphia. The Philadelphia group had not only taken the lead in this movement in America, but had also spared no pains in advertising its program. Roberts Vaux notes that as early as 1794 the prison society resolved to make its effect felt outside of the local municipality and state, and maintains that "an extensive correspondence was opened and carried on between the society and the executives of several of the states of the union, which tended to diffuse much information relative to its labors, and led to the adoption of reform in the penal laws in other parts of the continent.[43] It may have been as a

[43] *Notices*, p. 34.

direct result of this communication from Philadelphia that in his first message to the legislature Governor John Jay recommended the reform of the criminal code. Again, Thomas Eddy, one of the most energetic of the New York reform group, had been born in Philadelphia and had remained in intimate touch with the Society of Friends in that city. Professor Griscom was also a member of the Society of Friends. In 1794 Mr. Eddy and General Schuyler visited Philadelphia, were received by *The Philadelphia Society for Alleviating the Miseries of Public Prisons,* were told more of the reforms which had just been achieved in the criminal code and prison administration of Pennsylvania, and were shown what then seemed the highly successful new system in operation in the Walnut street jail. Study and further reflection convinced them that Pennsylvania had provided the desirable reform pattern for New York to emulate.[44] Aided by the legal sagacity of Spencer and the political support of Governor Jay, they introduced a bill into the New York Legislature designed to reduce the list of capital crimes to murder and treason, to substitute imprisonment for corporal punishment for non-capital crimes, and to provide for the erection of two state penitentiaries, one at Albany and one in New York City. This became law as the act of March 26, 1796.[45] Only one of the two prisons contemplated in the law was erected, the so-called Newgate Prison, which was built in Greenwich Village under the direction of a commission consisting of Matthew Clarkson, John Murray, Jr., John Watt, Thomas Eddy and Isaac Stoutenburgh, and was opened for the reception of inmates on November 28, 1797.

There were, however, two fatal initial defects in this

[44] Cf. J. L. Sullivan, "Note on the Penitentiary System of New York State," in G. E. Baker's edition of *The Works of William H. Seward,* Vol. II, pp. 173-80. C. G. Haines, *Report on the Penitentiary System of the United States,* 1822.

[45] *Laws of the State of New York, from the First to the Twentieth Session of the Legislature,* Greenleaf edition, 1797, Vol. III, pp. 291-99.

institution which led to its speedy abandonment. It was erected according to the unscientific congregate method of confinement, as practiced in the greater part of the Walnut street jail at Philadelphia, which made effective classification and discipline impossible. Moreover, it was so small that it very rapidly became overcrowded and the demoralizing practice arose of pardoning each year nearly as many convicts as were admitted, in order to keep the prison population down to a number which it was possible to house even under crowded conditions. According to statistics gathered by Senator Hopkins in 1824, 198 prisoners were received in 1813 and 134 were pardoned, and in 1814, 213 were received and 176 pardoned. Mr. Sullivan reports contemporary evidence as stating that between 1797 and 1822, 5,069 convicts were admitted and 2,819 pardoned.

The situation became so intolerable that on April 12, 1816, a law was passed authorizing the erection of a new state prison at Auburn in Cayuga County, and a commission consisting of Elijah Miller, James Glover and John H. Beach was appointed to direct operations. They were authorized "to build a state prison similar to the one now in use in the City of New York with such variations as they think will best promote the interest of such institution." [46] The immediate control of building operations was handed over to William Brittin, a carpenter by trade and the first warden of the institution.[47] The evils of the congregate system of confinement do not appear to have been fully grasped in New York State as late as 1816, for the first wing of the new structure at Auburn, the south wing, was erected with both double cells and large rooms or apartments capable of receiving ten or more convicts in each. By 1819 the influence of the sentiment for solitary confinement had become dominant, and an act

[46] *Laws of the State of New York, Thirty-ninth to Forty-first Sessions,* Albany, 1818, pp. 79-80.

[47] Ibid., 45th to 47th Sessions, Albany, 1825, pp. 134-135.

was passed on April 2nd of that year directing the inspectors to confine certain classes of prisoners in separate cells and to construct the north wing according to the principle of solitary confinement of each prisoner.[48] The outside cell construction, later followed in the Eastern Penitentiary of Pennsylvania, was not employed, but rather what came to be known as the Auburn, or inside cell, method of construction. After consultation with the Pennsylvania exponents of the system of solitary confinement, the New York reformers succeeded in securing the act of April 2, 1821, directing the prison inspectors to select a number of the "oldest and most heinous offenders" and put them in solitary confinement, with the end in view of observing its disciplinary effects. A second class was to be put in separate cells for three days each week, while the younger offenders were to be allowed to work in the shops six days each week.[49] Eighty convicts were awarded as a Christmas present, in 1821, the privilege of furnishing the material for this experiment in prison discipline and administration. The method employed was not what became a few years later the developed Pennsylvania system of solitary confinement at hard labor in two large roomy cells and a small outside yard, but solitary confinement in a single small inside cell without any labor or other adequate provisions for physical exercise. The experiment continued during the year 1822 and 1823, and it is not surprising that it proved a hopeless failure and led to a marked prevalence of sickness and insanity on the part of the convicts in solitary confinement. It should be remembered, however, that this crude experiment throws no light upon the disciplinary and reformative potentialities of the perfected Pennsylvania system.

The collapse of the experiment with solitary confine-

[48] *Laws of the State of New York,* 42nd to 44th Sessions, Albany, 1821, pp. 87-90.

[49] Ibid., pp. 215-18. *Sketch of the Principal Transactions,* p. 12; *Pennsylvania Journal of Prison Discipline and Philanthropy,* Vol. II, Number 2, 1846, p. 116.

ment at Auburn led to the complete abandonment of this type of discipline. In 1823 and 1824 Governor Yates pardoned most of those remaining in solitary confinement, and a majority of the legislative committee of investigation, appointed by the act of April 12, 1824, and consisting of Stephen Allen, Samuel M. Hopkins and George Tibbits, reported that nothing more could be hoped for from this type of procedure. The committee summarized their opinion as follows:

> A majority of the Board respectfully recommend to the Legislature the repeal of the laws for solitary confinement, in connection with the full adoption of an effectual government and discipline; and a majority of us would not recommend the same as a separate measure, nor in any case except in connection with such effective system of government and discipline.[50]

In the meantime the local prison authorities at Auburn had been working out a disciplinary and administrative scheme which was destined to become one of great historic significance—the Auburn system of congregate work by day and separation by night, with enforced silence at all times. Warden Brittin died in 1821 and his place was taken by Captain Elam Lynds, who, with the aid of his deputy and architect, John Cray, and with the encouragement of Gershom Powers, of the Board of Inspectors, worked out the new plan. The weight of evidence seems to warrant assigning the credit for originating and applying the new system of discipline to Mr. Cray.[51] The old system of congregate confinement having proved a failure and the alternative procedure of solitary confine-

[50] *Journal of the Assembly of the State of New York*, 48th Session, Albany, 1825, pp. 91-133. See especially pp. 121-126. For a statistical summary of the scandalous prevalence of pardoning in the Newgate Prison, see pages 126-7 of this report. This report is the best documentary source relative to the status of New York penology at the close of the first quarter of the last century.

[51] *Letter of Gershom Powers, Esq., in Answer to a Letter of the Hon. Edward Livingston in Relation to the Auburn State Prison*, Albany, 1829, pp. 5-11.

ment as applied at Auburn appearing likewise to promise nothing better, a compromise was reached between the two plans. The prisoners were allowed to work in groups in the prison shops and yards during the day, and were then locked singly in separate cells by night. Silence was enforced at all times, and the discipline was further extended by such devices as the lockstep, special regulations in the dining-hall, and the undeniable cruelty of Warden Lynds in his employment of whipping as a means of preserving order and securing obedience. Louis Dwight, the most powerful champion that the Auburn system ever had, describes in the following manner the operation of the new system. It is both an eloquent defense of this type of discipline and an excellent proof of the great transformation of disciplinary and administrative ideals held by prison reformers between 1826 and 1920:

At Auburn we have a more beautiful example still of what may be done by proper discipline, in a prison well constructed. It is not possible to describe the pleasure which we feel in contemplating this noble institution, after wading through the fraud, and the material and moral filth of many prisons. We regard it as a model worthy of the world's imitation. We do not mean that there is nothing in this institution which admits of improvement; for there have been a few cases of unjustifiable severity in punishments; but, upon the whole, the institution is immensely elevated above the old penitentiaries.

The whole establishment, from the gate to the sewer, is a specimen of neatness. The unremitted industry, the entire subordination and subdued feeling of the convicts, has probably no parallel among an equal number of criminals. In their solitary cells they spend the night, with no other book but the Bible, and at sunrise they proceed, in military order, under the eye of the turnkeys, in solid columns, with the lock march, to their work-shops; thence, in the same order, at the hour of breakfast, to the common hall, where they partake of their wholesome and frugal meal in silence. Not even a whisper is heard; though the silence is such that a whisper might be heard through the whole apartment. The convicts are seated, in single file, at narrow tables, with their backs towards the center, so that there can be no interchange of signs. If one has more food than he wants, he raises his left hand; and if another has less, he raises his right hand, and the waiter changes it. When they have done eating, at the ringing of a little bell, of the softest sound, they rise from the table, form the solid columns, and return, under the eye of the turnkeys, to the work-shops. From one end of the shops to the other, it is the testimony of many witnesses, that they have passed more than three hundred convicts, without seeing one leave his work, or turn his head to gaze at them. There is the most perfect attention to business from morning till night, interrupted only by the time necessary to dine, and never by the fact that the whole body of prisoners have done their tasks, and the time is now their own, and they can do as they please. At the close of the day, a little before sunset, the work is all laid aside at once, and the convicts return, in military order, to the solitary cells; where they partake of the frugal meal, which they were permitted to take from the kitchen, where it was furnished for them as they returned from the shops. After supper, they can, if they choose, read Scripture undisturbed and then reflect in silence on the errors of their lives. They must not disturb their fellow prisoners by even a whisper.[52]

About the time that the Auburn system was emerging into practice the legislature, by an Act of March 7, 1825, authorized the erection of another state prison near New York City to displace finally the Newgate Prison in Greenwich Village. The building commission was composed of Stephen Allen, George Tibbits and Samuel M. Hop-

[52] It was the emphasis on silence at Auburn which led to the frequent designation of the Auburn system as the "silent system." For the best analysis of the Auburn system at an early date, see Gershom Powers, *A Brief Account of the Construction, Management and Discipline of the New York State Prison at Auburn*, Auburn, 1826.

kins,[53] who had recommended the erection of an additional prison in their famous report of 1825 on the state prison system in New York. This new state prison was built in the three years following under the direction of Captain Lynds, and in May, 1828, was ready for occupancy. Christened at first the Mount Pleasant Prison, it has come to be known in our day as the Sing Sing institution. From the beginning it operated according to the Auburn system.

IV. THE STRUGGLE BETWEEN THE AUBURN AND PENNSYLVANIA SYSTEMS

Though the series of advances in New York State penology which led to the completed Auburn system should be regarded as primarily an adaptation and imitation of the Pennsylvania reforms, and the Auburn system a variant of the Pennsylvania system, once the Auburn type of discipline had assumed an independent position a vigorous competition sprang up between the two systems and a bitter controversy was waged between the partisans of each. While the Pennsylvania system was temporarily adopted by a number of Eastern states, it was speedily abandoned by all except New Jersey, which persisted in the experiment until 1858.[54] Owing to the economic advantages of the Auburn system, and, above all, to the tireless propaganda of Louis Dwight of the *Prison Discipline Society of Boston* in the interest of

[53] *Laws of New York*, 1825, Chap. XXV, pp. 16-17.

[54] The following data indicate the degree and period of adoption and abandonment of the Pennsylvania system in the United States. Maryland introduced solitary confinement in 1809 and abolished it in 1838. Massachusetts authorized solitary confinement in 1811 and did away with it in 1829. Maine experimented with solitary confinement from 1824 to 1827. New Jersey introduced solitary confinement in 1820, abolished it in 1828, reintroduced it in 1833 and finally abolished it in 1858. Virginia introduced solitary confinement in 1824 and practically abolished it in 1833. Rhode Island introduced solitary confinement in 1838 and abolished it in 1844. Except for these instances the Auburn system prevailed in the early state prisons of this country.

the Auburn system it triumphed almost completely over its rival in this country. On the other hand, most of the official European investigators of the two systems of prison discipline reported to their respective governments in favor of the Pennsylvania system of solitary confinement and the Pennsylvania system was much more widely adopted in Europe from 1830 to 1860 than the Auburn.

An adequate account of the bitter controversy that was waged from 1825 to 1860 between the exponents of the rival Pennsylvania and Auburn systems would occupy a large volume in itself and it can only be briefly touched upon in this place. The struggle began before either system was thoroughly established. As early as 1826-7 the commissioners who were appointed to devise the system of administration for the new state penitentiaries in Pennsylvania were approached by advocates of the Auburn system and were converted to an advocacy of its adoption. The main conflict was waged between the *Prison Discipline Society of Boston,* for the Auburn system, and the *Philadelphia Society for Alleviating the Miseries of Public Prisons,* for the Pennsylvania system. After its organization in 1845 the *Prison Society of New York* supported the Boston society in urging the adoption of the Auburn system. The *Prison Discipline Society of Boston* was organized by Louis Dwight (1793-1854). Dwight had originally prepared for the ministry, but was prevented from preaching by an injury to his lungs in an accident in a chemical laboratory. In 1824 he rode on horseback throughout the eastern part of the country distributing Bibles to prisoners. He was horrified by the appalling abuses in the contemporary penal institutions and he determined to devote his life to an improvement of their condition. He organized and directed the *Prison Discipline Society of Boston* from 1825 to his death in 1854. As secretary of the society he wrote its reports, which are much the best single source for the study of

American penology during this period, though they are disfigured by a violent opposition to the Pennsylvania system. He was repeatedly accused of unfairness and dishonesty by members of the *Philadelphia Society for Alleviating the Miseries of Public Prisons,* but a careful examination of the polemic pamphlets of both parties to the conflict cannot fail to impress an impartial reader with the fact that neither was qualified to "cast the first stone." Both were fiercely partisan and both were disgracefully unscrupulous in their use of statistics designed to support their cause or damage that of their opponents. The only gratifying feature of the controversy was that both systems were so greatly superior to the unspeakable congregate system which they displaced that their competition inevitably worked for the betterment of penal conditions. That Dwight and the Auburn system triumphed was not as much due to superior ability on his part as to the undoubted advantages in his position. The Pennsylvania system had been unfairly discredited by the failure of its imperfect application before 1829, and the Auburn system was free from this initial handicap. Further, the Auburn type of administration required less expenditure for introduction and the economic arguments in its favor were, at least superficially, much more attractive than for the Pennsylvania system. Added to these advantages was the superior and more widespread organization of the Boston Society throughout the country.[55]

[55] The controversy conducted in the reports and publications of these societies can be followed further in the controversial pamphlets which were issued by the exponents of the two systems during this period. The following are among the most important:

The Pennsylvania system is upheld and defended in the following articles and pamphlets:

Roberts Vaux, *Letters on the Penitentiary System of Pennsylvania, Addressed to William Roscoe, Esquire,* Philadelphia, 1827; George W. Smith, *A Defense of the Pennsylvania System of the Solitary Confinement of Prisoners,* Phil., 1833; Edward Livingston, *Introductory Report to the Code of Prison Discipline,* Philadelphia, 1827; and by the same writer, *Letters on the Pennsylvania System to Roberts Vaux,* 1828; Francis Lieber, *The Penitentiary System of Pennsylvania,* in the appendix to his translation of Beaumont and De Tocqueville; and by the same author, *A Popular Essay on the Subjects of Penal Law and*

In addition to the conflict between these prison reform societies, most of the leaders in the improvement of criminal jurisprudence and penal administration in this country took a decided stand on one side or the other of the controversy. The Pennsylvania system was defended by Roberts Vaux, Edward Livingston, Francis Lieber, Dorothea Lynde Dix, William Parker Foulke and Richard Vaux. The Auburn plan of administration was warmly favored by DeWitt Clinton, Gershom Powers, Amos Pillsbury, William H. Seward, E. C. Wines, Theodore W. Dwight, Frank Sanborn and Gideon Haynes. The controversy gradually died out after 1860. With an introduction of a knowledge of the Irish system into the United States, through the efforts of Frank Sanborn and others, about 1865, and its later development into the Elmira Reformatory system by 1875, the advocates of both older types of administration soon came to see that they had been supporting a hopelessly crude and elementary penal system and few possessed the audacity or stupidity to prolong the dispute.

on Uninterrupted Solitary Confinement at Labor, Philadelphia, 1838; John Sibley, *A Letter on the Superior Advantages of Solitary Confinement,* London, 1838; L. M. Moreau-Christophe, *Emprisonnement Individuel,* Paris, 1842; W. H. Suringar, *Considerations sur la réclusion individuelle,* Paris, 1843; *Report of a Minority of the Special Committee of the Boston Prison Discipline Society,* Boston, 1846; F. A. Packard, *A Vindication of the Separate System of Prison Discipline,* Philadelphia, 1839; *An Inquiry into the Alleged Tendency of the Separation of Convicts One from the Other to Produce Death and Derangement,* Philadelphia, 1849; W. P. Foulke, *Remarks on Cellular Separation,* Philadelphia, 1860; *The Pennsylvania System of Separate Confinement Explained and Defended,* Philadelphia, 1867; and the many and diverse writings of Richard Vaux from 1850 to 1875.

The Pennsylvania system is condemned in the writings given below: William Roscoe, *A Brief Statement of the Causes which Have Led to the Abandonment of the Celebrated System of Penitentiary Discipline in Some of the United States of America,* London, 1826; *The North American Review,* July, 1839, pp. 1-43; Ibid., January, 1848; Sir Peter Laurie, *A Letter on the Disadvantages and Extravagance of the Separate System of Prison Discipline,* London, 1848; and by the same author, *"Killing No Murder," or the Effects of Solitary Confinement on Prisoners,* London, 1846; George Combe, *Notes on the United States of North America,* 1838-40 (1841), especially, pp. 220-224; F. C. Gray, *Prison Discipline in America,* 1847; and *The Christian Examiner,* March, 1848.

On Louis Dwight see the chapter in O. F. Lewis, *Early American Prisons,* pp. 289-93.

V. LEADING PHASES OF NEW YORK PENOLOGY SINCE 1830

As this paper deals only with the historical background of the beginning of prison reform in New York State, it will be necessary to refrain from describing in detail the interesting and important progress made subsequent to the establishment of the Auburn system. Here would fall the development of the principle of differentiation in the treatment of the criminal population through the provision of institutions for delinquent children, reformatories for young first offenders, hospitals for the criminal insane and custodials for the feeble-minded and idiotic, all of which classes were incarcerated in jails and prisons in 1825 when guilty of criminal acts.[56] The first institution for juvenile delinquents in this country was opened at Madison Square on January 25, 1825, due to the efforts of local philanthropists, such as Thomas Eddy, Charles G. Haines, and Cadwallader D. Colden. They were led by Professor John Griscom, a member of the Society of Friends, who had just returned from a visit to Europe, during which he had noted the progress being made towards the provision of child-caring institutions in England and Continental Europe.[57] Even more significant was the birth of the modern reformatory with the opening of the Elmira Reformatory in 1877. This institution, the product of the energy and synthetic genius of E. C. Wines, Theodore Dwight, Frank Sanborn, Gideon Hubbell and Z. R. Brockway, embodied in its disciplinary and administrative procedure nearly all of the progressive phases of nineteenth-century penology, including Sir Charles Lucas' emphasis on reformation, Maconochie's practice of commutation of sentence for good behavior, the grading and classifying system of Sir Walter Crofton and his Irish system, the indeterminate sentence of Whatley, Combe and the brothers Hill, Marsangy's parole system and the emphasis on pro-

[56] On this diversification of institutions see Philip Klein, *Prison Methods in New York State,* Chap. II.

[57] B. J. Lossing, *History of New York City,* pp. 348 ff., 398.

ductive labor by Montesinos and Obermaier.[58] Nor should one forget Mr. Thomas Mott Osborne's *Mutual Welfare League,* recently originated in Auburn and tried out more thoroughly in Sing Sing, and which, in spite of being based on too enthusiastic an optimism as to the innate goodness of the average convict and marred by the lack of sufficient discrimination between different types of convicts, bids fair to be recognized as one of the epoch-making steps in the history of penology and reformation.[59] Finally, one must note the extremely significant step recently taken in the establishment of a psychological clinic at Sing Sing under the direction of Dr. Bernard Glueck.[60]

VI. SUMMARY

We have here attempted to show the relatively recent origin of prisons and the persistence until recent times of atrociously severe criminal codes and of the barbarous methods of corporal punishment which accompanied them. There was a general European movement towards the moderation of criminal codes and towards the adoption of imprisonment as the typical method of imprisonment during the late eighteenth and early nineteenth centuries. Among the European leaders in these reforms were Beccaria, Romilly, Howard and Elizabeth Fry. The initiative in America was taken by the Philadelphia reformers under the leadership of the Society of Friends. The program was based in part upon an imitation of the colonial precepts and practices of William Penn and in part upon an imitation of the European movements. They succeeded in introducing into America in a permanent fashion humane criminal jurisprudence and the modern prison

58 Wines, *Punishment and Reformation,* Chaps. IX-X.

59 Osborne, T. M., *Society and Its Prisons; Prisons and Common Sense.*

60 *Mental Hygiene,* January, April and October, 1918. For a comprehensive survey of the progress in criminology which has accompanied these advances in penology, see B. De Quiros, *Modern Theories of Crime.*

system. The New York reformers found in the Pennsylvania precedent the model for imitation. After a faulty trial of the Pennsylvania plan the New York authorities devised a disciplinary variation which soon assumed the proportions of an independent competing system and ultimately displaced its contender as the typical prison system of this country. Though the Auburn system has long since become antiquated, New York has maintained a leading place in progressive penology in this country through the priority which she can claim in the introduction of the first institution for juvenile delinquents, the first modern reformatory, the first notable experiment with prison democracy and the first thorough application of medical psychology to a study of the causes and treatment of crime.

SELECTED REFERENCES

Barnes, H. E. *History of the Penal, Reformatory and Correctional Institutions of New Jersey.*

Barnes, H. E. *The Evolution of Penology in Pennsylvania.*

De Quiros, B. *Modern Theories of Criminality.*

Ives, G. *A History of Penal Methods.*

Klein, P. *Prison Methods in New York State.*

Lewis, O. F. *The Development of American Prisons and Prison Customs, 1776-1845.*

Lindsley, J. B. *Prison Discipline and Prison Legislation.*

Phillipson, C. *Three Criminal Law Reformers: Beccaria, Bentham and Romilly.*

Robinson, L. N. *Penology in the United States.*

Vaux, Richard. *Sketch of the Origin and History of the Eastern Penitentiary.*

Webb, S. and B. *English Prisons Under Local Government.*

Wines, E. C. *The State of Prisons and Child-saving Institutions.*

Wines, F. H. *Punishment and Reformation* (New Ed.).

CHAPTER IV

The Place of the Pennsylvania Prison Society in American Prison Reform

I. THE ORIGINS AND ANTECEDENTS OF THE SOCIETY

At first sight any detailed survey of the activities of a local prison reform society might seem to be of only technical or esoteric significance or interest, but such is distinctly not the case with the *Pennsylvania Prison Society.* The Friends of Philadelphia, who made up the greater part of the active members of this society, actually brought into existence the modern prison system, and the reform of criminal jurisprudence upon which this rested. Therefore, an account of the activities of the *Pennsylvania Prison Society* is in reality the history of the specific manner in which we passed in this country from the barbarities of the colonial system of punishments into the next great stage of social methods of dealing with delinquents.

The antecedents of the *Pennsylvania Prison Society* go back to the ideals and practices of the founders of the province and to the reform movements of the eighteenth century. Such was its general background; it had no direct predecessor, as it was the first of the great prison reform societies.[1]

The beginnings of private prison reform movements in Pennsylvania are generally associated with the name of

[1] The other early prison reform societies in the order of their formation were: *The London Society for the Improvement of Prison Discipline,* 1815; *The Royal Prison Society of France,* 1819; *The Boston Prison Discipline Society,* 1824; *The Prison Association of New York,* 1845, to which may be added a society in Holland organized about 1812.

Richard Wistar, a member of the Society of Friends, who, just prior to the outbreak of the Revolutionary War, was attracted by the abject misery of the inmates of the provincial jail and had soup prepared at his own house and taken and distributed among the inmates of the jail. Others became interested in the situation, and, on February 7, 1776, there was formed *The Philadelphia Society for Assisting Distressed Prisoners,* the parent society of *The Philadelphia Society for Alleviating the Miseries of Public Prisons* and of *The Pennsylvania Prison Society.* This society had an existence of only nineteen months when it was broken up by the British occupation of Philadelphia. Of its work no official record remains. If one may believe the statement made a century later, without any evidence as to the sources of information, the society was organized to carry on more effectively the work of actual relief of prisoners which had been begun by Mr. Wistar. It is said that members of the society went from house to house with wheelbarrows gathering food and clothing for the convicts. In view of the fact that definite knowledge exists that there were several deaths from starvation in the jail in the period from 1770 to 1776, and that the inmates were in many cases almost entirely without clothing or bedding, there seems to be little reason for doubting that the purpose and activity of the society centered about improving the physical comforts of the prisoners. The only official notice of its activities which has been preserved is the following account of the termination of its existence: [2]

The British army having entered the city of Philadelphia in September, 1777, and possessed themselves of the public jails, no further service could be rendered, nor was any election held this month, for the appointment of new managers,

[2] Roberts Vaux, *Notices of the Original and Successive Attempts to Improve the Discipline of the Prison at Philadelphia and to Reform the Criminal Code of Pennsylvania,* 1826, p. 9.

so that the Philadelphia Society for Assisting Distressed Prisoners was dissolved during this memorable period.

Signed, RICHARD WELLS, *Secretary*.

Immediately after the peace of 1783 a number of prominent citizens of Philadelphia, led by Benjamin Franklin, Benjamin Rush, William Bradford and Caleb Lownes, organized a movement for the reform of the barbarous criminal code of 1718, which was still in force. Dr. Rush went as far as to advocate the total abolition of the death penalty. Their efforts resulted in the law of September 15, 1786, which substituted for the death penalty, in the case of some of the lesser felonies, "continued hard labor, publicly and disgracefully imposed." The results of this reforming law were not as satisfactory as were anticipated, while the public exposure of the convicts in their labor brought their distressing condition before the attention of a larger number of persons than could have been the case when secluded in the gloomy High street and Walnut street jails. The continued evils of the penal administration, together with this added publicity given to these deplorable conditions, prompted the formation of *The Philadelphia Society for Alleviating the Miseries of Public Prisons* in 1787.[3] This society, the first of the great modern prison reform societies, was organized on Tuesday, May 8, 1787, in the German School House on Cherry street.[4] The fundamental impulses, conceptions and purposes of the society are set forth in the preamble of the constitution:[5]

[3] The name was changed to that of The Pennsylvania Prison Society in 1887.

[4] The original members of the society were Francis Bailey, John Baker, Gerardus Clarkson, Tench Coxe, George Duffield, Samuel P. Griffiths, Henry Helmuth, Thomas Harrison, Joseph James, John Jones, John Kaighn, George Krebs, Thomas Lloyd, Caleb Lownes, Charles Marshall, Joseph Moore, John Morris, Thomas Morrison, John Olden, Thomas Parkinson, Isaac Parrish, Jonathan Penrose, Zachariah Poulson, James Reynolds, Thomas Rogers, William Rogers, Benjamin Rush, Lawrence Seckel, William Shippen, Jacob Shoemaker, John Swanwick, Richard Wells, William White, James Whiteall, Thomas Wistar, Benjamin Wynkoop, and William Zane.

[5] Roberts Vaux, *Notices*, pp. 10-11.

I was in prison and ye came unto me.

. . . And the King shall answer, and say unto them, verily I say unto you, inasmuch as ye have done it unto one of the least of these my brethren, ye have done it unto me.

Matthew xxv, 36, 40.

When we consider that the obligations of benevolence, which are founded on the precepts and example of the Author of Christianity, are not cancelled by the follies or crimes of our fellow creatures; and when we reflect upon the miseries which penury, hunger, cold, unnecessary severity, unwholesome apartments; and guilt (the usual attendants of prisons), involve with them; it becomes us to extend our compassion to that part of mankind, who are subjects of these miseries. By the aids of humanity, their undue and illegal sufferings may be prevented; the links which should bind the whole family of mankind together, under all circumstances, be preserved unbroken; and such degrees and modes of punishment may be discovered and suggested, as may, instead of continuing habits of vice, become the means of restoring our fellow creatures to virtue and happiness. From a conviction of the truth and obligation of these principles, the subscribers have associated themselves under the title of THE PHILADELPHIA SOCIETY FOR ALLEVIATING THE MISERIES OF PUBLIC PRISONS.

The remainder of the constitution of the society relates to its official organization, and only the sixth article is worthy of special notice. This describes the nature and duties of the so-called "Acting Committee," in which was vested wide authority, and which apparently constituted the body which carried on the real work of the society. It was specified that:

The Acting Committee shall consist of the President, two Vice Presidents, two Secretaries, two Counsellors, Treasurer, and six other members, three of whom to go off at the meetings in the months called January and July.[6] They shall

[6] In 1922 the Acting Committee had increased to sixty members.

visit the Prisons at least once a month, inquire into the circumstances of the Prisoners, and report such abuses as they shall discover to the proper officers appointed to remedy them. They shall examine the influence of confinement or punishment upon the morals of the Prisoners. They may draw upon the Treasurer for such sums of money as may be necessary. They shall keep regular minutes of their proceedings, to be read at the Quarterly Meeting of the Society.

While the importance of a precedent should not be underestimated, there seems no reason for doubting that the society of 1787 would have originated without the example of the organization of 1776. Only one member of the older society belonged to the second association (namely, Mr. Richard Wells), and the latter had a far wider program than the former. While still occupied with eliminating some of the physical suffering of the prisoners, it was primarily interested in a thoroughgoing reformation of the whole system of criminal jurisprudence and penal administration, which would cause the incidental evils and sufferings of the old system to disappear with the abolition of the causes for their existence.

II. THE EARLY COMPOSITION AND MEMBERSHIP OF THE PHILADELPHIA SOCIETY FOR ALLEVIATING THE MISERIES OF PUBLIC PRISONS

On account of the similarity between the aims and principles of the *Philadelphia Society for Alleviating the Miseries of Public Prisons* and the juristic and penological theories of the Quakers, and because of the fact that some of the most active members of the prison society were members of the Society of Friends, it has been customary, even for writers of authority, to represent the *Society for Alleviating the Miseries of Public Prisons* as identical with the Society of Friends. As a matter of fact, however, it is impossible to identify more than one hundred and thirty-six out of a total of three hundred and forty members in the crucial period from 1787 to 1830 as being also affiliated with the Society of Friends. The president of the society during the first forty-nine years of its existence was William White, Bishop of the Protestant Episcopal Church of Philadelphia. These facts, however, are in themselves no reflection upon the Society of Friends, nor do they detract in any manner from the degree to which society is indebted to the Friends for their services to juristic and penal reform. Rather, they are a compliment to the Quaker element in Pennsylvania, and the reform movement was both a triumph and a vindication of Quaker principles. When they became interested in prison reform the Episcopalians were compelled, in the period following 1787, to accept those Quaker conceptions and practices which they had spurned with contempt seventy years before. On the whole, then, it is not inaccurate in a general sense to regard those reforms which constituted the new penal code and the Pennsylvania system of prison administration as fundamentally the product of a Quaker movement.

The ideas and theories of the reformers were wholly in harmony with Quaker precedents, even if they were to some slight degree affected by the contemporary reform currents in Europe. Solitary confinement was the only element which needed to be added to Penn's juridical and penal practices in order to constitute the Pennsylvania system as it was known after 1830. The Quaker antecedents in the early provincial days were most important in making the reform movement "respectable" and in lessening popular prejudice. Finally, Roberts Vaux and his son, Richard, both Quakers, were for three-quarters of a century the most active members of the prison society in the cause of prison reform, in general, and in the exposition and defense of the Pennsylvania system, in particular. Nor should it be forgotten that there were many eminent citizens of Philadelphia, such as Benjamin Franklin and William Bradford, who, while not active participants in the prison reform society, were sympathetic with the cause of prison reform and co-operated with the society on all occasions.

III. THE WORK OF THE SOCIETY IN ADVANCING THE CAUSE OF REFORM IN CRIMINAL JURISPRUDENCE AND PRISON ADMINISTRATION, 1787 TO 1835

1. *The Origin of Prison Reform in Philadelphia*

While it is true that the impetus to reform came from many sources and there were many influential reformers not directly connected with the society, it is equally undeniable that there was no important reform legislation which was not secured in large part because of the efforts of the society. Therefore, a study of the work of the *Philadelphia Society for Alleviating the Miseries of Public Prisons* is little less than a survey of prison reform in Pennsylvania.

The first recorded activity of the society was the introduction in 1787 of religious services into the Walnut street jail. The keeper of the jail did all in his power to prevent the innovation and gave a sullen consent only on the written command of the sheriff of the county. The prisoners were assembled in a long column in the jail yard. A cannon was placed beside the improvised pulpit and a gunner stood by with a lighted match ready to fire into the mass of convicts at any sight of a riot. In spite of this unfavorable setting, the first sermon was delivered by Dr. William Rogers, a member of the society, with considerable effectiveness and very little disturbance. It is authoritatively asserted that this was the first religious service ever conducted in an American penal institution.[7]

[7] An interesting and probably not inaccurate attempt of an artist to reproduce this scene is to be found as a frontispiece to the Supplement to Number 49 of the *Journal of Prison Discipline and Philanthropy*, 1910.

As the society came into existence exactly when the effects of the operation of the law of September 15, 1786, were first becoming perceptible, it was but natural that the first systematic campaign of the society should be directed against the evils which were thereby revealed. Roberts Vaux thus describes the situation as it existed in the year 1787:[8]

> The law of 1786, although in many respects less sanguinary than the former enactments, contained some provisions, the execution of which led to the most injurious consequences. It directed that a certain description of convicts should be employed in cleaning the streets of the city and repairing the roads in the neighborhood; and authorized the keeper of the jail to shave the heads of the prisoners, and otherwise to distinguish them by an infamous dress. In this very objectionable manner they were brought before the public. The sport of the idle and the vicious, they often became incensed, and naturally took violent revenge upon the aggressors. To prevent them from retorting injuries still allowed to be inflicted, they were encumbered with iron collars and chains, to which bomb-shells were attached, to be dragged along while they performed their degrading service, under the eyes of keepers armed with swords, blunderbusses, and other weapons of destruction. These measures begot in the minds of the criminals and those who witnessed them disrespect for the laws executed with so much cruelty, and did not fail to excite the early notice of the society.

A committee of the society was immediately appointed "to inquire into the effects of the lately enacted penal law upon the criminals, now at work in our streets, and also its influence on society." The result of this inquiry was the following memorial of January, 1788, to the general assembly, the first public recommendation of the society. It will be noted that its chief recommendations were "more private and even solitary labor," separation of

[8] Roberts Vaux, *Notices*, pp. 21-2.

hardened criminals from first offenders, segregation of the different sexes, and the "prohibition of spirituous liquor among the criminals." The following is the text of this first memorial:[9]

To the Representatives of the Freemen of the Commonwealth of Pennsylvania, in General Assembly met.

The representatives and Petition of the subscribers, citizens of Pennsylvania:—

Your petitioners have viewed with pleasure the act of a former Assembly, for the reforming of the penal laws of the state by rendering them "less sanguinary and more proportionate to crimes," and though your petitioners conceive that the good ends thereby intended, have not hitherto been fully answered, yet they presume to suggest that the mode of punishment adopted in the "act for amending the penal laws," will be more likely to answer the desired purpose, by means of some amendments; a few of which your petitioners beg leave to lay before the house.

The punishment of criminals by "hard labor publicly and disgracefully imposed," as indicated in the preamble to the law, your petitioners wish the house would be pleased to revise, being fully convinced that punishment *by more private or even solitary* labor, would more successfully tend to reclaim the unhappy objects, as it might be conducted more steadily and uniformly, and the kind and portion of labor better adapted to the different abilities of the criminals; the evils of familiarizing young minds to vicious characters would be removed, and the opportunities of begging money would be prevented; for although the criminals are forbidden to have money in their possession, yet no penalty is inflicted on persons furnishing them therewith.

Your petitioners also wish to recommend to the attention of the house the very great importance of a separation of the sexes in the public prisons—and that some more effectual provision be made for the prohibition of spirituous liquor amongst the criminals, the use of which tends to lessen the

[9] *Sketch of Principal Transactions,* p. 6; Roberts Vaux, *Notices,* pp. 22-3.

true sense of their situation, and prevent those useful reflections which might be produced by solitary labor and strict temperance.

Your petitioners therefore respectfully request the house will be pleased to take the penal law under their consideration, and make such provision thereon as may more effectually answer the good and humane purposes thereby originally intended.

The legislature's attention and interest were attracted by this preliminary statement of defects and remedies and, on November 20, 1788, the supreme executive council sent a "minute" to a special meeting of the society asking more specific detailed information on the subject. In answer to this request, the society prepared its long memorial of December 15, 1788. This gave an account of the labors of the society in the Philadelphia jail; set forth notorious defects of the jail administration with respect to food, clothing, bedding, excessive use of alcoholic drinks, the herding of all classes of criminals and debtors and the evils of the system of public labor of the convicts; and concluded with its recommendations of separation of debtors from criminals, segregation of the sexes, total abolition of use of liquor in the jail, and, most important of all, *"solitary confinement to hard labor."*

This is the first recorded recommendation of what became the basic principle of the Pennsylvania system of prison administration and discipline. This epoch-making memorial of 1600 words presented the following indictment of the conditions in the city jail: [10]

1. Clothing of many prisoners is scant or lacking often owing to the length of time before trial. Sometimes exchanged for spirituous liquors. Even clothing furnished by the Society has been sold for rum. They suggest a prison dress which may not be sold or bartered.

10 Roberts Vaux, *Notices,* pp. 26-30.

2. Working criminals have made little complaint about food. Those committed for trial receive only a two-penny loaf daily. Persons held as witnesses receive no food, and must depend on their friends or other prisoners.

3. Innocent persons held for trial, when acquitted, may be detained for non-payment of jailer's fees.

4. Women with very young children receive the allowance of a single person. The Society had furnished soup to such prisoners.

5. No bedding whatever furnished by the authorities. Prisoners lie on the bare floor unless supplied by their friends.

6. Scanty supply of fuel burned in open fireplaces. Stoves are suggested.

7. Rum and other intoxicants sold to the prisoners by the jailers, who reap a rich profit from the transaction.

8. An old custom of partly stripping incoming prisoners of much of their clothing to be sold for rum for general use tolerated.

9. Sexes not separated.

10. Debtors confined with hardened criminals.

11. Unanimous in recommending solitary confinement to hard labor.

12. Unanimous in recommending total abstinence from spirituous liquors.

The document was signed by William White, Thomas Wistar and thirteen other members of the Society.

2. *The New Prison System in the Walnut Street Jail*

The effect of the memorial of December, 1788, was sweeping. The law of March 27, 1789, enacted all of the chief recommendations of the memorial. The society was further requested to aid the general assembly in preparing a bill which would provide for a thorough reconstruction of the prison system and a systematic revision of the criminal code. In addition to this specific co-operation with the legislature, the society considered it wise to make the minds of the members of the assembly more susceptible to the aims of the reformers by publishing a pamphlet entitled, "Extracts and Remarks on the Subject of Punishment and Reformation of Criminals," five hundred copies of which were distributed among members of the legislature and other public officers. The chief purpose of the pamphlet was to allay the fear that the proposed reforms in Pennsylvania would not prove workable or economical. A considerable collection of extracts from letters and prison regulations was reproduced, which demonstrated that the very measures proposed for Pennsylvania had already been successfully put into practice in a number of recently reformed English county jails or prisons. It was contended that experience had shown that imprisonment at hard labor was profitable even in England "where labor is cheaper and provisions much dearer than in the United States."

Most of the proofs of the success of the new system were drawn from the experience of Sir Thomas Beevor in the newly constructed prison at Wymondham in Norfolk, which had been erected as a result of the inspiration derived from a reading of John Howard's "State of Prisons." In this "model" jail were to be seen in actual successful operation all of the new principles which it was hoped might be introduced into Pennsylvania. Cells were provided to keep the different types of offenders separate, and the sexes were segregated in different parts of the building. Separate cells were provided for each prisoner "in which they sleep, and when necessary work the whole day alone." This solitary confinement was said by Sir Thomas to be more effective than whipping, and "that part of their punishment from which reformation is chiefly expected." This new system was found effective in every way. By providing hard labor for all on six days of every week, it was found that many prisoners earned more than double the cost of their maintenance. As a reformative agency the results were not less satisfactory. It had not yet been found necessary to punish any inmates by confinement in irons. The deterrent effects of the system were also alleged to be most gratifying. The judges on the circuit reported that never in their experience had there been so few commitments to the jail.

The Philadelphia society declared that exactly what was needed at home was to follow this English example and "make our prisons penitentiary houses and places of correction." [11] They pointed to the fact that the success of the Norfolk jail had led to its being imitated in other English jails. The remainder of the pamphlet was chiefly devoted to quotations from Howard's printed works as substantiating the following reform principles, which the society desired to introduce in Pennsylvania: "that reformation has become a principal object with the magistracy and rulers;" that murder, arson and burglary should be the only capital crimes; that drunkenness is the chief cause of crime; that solitary cells, ten feet high, ten feet long and eight feet wide furnish the best mode of confining convicts; that where labor is consistently provided for prisoners they are able to defray the expense of incarceration. From the whole pamphlet the society arrived at the following conclusion and recommendation: [12]

> From the foregoing extracts we learn that the miseries of the unfortunate prisoner have become subjects of deep investigation in Europe, and that by an observance of wholesome rules, gaols may prove the happy means of reformation, and that the criminals instead of being a burden may be transformed into serviceable members of the community.

[11] An exact return to Penn's provisions of a century earlier.

[12] *Extracts and Remarks on the Subject of Punishment and Reformation of Criminals*, p. 23.

Under these impressions the Society established in the city of Philadelphia for alleviating the miseries of public prisons, wish to present the subject to the Legislature of Pennsylvania, hoping that the penal laws of the state may be so modelled as to promote reformation in the criminal and safety to the people.

The results of these multifarious activities of the society from 1788 to 1790 appear in the famous law, passed on April 5, 1790, which marks the legal origin of the Pennsylvania system of prison administration. It provided for a revision of the penal code which went further than the revision of 1786 in substituting imprisonment at hard labor for the punishment of crimes; directed the separation of witnesses and debtors from convicts, and the proper segregation of the sexes; and ordered the erection of a block of cells in the yard of the Walnut street jail for the solitary confinement of the "more hardened and atrocious offenders."

3. *Reform of Criminal Code*

From 1790 to 1801 the activities of the society centered mainly in urging the further reform of the criminal code; in attempting to improve the condition of debtors in the jails; in opposing extortion in the fee system in the jail; in recommending and offering to pay for a system of "instruction in useful knowledge" in the jail; and in watching the operation of the new criminal code and penal system and reporting delinquency in its administration. The results appear in the law of September 23, 1791, abolishing the death penalty for witchcraft; the law of April 4, 1792, putting the keeper of the debtors' apartment in the jail on a salary rather than on a fee basis; the act of April 22, 1794, abolishing the death penalty for all crimes except murder in the first degree; and the laws of April 15, 1795, and February 15, 1799, extending and perpetuating the operation of the criminal and penal codes of 1790 and 1794.

By the end of the first decade of the operation of the new criminal code and penal system so great a degree of laxity had developed in the administrative system that it destroyed the benefits of the newer practices, which had proved very successful immediately after 1790. Accordingly, on December 14, 1801, the society addressed the following memorial to the legislature asking for a strict enforcement of the new system:[13]

To the Senate and House of Representatives of the Commonwealth of Pennsylvania:

The Memorial of the Philadelphia Society for Alleviating the Miseries of Public Prisons, Respectfully Represents:

That your Memorialists have contemplated with pleasure the progress made by former legislatures in preventing crimes, and reforming criminals, and, encouraged by the ready attention heretofore shown to their applications, are emboldened to call the notice of the legislature to the present state of our Prisons.

When the reform was made in our penal laws in the year 1790, although the principles were plainly laid down, yet it was not expected that the practical part could be suddenly or completely effected. It was then in some degree a matter of experiment. An experiment, however, though imperfectly made, which has not only increased our internal security, but has been so far approved of as to be adopted in several of our sister states.

Being ourselves fully convinced of the propriety both of these principles and this practice, we now wish briefly to solicit your attention to a most essential part of this humane and rational plan for preventing crimes and reforming criminals. Ever since the present establishment of the Prisons we have wished to make the fair experiment of solitude and labor on the convicts. Every year's experience has shown

13 Roberts Vaux, *Notices,* pp. 36-7.

us that in the present state of the Prison, such an attempt, however desirable, is impracticable.

We are therefore induced to request that you will devise such means as may appear to you most adequate, to separate the convicts from all other descriptions of prisoners, in order that a full opportunity of trying the effects of solitude and labor may be afforded.

Signed by direction of the Society,

WM. WHITE,

President.

Philadelphia, 12th mo. 14, 1801.

4. *The Agitation for a State Prison System and the Establishment of the Pennsylvania System of Prison Administration*

Two years more of observation, however, led the society to conclude that the architectural limitations of the old Walnut street jail were in large degree responsible for the degeneration of the administrative mechanism of the prison system, and they sent to the legislature, in 1803, a memorial urging the building of a new prison in Philadelphia. In this address they were joined by the inspectors of the Walnut street jail:[14]

To the Senate and House of Representatives of Pennsylvania:

The Memorial of the Philadelphia Society for alleviating the miseries of Public Prisons, and of the Inspectors of the Prison of the City and County of Philadelphia,

Respectfully Represents:

That in reforming the penal laws of this state the legislature of Pennsylvania contemplated the reclaiming of criminals, as well as preventing crimes; and with this view, adopted the mode of punishing criminals by solitary confinement at hard labour, under such regulations as appeared best calculated to impress strongly on the minds of the con-

[14] Roberts Vaux, *Notices*, p. 37.

victs the connexion of suffering with the transgression of the laws. At the time of this reform, the jail of the city and county of Philadelphia was considered as sufficiently large to carry this benevolent design of the legislature into effect, and to leave suitable room for the confinement of vagrants, prisoners for trial, etc. A period of more than twelve years has elapsed since this reform came into operation, and in the course of that time the number of prisoners of various descriptions has increased to such a degree, owing to the jail of Philadelphia being by law the general place of custody for all the convicts of the state, and likewise to the substitution of long periods of confinement instead of capital punishment, that the said prison is no longer capable of containing them in such a way as to answer the intention of the legislature. The number of vagrants, etc., has so much increased, that it is a matter of great difficulty to keep them in order, and impracticable to keep them regularly at labour. The prisoners who are detained for trial, run-away servants and apprentices, are through necessity confined in the same apartment with the vagrants, and the intercourse between such persons crowded together may easily be conceived to be most destructive to the morals of the whole, insomuch that when they are released from prison they are likely to come out intimately acquainted with the arts of villainy, and combined with an extensive association of persons of similar character to make depredations on the public. The great number of vagrants, untried prisoners, etc., produces hurtful effects on the convicts, as the latter are, for want of room, obliged to be kept in too large numbers in one apartment, by which the amelioration of their morals is either prevented or greatly impeded, the keeping of them attended with great hazard; and they have more opportunity of laying plans of escape; their labour is rendered less productive than it might be, and the idea of solitude is nearly obliterated.

The health of the city is much endangered by having so many people crowded together in one house. Notwithstanding the great attention to cleanliness, the jail fever made its appearance there during the last winter. Whether under the present arrangements, it will be practicable to prevent its breaking out again, and in case of such an event, extending its effects beyond the prison walls, it is impossible to determine.

Another house or set of buildings appears to be necessary, where the vagrants might be suitably classed and compelled to hard labour. In such proper apartments these prisoners might, under suitable regulations, be kept at labour so productive as might at least defray the expense of their keeping or maintenance: this, to the idle and disorderly would be such an object of terror, that the number of them would probably soon be lessened.

By such an arrangement also, the prisoners for trial, servants, and apprentices, could be suitably classed and taken care of, without being made necessary companions of abandoned characters; which is unavoidable in the present state of the prison; whilst the convicts, by having the whole of the present building allotted to them, could be subdivided into smaller classes—more effectually secluded from any confederacy with those out of doors—more easily managed, and have a fairer chance of improving their morals; and while their minds would have fewer objects to distract them, they might become more docile; and while their labour would be rendered more productive, they would be confirmed in those habits of industry which are calculated to render them useful, both to themselves and society. . . .

Placed as we are, in a situation to observe the salutary effects of solitude and labour, in preventing crimes and reforming criminals, we trust you will, as heretofore, receive our application with indulgence, and therefore again respectfully submit to your consideration, the propriety of granting another building, for the purpose of making such separation amongst the prisoners as the nature and wants of this truly benevolent system require.

As a result of this memorial, an act was passed on April 2, 1803, authorizing the raising of money for the erection of a new prison on Arch street. This was not opened, however, until 1817 and then it was used until

1823 solely for the detention of debtors. Not until the Eastern Penitentiary was opened at Cherry Hill on October 25, 1829, was any systematic provision made for relieving the ridiculous and demoralizing overcrowding of the Walnut street jail.

During the years 1809 to 1811, the society made a beginning of the establishing of a library in the Walnut street jail, but it would seem from the following report of the library committee that only Bibles were included in the first literary equipment of a Pennsylvania penal institution:[15]

> Bibles and Testaments have been furnished, and some of the prisoners seem inclined to peruse them; it is hoped benefit has resulted from the measure, but the committee is not prepared to give an opinion as to the utility of introducing any other books.

By 1816 the overcrowding of the Walnut street jail had become so serious that the society prepared a pamphlet entitled, *A Statistical View of the Operation of the Penal Code of Pennsylvania, to Which Is Added a View of the Present State of the Penitentiary and Prison of Philadelphia.* The pamphlet, aside from statistical information relative to convictions, was devoted to pointing out the "melancholy and striking contrast" between the "happy effect" of the system, as early administered, and the deplorable situation in 1816. The decline was held to be a result of overcrowding the Walnut street jail, which had not been enlarged since 1795, and had become so deficient in housing facilities for the increased number of convicts that from thirty to forty prisoners were normally locked up for the night in a room eighteen feet square. While there is no doubt that this memorial may have had some effect in hastening the opening of the Arch street prison for debtors in the following year, the

15 Roberts Vaux, *Notices,* pp. 39-40.

society became convinced that the system of sending all the more hardened types of prisoners from the entire state to the county prison of Philadelphia was no longer wise or tolerable, owing to the increasing population of the state and the failure to expand the prison plant in proportion. Consequently, in 1818, they sent their first memorial to the legislature urging the erection of State penitentiaries. This was the beginning of the agitation that led to the erection of the Eastern and Western State Penitentiaries:[16]

To the Senate and House of Representatives, etc.

The Memorial, Etc.

Respectfully Showeth:

That in the year 1787, an association was formed by a number of the inhabitants of Philadelphia, for the purpose of lessening the evils and miseries of prisons, and of promoting an amelioration of the penal laws of this state, under the title of "The Philadelphia Society for Alleviating the Miseries of Public Prisons," which society have continued their attention to the subject until the present time, and have the satisfaction, in common, with their fellow citizens, of witnessing considerable improvement in the management of the prison in this city. But the progress of which, they apprehend, is obstructed, and many other evils experienced by the necessity of crowding into that establishment great numbers of convicts from all parts of this populous state. They therefore respectfully request the legislature to consider the propriety and expediency of erecting penitentiaries in suitable parts of the state, for the more effectual employment and separation of the prisoners, and of proving the efficacy of solitude on the morals of those unhappy objects.

Signed on behalf of the Society,

William White,
Thomas Wistar,
Samuel P. Griffitts,
Joseph Crukshank.

16 Roberts Vaux, *Notices,* p. 41.

5. *The New Penitentiary*

It was due in large part to this memorial of 1818 that an act was passed on March 3, 1818, appropriating sixty thousand dollars for building a penitentiary at Allegheny on the principle of solitary confinement. This same act authorized, but did not command, the sale of the Walnut street jail, the removal of the prisoners to the Arch street prison, and the erection of a new penitentiary in Philadelphia from the proceeds of the sale of the Walnut street plant. As no definite action was taken on this authorization of 1818 with respect to building a new penitentiary in Philadelphia, the society came forward with the following final memorial of 1821, which succeeded in securing the passage of the act of March 20, 1821, appropriating one hundred thousand dollars for the erection of a state penitentiary in the county of Philadelphia capable of receiving two hundred and fifty convicts: [17]

To the Senate and House of Representatives of the Commonwealth of Pennsylvania, in General Assembly met.

The Memorial of the Philadelphia Society for Alleviating the Miseries of Public Prisons,

Respectfully Represents,

That it is now nearly forty years since some of your Memorialists associated for the purpose of alleviating the miseries of public prisons, as well as for procuring the melioration of the penal code of Pennsylvania, as far as these effects might be produced through their influence.

In the performance of the duties which they believed to be required of them by the dictates of Christian benevolence, and the obligations of humanity, they investigated the conduct and regulations of the jail, and likewise the effects of those degrading and sanguinary punishments, which were at that period inflicted by the laws of this Commonwealth. The result of these examinations was a full conviction, that not only the police of the prison was faulty, but the penalties

[17] Ibid., pp. 43-5.

of the law were such as to frustrate the great ends of punishment, by rendering offenders inimical, instead of restoring them to usefulness in society.

With these impressions, alterations in the modes of punishments, and improvements in prison discipline, were from time to time recommended to the Legislature, by whose authority many changes were adopted, and many defects remedied.

These reforms, from the nature of existing circumstances, were, however, of comparatively limited extent, but as far as the trial could be made, beneficial consequences were experienced.

Neighboring states, and remote nations, directed their attention to these efforts, and in many instances, adopted the principles which had influenced the conduct of Pennsylvania.

At the time of making the change in our penal code, substituting solitude and hard labour for sanguinary punishments, the experiment was begun in the county jail of Philadelphia, rather than the execution of the laws should be deferred to a distant period, when a suitable prison might be erected. Under all the inconveniences then subsisting, the effects produced were such as to warrant a belief that the plan would answer the most sanguine wishes of its friends, if it could be properly tried. But the construction ot the prison, and its crowded condition, being the only penitentiary used for all the convicts of the state, leave but slender hopes of the accomplishment of the humane intentions of the Legislature.

Your Memorialists believe, that they discover in the recent measures of the Commonwealth, a promise, which will fulfil the designs of benevolence in this respect. The edifice now in progress at Pittsburg for the reception of prisoners, constructed upon a plan adapted to strict solitary confinement, will go far towards accomplishing this great purpose; and your Memorialists are induced to hope, that the same enlightened policy which dictated the erection of a state prison in the western, will provide for the establishment of a similar one in the eastern part of the state.

Reasons of the most serious and substantial nature might

be urged to show the absolute necessity which exists for a penitentiary in the city and county of Philadelphia, whether we regard the security of society, or the restoration of the offenders against its laws. It will not be necessary here to recite the alarming proofs which might be adduced in support of their opinions, but refer to the documents herewith furnished, which exhibit the actual condition of the prison.

Your Memorialists, therefore, respectfully request, that you will be pleased to take the subject under your serious consideration, and if you judge it right, to pass a law, for the erection of a penitentiary for the eastern district of the state, in which the benefits of solitude and hard labour may be fairly and effectually proved.

Signed by order and on behalf of the Society.

William White, President.
William Rogers, Vice-President.
Thomas Wistar, do
Nicholas Collin,
Samuel Powel Griffitts,
Jos. Reed,
Roberts Vaux.

Attest.
Caleb Cresson, Sec'y.

The confidence reposed by the legislature in the information and achievements of the society is shown by the fact that a majority of the board of commissioners named in the act to supervise the building of the penitentiary were members of the prison society.[18]

In spite of all their labors in this direction, however, the society came very near to losing the opportunity of testing their penological principles, based upon the fundamental doctrine of solitary confinement at hard labor. By a resolution of March 23, 1826, the legislature appointed Charles Shaler, Edward King, and T. J. Wharton as com-

[18] The members of this board were Thomas Wistar, Samuel P. Griffitts, Peter Miercken, George N. Baker, Thomas Bradford, Jr., John Bacon, Caleb Carmalt, Samuel R. Wood, Thomas Sparks, James Thackera and Daniel H. Miller.

missioners to revise the penal code. They were directed to carry out the revision according to the system of imprisonment at hard labor with solitary confinement. While engaged on their labors they came under the influence of Louis Dwight, secretary of the Boston Prison Discipline Society, and the most zealous and energetic supporter of the Auburn system of prison administration based upon congregate workshops and separation at night. As a result of Mr. Dwight's advocacy of the Auburn system, and the favorable impression of it derived from a personal visit and study by the commissioners, the latter recommended in their report that the new penitentiaries at Allegheny and Philadelphia be altered in construction, so that they might be administered according to the Auburn plan. *The Philadelphia Society for Alleviating the Miseries of Public Prisons* became alarmed at the prospect of losing the benefit of all their efforts in behalf of the system of solitary confinement, and they sent one of their members, Mr. Samuel R. Wood, to labor with the chairman of the judiciary committee of the legislature. Mr. Wood's arguments were sufficiently effective, so that when the law of April 23, 1829, was passed, finally establishing the system of penal administration for Pennsylvania, it provided for solitary confinement at hard labor.[19]

6. *Diverse Activities of the Society, 1820-1835*

As soon as the new state prison system was established, the society renewed the agitation for the abandonment of the Walnut street jail and the building of a new county jail in Philadelphia. In this they were in part successful. A new county prison, known as the Moyamensing Prison, was erected, but its construction was not wholly

[19] The acts of 1821 and 1829 were drawn up by Roberts Vaux, Thomas Bradford, Jr., and Samuel R. Wood.

in accordance with the principle of solitary confinement.

Not only did the society labor strenuously in this period for the improvement of the prison system, but they also were the first to point out a need for the differentiation of penal and correctional institutions on the basis of the age of the offenders. Accordingly, in 1823, a committee of the society was appointed to investigate the need for an institution for juvenile delinquents in Pennsylvania. In 1826, in an able memorial written by Roberts Vaux, the committee reported in favor of the immediate construction of such an institution. With the aid of other enlightened citizens of Philadelphia, the society was able to secure the erection of the Philadelphia House of Refuge in 1828.

In spite of this formidable list of local achievements, the activities of the *Philadelphia Society for Alleviating the Miseries of Public Prisons* were not limited to the state of Pennsylvania. A knowledge of the prison reform movement which they promoted and advanced had spread throughout the United States and Europe by 1830. The society was early attracted by John Howard's work in Europe, and at the fourth meeting of the members they listened to a letter from Dr. Lettsom, of London, describing Howard's journeys on the Continent in the investigation of prison conditions.

While the Philadelphia society gained an early inspiration from the work of the English reformers, it was not long before the English began to seek advice from the sponsors of prison reform in Pennsylvania. In 1818, Dr. Stephen Lushington, of the *London Society for the Improvement of Prison Discipline,* wrote to the Philadelphia society inquiring as to the effect of the new system of solitary confinement with labor. He was answered by President White, in a letter which set forth the difficulties under which the system had been compelled to operate, owing to the overcrowded condition of the Walnut street prison, and expressed the optimistic hopes of the society with regard to the future, when the new system could be carried out under architectural surroundings which would not defeat its fundamental principles. The last paragraph of the letter is worthy of quotation:[20]

We feel great satisfaction in your exertions in this dignified cause; and hope you will not be discouraged by any partial considerations, from continuing to co-operate with us, in endeavoring to establish the beneficent principle, that the prevention of crime, and the reformation of the offender, is the object of punishment. And whatever may have been the fears and resentments of those times, which produced the too generally prevailing system of lightly multiplying criminal offences, and of inflicting death, and other odious punishments; let us indulge in the pleasing hope, that this system of ignorance and barbarism will no longer continue to the disgrace of the nations and governments, who are now arrived at the highest state of civilization, and who profess to be actuated by the benign and salutary influences of Christianity.

The list of corresponding members of the society up to 1830 furnishes a valuable means of estimating the extent of the influence of this Philadelphia society. Among the corresponding members in Europe were such distinguished names in the history of legal and penal reform as Sir Samuel Romilly, Thomas F. Buxton, William Crawford and William Roscoe, of England; Henri Grégoire and Charles Lucas, of Paris; and Prince Gallitzin, of Russia.[21]

The contributions of the society to the growth of prison reform movements in the United States in the half century following the Revolution can scarcely be exaggerated. As early as 1794 the society resolved to make its work broader than a local effort in Philadelphia, and "an

20 Roberts Vaux, *Notices,* pp. 42-3.

21 Roberts Vaux's writings on the Pennsylvania prison reform movement were well known in Europe in 1830.

extensive correspondence was opened and carried on between the society and the executives of several of the states of the union, which tended to diffuse much information relative to its labors, and led to the adoption of reform in the penal laws in other parts of the continent." The effect of this missionary effort is particularly evident in the law of March 26, 1796, passed in New York, reducing the capital crimes from sixteen to two and providing for the erection of two state prisons. New Jersey also reformed its criminal code by the law of March 18, 1796, and directed the erection of a state prison by the law of March 1, 1797. In 1813 the secretaries of the society were directed to correspond with those in charge of the new system of penitentiary administration in the other states and to make inquiry as to the extent of the progress already made. It was found that some ten states had established improved penitentiary systems with at least moderate success. There is no reason to doubt that the impulse to reform in each instance came to some extent from the Pennsylvania movement. It is definitely known that before 1825, Maine, Maryland, Massachusetts, New York, New Jersey and Virginia had adopted for trial the Pennsylvania system of solitary confinement.

Especially interesting was the influence of the Pennsylvania system upon New York state, for it can readily be shown that the great contending prison system—the "Auburn system"—was but the result of an alteration of the Pennsylvania system of solitary confinement. During the second decade of the nineteenth century there was a wave of imitation, throughout the eastern states, of the Pennsylvania system of solitary confinement, and New York, in common with others, decided in 1819 to build a block of cells for solitary confinement in the yard of the newly constructed prison at Auburn. In 1820 the New York authorities sent an inquiry to the *Philadelphia Society for Alleviating the Miseries of Public Prisons,* asking for advice as to the new method of administration. The society deputed Roberts Vaux to write the reply and he answered, giving the desired information and enjoining the New York reformers to persist in their intentions. In 1821 the cell block was opened and eighty hardened criminals were locked in separate cells without labor or exercise. By 1823 this procedure had become so detrimental to the physical and mental health of the prisoners thus confined that it was practically abandoned, and in the following year Elam Lynds, the head keeper, and John Cray, the head architect, devised the world-famed "Auburn Prison system," which consisted of solitary confinement at night and silent but congregate work in a common workshop by day. It can readily be seen that this was but a modification of a direct imitation of the Pennsylvania example—a modification which was considered by its exponents to mark a great advance in prison administration, but which was regarded by the adherents of the Pennsylvania system as a retrogressive step towards the corrupting influence of the former promiscuous association of convicts. It is scarcely necessary to mention the fact that for more than a quarter of a century nearly all the controversy over prison administration centered about the respective merits of the Auburn, as opposed to the Pennsylvania, system.[22]

It is not necessary to summarize at this point the early achievements of the *Philadelphia Society for Alleviating the Miseries of Public Prisons.* It has been shown that they played a dominating part in bringing about all of those progressive changes which characterized the origins of modern penology, and that the society constituted what Tarde would call the "radiant point of imitation" for the

[22] This controversy can best be followed in the publications of *The Philadelphia Society for Alleviating the Miseries of Public Prisons* and of the *Boston Prison Discipline Society* from 1825 to 1855. See above, Chap. III.

early developments of prison reform in America, and, to a lesser extent, in Europe.

IV. THE WORK OF THE PHILADELPHIA SOCIETY FOR ALLEVIATING THE MISERIES OF PUBLIC PRISONS (THE PENNSYLVANIA PRISON SOCIETY) SINCE 1835

The part played by the *Philadelphia Society for Alleviating the Miseries of Public Prisons* in the reconstruction of penal conditions in Pennsylvania at the close of the colonial period and in the creation of the Pennsylvania prison system has been described. At the close of nearly a century after these reforms had been achieved the society still exists as the most powerful agency for prison reform in the state, and its labors in this field since 1835 have been more productive of permanent good than the combined efforts of other critics and investigators. Very little has been achieved in improving the conditions in penal and reformatory institutions in Pennsylvania which has not been due in a very large degree to the activities of this organization. And, as in the beginning, the majority of the most active members since 1835 have belonged to the Society of Friends.[23]

The following summary review of the work of this organization cannot be regarded as anything more than an account of a few of its more conspicuous achievements and activities. A full account of their multifarious labors would constitute a treatise in itself.[24] The first notable service rendered by the society following 1835 was the aid it gave to Dorothea L. Dix in agitating for the estab-

[23] Its name was changed to that of *The Pennsylvania Prison Society* in 1887.

[24] The full account of the labors of the society can be obtained from the files of the *Journal of Prison Discipline and Philanthropy*, the organ of the society. It can be obtained in the society offices, and a full set has also been collected for the library of the Russell Sage Foundation in New York.

lishment of a hospital for the insane which would allow of the removal of insane convicts from the state penitentiaries. A vigorous memorial was sent to the legislature in 1845 urging such action. In 1850-1851 the society devoted its main efforts to an attempt to compel the practice of solitary confinement in the county jails of the state. The first law in Pennsylvania ordering the granting of commutation of sentence for good behavior—that of 1861—was passed as a result of the agitation of the society, especially of Townsend Sharpless. From 1853 to 1870 the society labored to have a workhouse provided for the city of Philadelphia. One of the most important achievements of this organization was the leadership that it took in securing the legislation creating the state board of public charities in 1869. In 1872 it secured the creation of the state board of pardons, thus taking the important pardoning powers out of the hands of the governor alone. It lent its aid after 1885 to the struggle for a special state hospital for the criminal insane. In the period of discussion accompanying the establishment of the Huntington Reformatory, the majority of the members of the society ranged themselves in favor of the adoption of the advanced Elmira system of prison administration. In the period from 1909 to the present, which has been characterized by the greatest penological progress of the last generation, the society has led in the program of education and agitation which secured such notable innovations as the introduction of probation, parole and the indeterminate sentence, has made vigorous attempts to remedy the intolerable industrial situation in the state penitentiaries, and obtained legislation creating a general prison investigating commission.

This commission made some specific recommendations which have led to the establishment of a Department of Public Welfare, one of whose departments is called the Bureau of Restoration. This commission has already almost doubled the industrial products of the prisons, and in addition has conducted an exhaustive survey of all the prisons of the commonwealth, the facts ascertained by which investigation will be made the basis for some remedial legislation. The Rev. J. F. Ohl, chairman of the Standing Committee on Legislation, rendered efficient service in securing for the prisoners the advantages of parole and probation.

Some notable humanitarian efforts of the society have been expended in aiding discharged prisoners and in visiting prisoners in both state and county institutions. Every year thousands of visits were made to the prisoners at the Eastern Penitentiary, and in this phase of the work doubtless the most active was Mr. John J. Lytle, the General Secretary of the Society from 1851 to 1909. When the state in 1895 discontinued an appropriation by which needy prisoners at the time of their discharge were furnished with decent clothing and temporary aid while searching for employment, Mr. Lytle by his personal efforts secured contributions for this purpose from philanthropic citizens. Although the state in 1911 granted funds to supply the discharged prisoners with clothing, the society still renders a decided service in securing employment for prisoners when released, in paying for transportation to their homes, and in giving temporary aid while looking for employment. In the more recent period, Mr. Albert H. Votaw, the successor of Mr. Lytle, has been active in giving attention to the legislative program and especially to the conditions at the county jails. While this study of jail conditions has been less uniform than the investigations by the board of public charities, it has been much more penetrating, especially in the last decade when the work of the state board has been rather perfunctory and mechanical, while that of the prison society has been especially thorough-going and conscientious. Though a considerable number of valuable recommendations, made by the state board, have been carried out, yet it is generally conceded by all investigators and by those who have given any attention to the investigations that nothing short of a complete revolution will remedy the intolerable conditions prevalent in the county jails, chief among which are the demoralizing effects of idleness. It now seems probable that the new Department of Public Welfare will recommend the abolition of the county jail and that all convicted prisoners, since they have offended "the peace and dignity of the Commonwealth," shall be placed under the authority of state officials on farms established for the care and treatment of delinquents.

BIBLIOGRAPHIC NOTE

There is no thorough history of the Quakers in American prison reform or of the work of the Pennsylvania Prison Society. The sources are in rare pamphlet literature, most of which is noted in footnotes 23-34 and 55 of Chapter III of the present work. My forthcoming work on the history of Pennsylvania penology will contain the most detailed account of these developments yet published. Much of interest will be found in Richard Vaux's *Sketch of the Origin and History of the Eastern Penitentiary;* and O. F. Lewis's *Development of American Prisons and Prison Customs, 1776-1845.*

CHAPTER V

Some Leading Phases of the Evolution of Modern Penology [1]

I. THE DEVELOPMENT OF PENOLOGY IN RECENT TIMES AS A PHASE OF GENERAL SOCIAL AND INTELLECTUAL HISTORY

In a preceding chapter we examined in some detail the progress in criminal jurisprudence and penal administration which brought about the termination of corporal punishment and the substitution therefor of imprisonment in this country between 1760 and 1840. In this chapter there will be presented a rapid and comprehensive survey of the whole field of the development of modern criminology and penology, with special reference to those phases of progress which have taken place since the establishment of the Auburn and Pennsylvania systems.

It is probably apparent to all thoughtful students of the progress of penology in modern times that its advance has been a product of the general growth of scientific knowledge concerning the individual and his social relationships. If it has shown a tendency to lag behind certain other phases of general intellectual progress, this has been because it is connected very closely with both ethical and metaphysical assumptions and legal concepts and processes which inevitably retard the free and natural progress of thought and procedure. A few examples of this intimate dependence of penological development upon the progress of thought and science in modern times will be sufficient to illustrate this introductory consideration.

[1] Eighth Annual Stuckenberg Lecture at Pennsylvania College, February 14, 1922.

Modern biology, for example, has made clear the characteristic animal traits which man has inherited from his ancestors and has opened the way for an understanding of the difficulties inherent in attempting to keep this primitive equipment controlled by modern laws and institutions. It has called attention to the frequent occurrence of organic defects in the criminal personality, which are an important cause of his criminal behavior, and which may, through ill-controlled heredity, lead to a transmission of these menacing defects to a multitude of descendants. It has also made plain the necessity of incarcerating the prisoner under healthful conditions if any effective effort at reformation is to be hoped for.

Equally significant has been the growth of scientific knowledge in the field of psychology. This has utterly destroyed the old notion of the criminal as a "perverse free moral agent," and has led to the analysis of the nature and significance of "criminal behavior." It has pointed out the psychopathic trends and characteristics in the disposition or mental constitution of the typical criminal. It has, at the same time, destroyed forever the belief that the criminal class is a uniform type, and it has made clear the necessity of differentiation in the study and treatment of the offenders against the law. It has proved to the satisfaction of all scientifically minded persons the utter hopelessness of attempting to reform a certain very considerable group of low-grade psychopathic criminals, and has demonstrated the necessity of a permanent detention and segregation of this type in the interest of social protection. But it has also made it equally apparent that the majority of the remaining element in the criminal class can be restored as safe members of society when they are subjected to proper educational and therapeutic treatment, according to the principles of modern psychiatry. More than this, it has aided the courts in providing a more scientific technique for detecting and convicting the criminal. The work of Hans Gross and Hugo Munsterberg is sufficiently well known to illustrate this field of psychological activity in its relation to criminology and criminal jurisprudence.

Nor have the natural sciences and the psychological sciences been alone in advancing penological concepts and methods. Sociology has shown that a criminal act is relative in the matter of its concrete form—what constitutes a heinous act in one society being an act of supreme virtue or real heroism in another. But it has shown that in all societies a criminal act has at least one uniform implication and significance, namely, that it is anti-social. This leads to the sociological theory of punishment and reformation. Punishment is regarded as the penalty exacted by the group for the violation of the rules prescribed for individual conduct within its limits. The basis for punishment must be social defense, and this may be achieved by securing the life-long segregation of the permanently unfit and degenerate and by the reformation of the reformable element. Finally, the sociologist insists that reformation must consist in preparing the convicted person for a normal type of socialized existence, and realizes that this can only be brought about by a system of social education during the period of incarceration and conditional release, and will only be obstructed by placing the individual in an environment widely different from that which exists in the daily life of the citizen. He realizes that any such procedure as solitary confinement or vindictive discipline will invariably result not in reformation, but in further deterioration of an already imperfectly developed personality. These are only a few of the more conspicuous aspects of the contribution of some of the phases of modern science to a more rational attitude towards crime and the treatment of the criminal.

II. CHANGING CONCEPTS AND ATTITUDES RESPECTING CRIME AND THE CRIMINAL

This is not the place to attempt an historical survey, however brief, of the evolution of present-day notions with respect to crime and the criminal, but it may be helpful to summarize the chief transformations in the attitude of society towards crime and the criminal class, as the logical introduction to the history of penal institutions and methods in modern times. In primitive society such acts as now fall under the head of criminal conduct were rather sharply divided into two general classes. Public crimes, or those which were punished by the group, consisted of such infractions of the *mores* as were believed to threaten the safety or prosperity of the whole group, such as violation of taboos, treason and sacrilege. These only were a matter of concern to the whole society and punished by its public agents. Private crimes, or those which involved injury or wrong to an individual, such as murder, assault or theft, were settled by the relatives of the interested parties according to the method of blood-feud. This extremely temporary, expensive and imperfect method of settling disputes and wrongs was soon superseded by the duel, or trial by battle, the ordeal, compurgation and compensation, all supervised by the elders or leaders of the group. In this way even the private crimes gradually came to be regarded as matters of common concern and were generally assimilated to public crimes under the single category of proscribed actions.

With the growth of the national state and royal absolutism, crime, as a menace to the public order, came to be regarded as an infraction of the "King's Peace," and its repression was brought under the control of the appropriate organs of the early state. The political and legalistic conception of crime prevailed for several centuries, but with the development of the modern sociological outlook there has come a tendency to view it as something more than a personal offense against the monarch or his symbolic power, or against the laws of the realm, namely, as an act which violates those institutions and practices upon which the integrity of the existing social order depends. As Arthur Cleveland Hall has made clear, the progress of civilization and the onward march of social evolution, with the ever-increasing volume and complexity of social relationships, have tended to increase the number and the types of acts which seem to threaten the social order and are, therefore, branded as criminal.

The attitude of society towards the criminal has undergone a parallel transformation. It has passed through exactly what Comte regarded as the stages of the mental evolution of humanity—the theological, the metaphysical and the scientific. In primitive and early political society the criminal was believed to be possessed by an evil spirit. Later he was viewed in a sort of metaphysical sense as a "perverse free moral agent." Finally, with the development of the scientific outlook, the criminal is now looked upon as a pathological unit of behavior, whose actions are determined by hereditary disposition and the experiences of life. The earliest scientific form of interpretation of the pathological behavior of the criminal was set forth by the group of anthropological or somatological theorists, mainly Lombroso and his followers, who believed that the typical criminal exhibited gross forms of physical defect and biological reversion. While careful students of criminal science have not been generally disposed to reject in their totality the views of Lombroso, a continually increasing number of criminal scientists, from the days of Maudsley onward, have come to believe that pathological psychic traits are much more important in the production of the criminal mind than are mere physical defects. Lastly, the sociological student of criminal behavior emphasizes the part played by a defective life experience, leading to a maladjustment to the conditions of a properly socialized existence. But enlightened advocates of all of these three major modern interpretations unite in opposing the older metaphysical and legalistic view of the criminal as a "perverse free moral agent," deserving only the savage revenge of the society whose rules and institutions he has outraged. All agree that the criminal is as truly a patient for the care of the scientist as is the victim of insanity or tuberculosis, and that the prison of the future must be regarded as a hospital for the isolation, treatment and cure of this class of diseased and maladjusted individuals. Of course, no scientific student of crime accepts the judicial test of criminality, but must hold that a large number of convicts are not, scientifically speaking, criminals, while probably a large minority of the criminal classes are never detected or convicted.

III. THE HISTORICAL METHODS OF TREATING THE CRIMINAL

In early society crimes against the public welfare were punished by summary execution of the culprit, by exile and outlawry, or by corporal punishment, according to the nature of the criminal act and the customary procedure of the group. Private crimes, avenged by kinsmen of the injured, were also punished in a variety of ways, most usually by death or enforced slavery, but as time passed and they were gradually brought under the supervision of the elders of the group for consideration, there developed the famous principle of *lex talionis,* or the often grotesque subjection of the convicted culprit to the identical treatment that he had given his victim, be it death or various forms of mutilation. When the state took over the function of dealing with crime it adopted these primitive varieties of retaliatory corporal punishment as the chief method of punishing criminals.

While prisons, or institutions for confining individuals, had existed in one form or another from the period of the prevalence of cannibalism, imprisonment, as the typical method of punishing the class of law-breakers, was not generally adopted until the beginning of the nineteenth century. When employed at an earlier date it was made use of to confine political prisoners, heretics, those held for ransom and debtors, or to hold pending trial those accused but not convicted of crime. It is futile to attempt to state with exactness just the date at which imprisonment as a punishment for crime became more general than the older practice of corporal punishment; all that can be said is that during the latter half of the eighteenth century the prevailing method of punishment gradually but surely shifted in western Europe and the North American colonies from corporal punishment to imprisonment.

From the beginning, four aims or purposes have been avowed in imprisonment, namely, the revenge of society upon the culprit, the deterrence of others from the commission of crime, the segregation of law-breakers for social protection, and the reformation of the convicted individual. It has been only in recent years, however, that social protection and reformation have been regarded as the all-important aims of punishment, in general, and of imprisonment in particular as the conventional mode of contemporary punishment. The earlier notions of how reformation could be effected during imprisonment were exceedingly crude, naïve and unscientific, the most notorious example probably being the so-called Pennsylvania conception that it could be produced most efficaciously by solitary confinement in a gloomy cell during the total period of incarceration. From this early view of the matter the situation has gradually improved, until to-day it is understood that where reformation is possible under any circumstances, it must be achieved by a careful preliminary isolation, study and differentiated treatment of the individual offender, with the aim in mind of eliminating his psychopathic traits, and by a proper system of socialized education gradually adjusting him to a state of normal group conduct, thereby preparing him for a safe resumption of social relationships.

But just as the progress of science has revolutionized the aims and methods of imprisonment, so now it seems to be threatening the very future of the prison itself. Beginning with the incarceration within one structure of individuals of both sexes, of all ages, those accused and those convicted of crime, those convicted of the most petty and the most heinous of crimes, those sound of mind and those suffering from neuroses and psychoses, as well as idiots and various grades of feeble-minded, the institutions for the reception and detention of these classes have gradually been differentiated into institutions for the training of juvenile delinquents, reformatories for young adult offenders, separate institutions for the sexes among all classes of offenders, state hospitals for the criminal imbeciles and the criminal insane, and detention jails for those accused of crime. At the same time, there has grown up the practice of outdoor treatment of the criminal class through probation and the suspended sentence, and conditional release from prison on parole. It would appear, then, that the prison is on its way towards ultimate extinction, except as a place for the permanent detention of the habitual criminal who defies all efforts at reformation, and that the prison is but another temporary episode in the history of society's experience in methods of repressing crime.

IV. THE DEVELOPMENT OF PENAL, REFORMATORY AND CORRECTIONAL INSTITUTIONS

1. *The Origins of the Modern Prison*

As we pointed out above, it is a purely scholastic and insoluble question as to when imprisonment, as a form of repressing crime, actually began. But it is very easy to answer such a part of this question as has any practical significance. While prisons, as places for the holding of human beings in confinement, have existed since the days of primitive cannibalism, the prison, as a distinct institution for the confinement of persons convicted of crime, is an institution which has developed almost entirely within the last hundred and forty years. Down to about 1780, in both Europe and America, the jails or prisons existed primarily for the confinement of heretics and debtors or for the safekeeping of those accused of crime pending their trial. Such as were convicted were normally sentenced either to corporal punishment, or, as became common after the colonial expansion began, to deportation.

To speak with strict historical accuracy, the introduction of the notion of employing confinement within a prison, as the general method of punishing crime, was due to William Penn and the Quakers of West Jersey, who provided for a system of work-houses in the penal code they drew up in 1681. Soon afterwards William Penn introduced the same system into his Pennsylvania colony. It is believed that Penn derived this novel practice, which he brought to West Jersey and Pennsylvania, from the English workhouse as employed in poor relief, and from his observation of the operation of the Dutch system of workhouses as applied to the treatment of youthful and aged paupers and vagrants. To this possible source of imitation there should, of course, be added the natural and inevitable tendency of any Quaker government to desire to avoid, as far as possible, the cruel and bloody types of corporal punishment then in vogue, and to substitute therefor a more human method of treating the convicted offender. But, interesting as these early historic instances may be to the student, in neither colonial Jersey nor provincial Pennsylvania was this Quaker method of imprisonment employed with any degree of permanence or uniformity. Its only effect upon posterity was to furnish a respectable precedent to which Quakers could turn a century later when they were groping about to discover some method of improving the barbarous prevailing methods of treating the criminal.

The real beginning of the systematic introduction of imprisonment as the prevailing method of punishment of the delinquent came in the last quarter of the eighteenth century, being prepared by the moral revival led by Wesley and Whitfield, the humanitarianism of the English and American Quakers, and the progress of rational and enlightened jurisprudence in the works of Montesquieu, Beccaria, Romilly and Bentham. Between 1773 and 1791 John Howard not only did much to improve the condition of imprisoned debtors in England, but also made a very thorough study of similar conditions on the continent of Europe and brought back to England a vast amount of interesting penological information which served to interest and instruct his contemporaries. Twenty years after Howard's death a Quaker humanitarian, Elizabeth Gurney Fry, began her work among the horribly treated women prisoners in London. In this same generation following 1775 there were distinct advances in certain local English jails which definitely anticipated the modern prison system. Little could be done in England, however, to produce a prison system until, between 1815 and 1835, Romilly, Mackintosh, Peel and Buxton had succeeded in having repealed the barbarous English criminal laws and in securing a substitution of imprisonment for corporal punishment or banishment as the most approved method of dealing with the criminal. In the period of the first Revolution, France also made certain marked advances towards the substitution of imprisonment for corporal punishment. Yet, in spite of these European advances which have been mentioned, as well as certain earlier or contemporary progress being made in the Papal prison at Rome and that of Ghent in Belgium, the real center from which the modern prison and its accompanying system of discipline and administration has spread was the system introduced in Philadelphia by the Quakers following 1776.

In 1776 the Philadelphia Friends formed an association, entitled the Philadelphia Society for Assisting Distressed Prisoners, for the purpose of relieving the conditions of the debtors and accused persons confined in the jail at Third and High streets. After the Revolutionary War this society was reorganized in the German School House at Philadelphia, as the Philadelphia Society for Alleviating the Miseries of Public Prisons. Between 1786 and 1795 the Society had secured the abolition of the barbarous criminal laws of Pennsylvania and the substitution of imprisonment for corporal punishment in the case of all crimes except murder. This necessitated the provision of a system of penal institutions which would make the confinement of the offender possible, and there was thus produced the modern prison. The Quakers derived their doctrines and reform proposals in part from the earlier precedents of Penn and his associates and in part from correspondence with Howard and other contemporary European reformers.

The Quakers in this manner not only originated the general practice of prison discipline, but they also brought into being a system of prison discipline which has had a tremendous influence upon the subsequent history of penal administration and of the theory of penology. Struck by the filth and debauchery which were then to be observed in all of the so-called congregate or promiscuous jails of the time, they conceived the notion that the prevention of further depravity through evil association, as well as the probable future reformation of the culprit, would be most surely obtained through the solitary confinement of the convict in an isolated cell, where he might in solitude and at his leisure contemplate the evils of his past life, and be thereby led to resolve "in the spiritual presence of his Maker" to reform his future conduct. To provide such a beneficent moral environment the Philadelphia reformers were able to persuade the Pennsylvania legislature to remodel the Walnut street jail in 1790-91, so as to permit of the solitary confinement of the worst types of offenders. With the growth of the population of the state it became necessary to provide more commodious penal institutions, and, in 1818-21, laws were enacted authorizing the erection of two state penitentiaries on the system of solitary confinement. The Western Penitentiary was opened at Pittsburgh in 1826, and the Eastern Penitentiary at Philadelphia in 1829. This Eastern, or Cherry Hill, Penitentiary immediately became the world's most famous penal institution, visited by prison reformers from every point of the Western World.

The originators and defenders of the system of solitary confinement alleged that it possessed the following virtues: the protection against possible moral contamination through evil association; the unusual invitation to self-examination and self-reproach in solitude; the impossibility of being visited by anyone except an officer, a clergyman or a reformer; great ease of administration of the government and discipline; the possibility of an unusual degree of individuality in treatment; little need for disciplinary measures; the absence of any possibility of mutual recognition of prisoners after discharge; and the fact that the horrors of loneliness made the prisoners unusually eager to engage in productive labor, during which process they might be taught a useful trade, preparatory to their attaining freedom. But, whatever its incidental advantages, the element uniformly and most vigorously emphasized by the founders of the Pennsylvania system was the allegation that solitude was most certain to be productive of earnest self-examination and a consequent determination to reform.

Distinguished visitors from abroad came to view this new system of penal administration and to recommend with general success its adoption in their home countries. In the decade of the 1830's Sir William Crawford from England, Dr. N. H. Julius from Prussia and Frédéric Auguste Demetz from France came to Philadelphia and recommended the immediate adoption of the Pennsylvania system in their respective countries. In America, however, the Pennsylvania system was much less popular than it was in Europe. In spite of temporary adoption in other states, most notably New Jersey and Rhode Island, the Pennsylvania system made little headway in the United States. It was even abandoned by the state of Pennsylvania in the Western Penitentiary in 1869 and in the Eastern Penitentiary in 1913, though as a matter of fact, it had practically ceased to exist in the Eastern Penitentiary a half a century before it was legally and formally abandoned.

The reason for the relative lack of popularity of the Pennsylvania system in America was primarily the rise in this country of another and a rival system of prison administration, namely, the Auburn system of combined isolation and association which, owing mainly to the indefatigable labors of Louis Dwight, came generally to dominate American penal administration until its popularity was threatened by the introduction of the Elmira system a half-century later.

In spite of the fact that the Auburn system became the great historical rival of the Pennsylvania system, it was in reality but a derivative or variant from the Pennsylvania type of prison administration. Imitating the precedent of Pennsylvania by substituting imprisonment for corporal punishment, New York state reformed its penal code in the last decade of the eighteenth century and thereby created the necessity for a system of prisons. The older institutions proving so unequal to the task of housing the larger number of prisoners confined under the new method of punishment that by 1810 the Governor had to pardon as many prisoners annually as were committed, the legislature, in 1816, authorized the building of a new prison at Auburn. Between 1817 and 1824 the system of discipline here enforced alternated between the old congregate system and the solitary or Pennsylvania system, but, by 1824, under the guidance of Elam Lynds, Gershom Powers and John Cray, the Auburn system of solitary confinement by night and associated labor by day had come into existence. This type of discipline and administration was soon introduced in the new Sing Sing prison, and into the state prisons of Connecticut and Massachusetts at Wethersfield and Charlestown, respectively.

This method of prison discipline and administration was alleged by its supporters to be superior to the Pennsylvania practice because of the greater cheapness of erecting a prison on the Auburn plan; its greater adaptability to the economic advantages of associated labor and mechanical methods of manufacturing; and the fact that it did not render the prisoner liable to what the exponents of the Auburn system regarded as the deleterious effects, both moral and physical, of complete solitude. It was believed that the Auburn practice of complete isolation at night and of silent association during the day was ample both to provoke moral reflection and to prevent contamination through evil association. But it is doubtful if the advantages, real and alleged, of the Auburn system would have been sufficient to secure its remarkable success had it not received the vigorous support of the greatest figure in early American prison reform, Louis Dwight, the active and alert secretary of the Prison Discipline Society of Boston. Possessing a firm conviction that the Auburn system was incomparably the best that human ingenuity had as yet devised, he gave unsparingly of his own energy and made what at times bordered on an unscrupulous use of the authority and prestige of his Society in order to urge everywhere and always the adoption of the Auburn system. So well did his efforts succeed that for a half-century after 1830 the Auburn system of prison administration was practically identical with American penal institutions.

In spite of their great prestige and reputation and their undoubted historical significance in the evolution of penology, however, both the Pennsylvania and the Auburn systems must be regarded as important chiefly through having originated the modern prison. Neither marks more than the first crude step taken in the effort to render more humane and more scientific the treatment of the violator of the law. In spite of the exaggerated pretentions and claims of their supporters, both of these methods of prison administration lacked almost entirely the provision of those deeper moral, psychological and social impulses and motives which must lie at the foundation of any effective reformation of the offender. There can be no doubt that whatever claims have been brought forward to the contrary, neither system actually advanced the cause of reformation to any degree comparable to the part that it played in carrying out the other conventional aims assigned to imprisonment, namely, social protection, revenge or retaliation, and deterrence. It is to that series of progressive reforms which culminated in the Elmira system that one must look for the first appearance of any even moderately successful machinery designed to supply the chief impulses which are necessary if it is hoped to create any widespread determination to reform in the minds of any large number of prisoners.

2. *The Origin and Development of the Elmira Reformatory System*

In his two works, *The Penitentiary Systems of Europe and America* (1828) and *The Theory of Imprisonment* (1836), that wise and progressive French penologist, M. Charles Lucas, had clearly taken the advanced position that a curative reformatory type of prison discipline ought to be substituted for the contemporary repressive prison system. It was a long time, however, before this aspiration was adequately realized. It was only achieved, and then imperfectly, in the Elmira Reformatory system introduced into New York State following 1870.

A number of significant currents of reform in penology converged in producing this system. An important element was contributed by the new methods of prison discipline introduced in the British penal colony in Australia. Captain Alexander Maconochie came to Norfolk Island in Australia in 1840, and was able to bring about a tremendous improvement in penal methods by eliminating the old flat-time sentence and introducing the beginnings of commutation of sentence for good behavior. Every convict, according to the seriousness of his offense, instead of being sentenced to a given term of years, had a certain number of marks set against him which he had to redeem before he was liberated. These marks were to be earned by deportment, labor and study, and the more rapidly they were acquired the more speedy the release.

At about the same time the notion of an indeterminate time sentence was originated and given popularity through the writings of Archbishop Whately of Dublin, the Scotchman George Combe, and especially the English reformers, Frederick and Matthew Davenport Hill. Its supplement, the famous parole system, while anticipated by a number of other reformers, was most systematically and effectively advocated by the French publicist, Bonneville de Marsangy. Maconochie's system of determining the period of incarceration upon the basis of the behavior of the convict was combined with the notion of the indeterminate sentence and parole in the famous Irish system of prison administration, which was introduced by Sir Walter Crofton in the decade following 1853. To these earlier progressive innovations he added the practice of classifying convicts in graded groups, through which each convict had to pass before obtaining his freedom on parole, his advancement being determined by his conduct.

The notion of productive and instructive prison labor, which goes back to the Pennsylvania Quakers, was also developed by a number of progressive penologists during the second quarter of the nineteenth century, especially by Montesinos in Spain and Obermaier in Bavaria.

All of these liberal and progressive innovations, which have been all too briefly and casually mentioned above, attracted the attention of the leading American reformers, most notably Theodore W. Dwight and E. C. Wines of the New York Prison Association, F. B. Sanborn of Concord, Massachusetts, Z. R. Brockway, Superintendent of the Detroit House of Correction, and Gaylord Hubbell, Warden of Sing Sing Prison. All of these men prepared able, vigorous and widely read public reports or private monographs, urging the adoption of these advanced methods in the American prison system, but they were only able to secure the introduction of these innovations for the treatment of younger first offenders. A law authorizing the creation of such an institution at Elmira, New York, was passed in 1869, and the institution was opened in 1877, with Mr. Brockway as its first superintendent. A decent preliminary approximation to the principle of the indeterminate sentence was secured, and the inmates were divided into classes or grades through which they might advance to ultimate parole by virtue of good conduct if they did not desire to remain in the institution for the maximum sentence.

The great advance which the Irish and Elmira systems mark over Pennsylvania and Auburn systems was the fact that in these later types of penal discipline the term of incarceration was at least roughly made to depend upon the observable progress made by the prisoner on the road to ultimate reformation. It was, thus, a system which chiefly stressed reformation rather than either retaliation or deterrence. As far as its application in the United States is concerned, however, even this method of discipline possessed serious and grave defects. In the first place, it was scarcely at all introduced into the prisons which confined the adult offenders, thus not being applied to the great bulk of the prison population. In the second place, while it was based primarily upon the idea of effecting the reformation of the convicts, it failed signally to provide the right sort of psychological surroundings to expedite this process. The whole system of discipline was repressive, and varied from benevolent despotism, in the best instances, to tyrannical cruelty in the worst. There was little, if anything, done to introduce into the mind of the individual convict, or into the groups of the convicts generally, any sense of individual or collective responsibility for the conduct of the prison community, nor was any significant attempt made to provide any education in the elements of group conduct and the responsibilities of the citizen. There was little, if any, grasp of that fundamental fact which is basic in the newer penology, namely, that a prisoner can be fitted for a life of freedom only by some training in a social environment which bears some fair resemblance in point of liberty and responsibility to that into which he must enter upon obtaining release. Finally, there was no wide acceptance of the present position that the general body of delinquents cannot be treated as a single unified group. There was no general recognition that criminals must be dealt with as individuals or as a number of classes of individuals of different psychological and biological types that must be scientifically differentiated through a careful psychiatric study, as well as a detailed sociological study of their environment, preliminary to the major part of their treatment while incarcerated. These last conditions have only been very recently and very incompletely realized in systems of convict self-government, such as those which Mr. Thomas Mott Osborne has introduced, and in such careful psychiatric studies of the criminal class as were attempted in the psychiatric clinic introduced in the Sing Sing prison by Drs. Thomas W. Salmon and Bernard Glueck, and have been more extensively employed in connection with juvenile courts.

3. *The Progress of Differentiation in Institutions for the Treatment of the Criminal Classes*

One of the most conspicuous and significant phases of the progress of prison administration in the last century has been the development of a scientific differentiation in the institutions designed to treat the criminal class. In the early modern prisons which prevailed before the Pennsylvania and Auburn prisons came into existence, all alleged and real delinquents were herded together in one enclosure, generally in one room or group of rooms, containing accused and convicted, debtors and criminals, male and female, young and old, insane, idiotic and those of normal mentality, first offenders and hardened recidivists. The reformation of the offender was rendered hopeless at the outset under such conditions.

The rise of the Pennsylvania and Auburn systems marked a great step in the way of progress. The accused were separated from the convicted, and separate portions of the prison were assigned to the male and female prisoners. The next step came in the erection of Houses of Refuge for young offenders, their condition in the prisons of the time naturally giving rise to much sympathy on the part of reformers. The historical background of their development is a long one. The origins of institutions for juvenile delinquents must be sought in the juvenile departments of the English workhouses of the sixteenth and seventeenth centuries. The movement reached its highest early development in Holland, where, by the seventeenth century, a famous system of such institutions for the neglected and delinquent youth had developed. From an observation of their operation William Penn is said to have derived in part his notion of imprisonment as a method of treating the criminal.

The beginning of the modern movement is normally taken to date from the building of the House of Refuge at Danzig, in 1813, under the direction of one John Falk. In London, also, similar institutions were developing, in part out of earlier progress there and in part from imitation of continental methods. The introduction of such institutions into the United States was due to the work of Professor John Griscom, a Quaker who traveled extensively in Europe in the early twenties and was struck with the importance of these "child-saving institutions." He brought back his impressions to New York City and Philadelphia, where they were appropriated by the reforming groups. The first House of Refuge for juvenile delinquents in this country was opened at Madison Square in New York City on January 25, 1825. It was built far north of the center of the city, in the hope that a century of municipal expansion would not disturb it. The second institution of the kind was opened in Boston in 1826, and the third in Philadelphia in 1828. But these were private institutions, though in part open to the use of the commonwealth. The first state institution for juvenile delinquents was opened at Westboro, Massachusetts, in 1847.

These early Houses of Refuge, however, were nothing more than prisons for young offenders. In neither architecture nor administration did they differ from the conventional prison, though an exception must be made in the case of the Boston House of Refuge, where, as early as 1831, Beaumont and De Tocqueville discovered the existence of a crude but real system of classification, promotion and inmate self-government. The origination of the more modern and humane method of handling juvenile delinquents in the cottage or family arrangement was due to the work of the French publicist and reformer, Frédéric Auguste Demetz. Looking upon the problem as a French judge, Demetz was shocked by the conventional method of handling juvenile delinquents. Aided by the Vicomte de Courteilles, a wealthy Touraine landholder, who gave Demetz the necessary farming land, the latter opened at Mettray in 1840 his first agricultural colony for juvenile delinquents administered according to the "Family system." His system spread rapidly, being first introduced into this country at the state reform school in Lancaster, Ohio, in 1855. But the family system of housing and administration, initiated by Demetz, was only a beginning in the right direction. Long hours and heavy work were prescribed for the inmates with the avowed aim of making them too tired to desire to play or engage in mischief. The progress has been a long and gradual one from these early "cottage institutions" to such a system as that of the George Junior Republic or that now practiced in such a reform school as the girls' institution at Sleighton Farms in Pennsylvania, where inmate self-government and an extremely close approximation to normal family life prevail.

The remaining step which has thus far been taken in differentiating penal institutions was introduced in the Elmira system mentioned above. Here provision was made for a class of first offenders midway in age between the juvenile and adult offenders. This specialization embodied in separating the younger prisoners marked a double differentiation, being not only one based on age, but also one which was founded upon the primary aim of reformation of inmates rather than chiefly incarceration and punishment, as in the prevailing type of prison. The other major type of differentiation in institutions for treating the groups that were once incarcerated in the older prisons has consisted in removing from prison those classes that admittedly have no place in a prison system. Perhaps the first step was the removal of the debtors. To those who have read of Oglethorpe's foundation of an American colony to furnish a refuge for European debtors it may seem strange that as late as 1830 Louis Dwight could find a wide prevalence of imprisonment for debt in this country, being carried out under atrocious conditions. It was not terminated until the decade of the thirties, when humanitarian agitation and the democratic wave that brought Jackson to the presidency succeeded in abolishing this archaic and oppressive practice.

About the same time there began a movement for transferring the insane and idiotic from penal institutions and poorhouses to the first crude hospitals for the insane. This important advance owes its origins almost wholly to the great work of Dorothea Lynde Dix, a name little known to-day, but one which is worthy to rank with any in the history of nineteenth-century philanthropy. For a generation following 1830 she labored incessantly in the cause of a better and more scientific method of handling the insane. She succeeded in getting reluctant state legislatures to appropriate sums for the establishment of the first hospitals for the insane in this country, and was also to some degree successful in getting the insane out of the prisons and almshouses and into these new hospitals. But the mechanism for effecting the transference was faulty, and it was not until long after her death that, at the very close of the nineteenth century, some progress was made in providing separate hospitals for the criminal insane. Only within the last decade, chiefly as the result of the work of H. H. Goddard and his associates, has there appeared any general recognition of the necessity of creating separate places for the care and treatment of the feeble-minded who have been guilty of a violation of the law. Finally, even the little that has been done in the way of a psychiatric study and classification of the criminal population, has, as Dr. Bernard Glueck has so convincingly demonstrated, proved the futility of hoping to treat even the classes which now remain in the conventional prison as a single group to be handled in a uniform type of penal institutions. Rather, the present adult convict population requires a very careful psychological, biological and sociological classification, differentiation and treatment in a specialized set of institutions equally well diversified. There is little doubt that in the scientific prison administration of the future the agencies for dealing with the socially sick, or the criminal class, will be as varied and scientifically adapted to their work as are the institutions which are now provided to deal with the physically and mentally sick.

V. CERTAIN ASPECTS OF PROGRESS IN PENAL METHODS

1. *Special Attempts to Bring about the Reformation of the Convict*

One of the earliest and certainly the most obvious method of attempting to produce an effort at reform on the part of the convict was the provision of rewards for good behavior. The most crude and elementary type of such rewards was to offer special privileges and favors to "trusties" who had earned the confidence of the prison authorities through good behavior. A more systematic and scientific method was to allow the prisoner to earn an earlier discharge through excellent deportment. Perhaps the first example of this practice was adopted in the Auburn prison in 1817, but it appears to have been a local curiosity introduced chiefly as a method of speeding up the prisoners in the shops and not to have been particularly closely connected with any notion of producing a changed attitude in the criminal with respect to his social behavior. The significant introduction of the method of commutation of sentence for good behavior seems to have been the work of Captain Maconochie in Australia and of Walter Crofton in Ireland between 1840 and 1860. It was sporadically introduced into this country in the period following the Civil War. The next logical progressive step was the introduction of the indeterminate sentence and the conditional release on parole. This came into the United States in the Elmira imitation of the Irish system of Crofton, but was here applied only to youthful first offenders. So far as adult criminals were concerned, this country followed the irrational method of adopting the parole system long before it did the indeterminate sentence. The method of paroling prisoners spread gradually in the decade of the 90's and the following years, when it was applied in conjunction with the maximum and minimum sentence laws and the prevailing systems of commutation. Not until about 1910 did the indeterminate sentence begin to make its way at all systematically into American courts. It was then aided by efforts of the American Institute of Criminal Law and Criminology, in co-operation with local sympathizers in various states. But even at the present time a thoroughgoing indeterminate sentence scarcely exists in this country except by subterfuge. Probably it is best that such should be the case until more scientific and impartial machinery can be provided to operate so flexible an instrument as a completely indeterminate sentence. The parole system is widespread, but is rarely effectively enforced because the states refuse to supply funds to maintain an adequate number of field workers to make the parole supervision at all effective. In many cases the parole system has meant nothing more than a general reduction of sentence for those whose behavior has legally entitled them to early release.

It is probable, however, that the most effective agency in advancing the cause of the reformation of the criminal has not been special rewards for good behavior, whether privileges while in prison or a shortening of the sentence, but rather the education of the prisoner for a normal life after his release. Perhaps the earliest type of education in prison administration was in the economic field. The exponents of the Pennsylvania system back in the 30's of the last century laid special stress upon the adaptability of their system to the teaching of a remunerative trade to each inmate. While trade instruction in prisons for adults has made certain sporadic progress in Europe, it has advanced but slightly in this country. Little has been done along this line here except in the reformatories, and even in these there has been a tendency to carry too far the element of high productivity in the shops, as at the Rahway Reformatory in New Jersey, or to go to the other extreme and develop a great trade school with no practical application, as at the Huntingdon Reformatory in Pennsylvania. Likewise the academic or literary education of adult prisoners, while present in some form in most American prisons since the middle of the last century, has rarely received any scientific and thoroughgoing application outside of the reformatories. In some of these, as at Rahway, it has, however, reached a level of excellence not equaled by most of the public school systems of the country.

Probably more important than either economic or academic education is the social re-education of the prisoner, namely, the attempt to readjust the personality of the convict to the necessities imposed by a normal social life through supplying him, as far as possible while in prison, with the inward motives and the external social environment which are required to meet the conditions of the life of the ordinary citizen. While some faint anticipation of this step might possibly be detected in the Irish and Elmira systems, it is probable that the first conscious and comprehensive attempt to provide an effective system of social re-education is to be seen in the *Mutual Welfare League* and the system of convict self-government introduced by Mr. Osborne at Sing Sing. The fundamental conception of Mr. Osborne's plan represents probably the greatest step in advance in prison administration since the origin of the modern prison system. Its real significance and ultimate promise justify a brief summary of the nature of the scheme. The rules of discipline of the institution were chiefly left to a body of delegates of fifty convicts elected by the inmates on the basis of the representation of the several work gangs. Infractions of discipline were dealt with by a board of five judges chosen by the delegates, though an appeal might be taken from their decisions to the warden. The decisions of the judges were carried out by the regular officers of the prison.

No keepers or guards were allowed in the shops, discipline here being wholly in the hands of the convicts. A system of token money was introduced in the shops. A convict commissary was organized from which inmates could purchase articles of comfort. An employment bureau was maintained by the members of the League. Outdoor recreation, lectures and entertainments were provided. The position and privileges of the inmates depend upon the degree and excellence of their adherence to the regulations of the self-governing system. It was further intended that released members of the League should make an effort to find employment for their fellow-members upon the expiration of their sentences and should attempt to sustain the efforts at reformation which has been initiated at Sing Sing. In this way it was hoped that an adequate system of social education might be provided which would restore to a normal life the great majority of convicts who had hitherto been released only to be returned for another offense after a brief period of freedom.

But Mr. Osborne's scheme possessed one fatal weakness, namely, that he attempted to apply it to the whole prison population, while it obviously could and should be applied only to those for whom there might be some decent probability of reclamation. What is yet needed is the establishment of psychiatric clinics at every prison, so as to make it possible to weed out at the beginning those hopeless defectives and degenerates whose reformation is obviously impossible and whose presence in any self-government scheme only lessens its effectiveness for those to whom it is legitimately serviceable. Yet even this is insufficient. A sociological study must be made of the social environment from which each criminal comes, with the end in view of attaining a better understanding of his past experiences and the type of treatment needed while in prison, as well as getting the proper information to aid in a thorough follow-up treatment after the prisoner has been released. Nothing could be more foolhardy than to terminate reformatory measures at the gate of the prison. It seems generally agreed that the penology of the future will demand as thorough after-care for the discharged prisoner as that which public hygiene now requires for patients discharged from the ordinary hospital or that which mental hygiene now prescribes for those returning from psychopathic hospitals.

2. *The Development of Prison Labor*

The history of the economic aspects of modern prison administration has not been more inspiring than the other phases of its development. The European situation is so varied and complicated that it must be passed by with the mere mention of the fact that Montesinos in Spain and Obermaier in Bavaria share with the Quakers of Pennsylvania the honor of having been the earliest advocates of productive labor as a part of a successful prison system. In general, the industrial phases of penal administration are far more highly developed in Europe than in America.

Our prisons started at the close of the eighteenth century either with no labor at all, or else with merely the crudest forms of tasks, such as breaking stone, grinding meal, or even manipulating a treadmill. With the development of the merchant capitalists in this country in the 1830's, there arose a demand for prison labor, and these men very generally contracted for the services of such convict labor as they desired, according to the "lease" system, whereby they took complete charge of the prisoners during working hours. This method became remarkably popular during the period of abnormal demand for prison labor in the Civil War. This crude lease system obviously possessed certain oppressive features, and it was gradually supplanted by the so-called "piece-price" variety of the contract system, according to which the contractor did not lease the bodies of the convicts, but agreed to pay for the product of their labor at a stipulated price per piece. Where willing contractors did not exist or where their methods were obnoxious, the "public-account" system was introduced, and the products made by the prisoners were sold by the state agents in the public market.

But, after the rise of the modern labor organizations in the 70's, violent opposition to convict labor arose on the part of the laborers outside the prison walls. Prison labor was branded an unfair type of competition, and free labor demanded a cessation of both the contract and public-account systems. Where the labor organizations were strong they either brought about the abolition of practically all prison labor, producing great suffering on the part of the prison population, as in Pennsylvania since 1897, or forced the states to adopt the "state-use" system, in which prison-made products were not sold to the public at all, but were used in various state institutions. More recently the progress of a more liberal attitude towards the criminal has allowed him to be employed outside the prison on roads or public improvements, and in this way there has developed that variant of the state-use system known as the "public works and ways" system. Particularly significant has been the recent movement to purchase large prison farms and to put the convicts at agricultural labor. Some feeble beginnings have been made toward instituting a system of compensation or wages for convicts.

3. *The Sterilization and Segregation of the Feeble-Minded and Idiotic Classes and the Habitual Criminal*

Owing to the alarming increase of these classes and their special menace to the community, much of the best social investigation in recent years has been devoted to a study of the defective and degenerate elements in the general population. A number of classic investigations of congenitally defective and degenerate families by Dugdale, Goddard, McCulloch and Blackmar have revealed, with a wealth of evidence, the disastrous results which attend the promiscuous and unrestricted breeding of defectives and degenerates. The general dissolution of the theological view of the causation of defective and degenerate personalities and the development of our scientific knowledge regarding the transmission of congenital defects has at last indicated the only possible method of ridding society of this small but ever-increasing degenerate element, from which a substantial proportion of the paupers, criminals and other social derelicts are recruited.

The sole manner of procedure whereby this class can be speedily eliminated, before it becomes so large as to drag down the normal population in a common destruction, is to segregate or sterilize all of its members. The former expedient, while arousing less traditional resistance and opposition and desirable with females, is attended with great expense, and the much simpler and more humane method of sterilizing those male members of the defective class that can be safely trusted outside of an institution has of late met with great favor among biologists and physicians. If this policy were systematically pursued it would be a conservative prediction to state that in fifty years the defective and degenerate classes would virtually disappear and the criminal class be reduced more than one-half. Most states have begun to make some pretense at custodial segregation of the worst types of the idiotic and the feeble-minded, and sixteen, following the Indiana precedent of 1907, have legalized the sterilization of the hopelessly defective and the habitually criminal, but the laws have not been applied with any thoroughness except in California. The plan suggested by McKim of painlessly exterminating the idiotic, hopelessly insane and habitually criminal classes is probably as remote from practical adoption as it is wise and desirable.

The progress in psychiatry in the last decade has, however, indicated that we can no longer indulge in the easy generalization that the majority of criminals are feeble-minded and that feeble-mindedness is a simple and uniform example of invariably inherited defect. The psychiatric study of criminality, particularly in the clinics devoted to this purpose, has shown that psychopathic criminals are more often suffering from psychoses and neuroses than from overt defect and dementia. And many of these mental disorders are purely functional without any physical basis and, hence, quite incapable of biological transmission. Therefore, any comprehensive plan for the prevention of crime would call for not only segregation and sterilization of the feeble-minded but also for the establishment of psychiatric clinics designed to discover and treat those psychopathic disturbances which are the potential cause of even the most serious crimes, such as those of Harry Thaw, Loeb and Leopold and Noel. And, while doubtless an extremist on the other side, Abraham Meyerson has shown that we must adopt a critical attitude towards the doctrines of Goddard and others with respect to the easy-going assumption of the hereditary derivation and biological causation of most types of feeble-mindedness.

4. *Probation and the Non-Institutional Care of Delinquents*

The beginnings of the non-institutional care of delinquents may be traced to the ticket-of-leave or parole system, which originated in the middle of the nineteenth century and has come to be a cardinal feature of advanced penological theory and practice. This, however, merely made possible the removal of the convict from imprisonment during the latter portion of his term and in no way attempted to do away with imprisonment altogether. With the gradual growth among careful students of penology of the conviction that in many, if not in most cases, the convict issues from prison a worse character than he was upon entry, especially in the case of young first offenders, there has arisen a determined movement to secure the introduction of a system of suspended sentence and probation, to be applied to those first offenders and others, who, it seems reasonable to believe, can be most effectively treated outside of a penal institution. As has been the case with nearly all of the radical innovations in penology, this progressive practice was first applied to juvenile delinquents, especially in connection with the creation of a juvenile court system in the more advanced municipalities of the country, a movement which originated in Rhode Island, Illinois and Minnesota in 1899, and in which Judge Benjamin B. Lindsey of Denver was a pioneer and the most picturesque figure. Forty-seven states now have juvenile probation laws. As has been the case with almost every progressive prison-reform practice in the past, so with probation its application to juvenile delinquents was soon followed by its introduction into the methods of treating adult delinquents not convicted of major crimes. At the present time, some thirty-five states now have probation systems which are applied to adult delinquents with a greater or less degree of thoroughness. Massachusetts, New York and New Jersey have led in this practice. Only in connection with the probation department of the Philadelphia municipal court under the direction of Chief Probation Officer, Louis N. Robinson, has any notable progress been made in Pennsylvania, but here the prospects for a successful application of the principle of the suspended sentence and probation to delinquents are unexcelled in this country. Whatever the shortcomings at the present time, there can be no doubt that it will come to be one of the vital features of the penology of the future.

5. *Differentiation in the Type of Institutions Designed to Deal with the Various Types of Adult Convicts*

The tendency to differentiate institutions receiving those convicted of crime seems designed to pass through another stage, after having gone through the elementary step of providing separate institutions securing a differentiation of convicts on the basis of age, sex, degree of criminality and gross mental qualities. There is general agreement among students of criminology and penology that the institutions dealing with adult convicts not adjudged insane by the court, must be differentiated upon the basis of both the stage of the treatment of the convict and the special characteristics and aptitudes of the chief groups of convicts. Such a system would call for a reception prison, where preliminary study and classification could be carried on by biologists, psychiatrists and sociologists, and where the economic capacity of the convicts could also be ascertained. On the basis of such a preliminary study of the convicts received, there could be a scientific ascertainment of the next stage in their disposition. As far as possible reformable first offenders should be treated outside of institutions in connection with the system of probation. Industrial prisons, of at least two different types, should be provided, as well as prison farms and arrangements for employing the convicts on roads and other public works. Provision must be made for gradual increase of liberty and self-control on the part of the convict before he is allowed to be released on parole. Most of the defects of the parole system in the past in this country have been due to the fact that prisoners have been kept under tyrannical discipline and then suddenly turned out without the slightest restraint. On the other hand, the state must be prepared to keep perpetually in custody that portion of the convict body which is revealed by investigation to be biologically, psychologically or sociologically permanently unfit to be at large. When such a system has been worked out the prisons will probably have disappeared, in fact as well as in name, and we shall have in their place social hospitals designed to treat the socially sick—namely, the so-called criminal class.

6. *Some Necessary Changes in Criminal Jurisprudence*

It is a fact well recognized by criminologists and penologists that any fulfilment of their progressive plans for reform must wait upon a radical reconstruction of our criminal law and criminal procedure. Our legal system for ascertaining guilt and dealing with the criminal is founded entirely upon medieval metaphysical and theological presuppositions, which antedate wholly modern biological, psychological and social science. The criminal is proceeded against as "a perverse free moral agent" and the court is charged with wreaking upon him the vengeance of society. For the average criminal the law recognizes no biological, psychic or social fact in the causation of the crime nor any biological, psychic or social condition of the criminal, when administering the sentence. The crime and not the criminal is what is theoretically punished, and the effort has been made in a crude and unscientific way to adjust the penalty to the crime, the possibility of which modern criminology and penology utterly denies. Further, the jury system renders the ascertainment of guilt difficult if not impossible. At least, one may say that it is little more scientific than the ancient ordeal and trial by battle and the element of chance involved is quite as large as in these outgrown practices. The jury system renders null and void most of the laws of evidence and other safegards of legal procedure, and destroys the whole machinery of justice by submitting the final decision as to guilt to a group of utterly untrained and usually quite unfit men, singularly responsive to rhetorical arguments by opposing counsel. Little is needed to condemn the jury beyond an honest examination of its historical development and its obvious and palpable legal, psychological and sociological defects and absurdities.

In the place of this anachronistic scheme of criminal law and criminal procedure, the criminologist and penologist of today would introduce a permanent body of experts drawn from the law, biology, psychology, sociology and economics to examine the evidence against the accused and to determine his guilt. There would be no flat sentence, but rather a truly indeterminate sentence, which would allow the convict to be properly studied, classified and treated under the supervision of another body of administrative experts in institutions for the treatment of convicts. Only such a body is competent to determine when a convict is fitted for freedom or to prescribe the treatment which can lead to any hope of differentiating and reforming the convict. It may well be conceded that such a system of criminal procedure and jurisprudence and penal administration is remote from enactment and popular acceptance, but this very remoteness is the measure of the time which must elapse before we can achieve anything like a scientific method of ascertaining guilt or treating and reforming those adjudged guilty of violating the basic legal rules of the social order.

SELECTED REFERENCES

Bacon, Corinne. *Prison Reform.*

Barnes, H. E. *The History of the Penal, Reformatory and Correctional Institutions of New Jersey.*

Barnes, H. E. "The Economics of American Penology," in *Journal of Political Economy,* October, 1921.

Barnes, H. E. "The Evolution of American Penology as Illustrated by the Western Penitentiary of Pennsylvania," in *Western Pennsylvania Historical Magazine,* October, 1921.

Barnes, H. E. "The Progress of American Penology as Exemplified by the State of Pennsylvania," in *Journal of Criminal Law and Criminology,* August, 1922.

Barrows, S. J. *The Reformatory System in the United States.*

Beaumont and De Tocqueville, *On the Penitentiary System in the United States* (1833).

Brockway, Z. R. *Fifty Years of Prison Service.*

Carpenter, M. *Reformatory Prison Discipline as Developed by the Rt. Hon. Sir Walter Crofton.*

Folks, H. *The Care of Destitute and Neglected Children.*

Gillin, J. L. *Criminology and Penology.*

Glueck, B. *Studies in Forensic Psychiatry.*

Glueck, B. "A Study of 608 Admissions to Sing Sing," in *Mental Hygiene,* January, 1918.

Glueck, B. "Concerning Prisoners," in *Mental Hygiene,* April, 1918.

Glueck, B. "Psychiatric Aims in the Field of Criminology," in *Mental Hygiene,* October, 1918.

Glueck, B. "Recent Progress in Determining the Nature of Crime and the Characteristics of the Criminal," in *Proceedings of the National Conference on Social Work,* 1917.

Glueck, S. S. *Mental Disorder and the Criminal Law.*

Goddard, H. H. *The Kallikak Family.*
Goddard, H. H. *The Criminal Imbecile.*
Hall, A. C. *Crime and Social Progress.*
Healy, W. *The Individual Delinquent.*
Henderson, C. R. (Ed.) *Penal and Reformatory Institutions* (Russell Sage Publications).
Henderson, C. R. *Modern Prison Systems.*
Hoag and Williams. *Crime, Abnormal Minds and the Law.*
Hobhouse, L. T. *Morals in Evolution,* Chap. III.
Howard, J. *The State of Prisons in England and Wales* (1777).
Ives, G. *A History of Penal Methods.*
Klein, P. *Prison Methods in New York State.*
Leonard, E. M. *The Early History of English Poor Relief.*
Lewis, B. *The Offender.*
Lindsley, J. B. *Prison Discipline and Penal Legislation.*
McKim, C. *Heredity and Human Progress.*
Marett, R. R. *Anthropology,* Chap. VII.
Myerson, Abraham. *The Inheritance of Mental Disease.*
Osborne, T. M. *Society and Its Prisons.*
Parmelee, M. *The Principles of Anthropology and Criminology in their Relation to Criminal Procedure.*
Parmelee, M. *Criminology.*
Parsons, P. A. *Responsibility for Crime.*
Parsons, P. A. *The Question of Crime.*
Pound, Roscoe (Ed.) *Criminal Justice in an American City* (Cleveland Foundation Publications).
Pound, Roscoe, "The Future of the Criminal Law," in *Columbia Law Review,* January, 1921.
Pound, Roscoe. *Criminal Justice in America.*
Report of the Commission on the Penal Code of Pennsylvania, 1828.
Robinson, L. N. *Criminal Statistics in the United States.*
Robinson, L. N. *The Employment and Compensation of Prisoners in Pennsylvania.*
Robinson, L. N. *Penology in the United States.*

Ruggles-Brise, E. *Prison Reform at Home and Abroad.*

Smith, M. H. *The Psychology of the Criminal.*

Snedden, D. S. *Administrative and Educational Work of American Juvenile Reform Schools.*

Spalding, W. F. (Ed.) *Parole and Probation* (Proceedings of the Annual Congress of the American Prison Association, 1916).

Stephen, J. F. J. *History of the Criminal Law in England.*

Sutherland, E. H. *Criminology.*

Tannenbaum, F. *Wall Shadows.*

Thayer, J. B. *The Development of Trial by Jury.*

Tiffany, F. *Life of Dorothea L. Dix.*

White, W. A. In *Journal of Criminal Law and Criminology,* Vol. VIII, pp. 499-501; Vol. IX, pp. 596-8.

White, W. A. *Insanity and the Criminal Law.*

Wines, E. C. *The State of Prisons and Child-Saving Institutions.*

Wines and Dwight. *Prisons and Reformatories in the United States.*

Wines, F. H. *Punishment and Reformation* (edition of 1919 by W. D. Lane).

Whitin, E. S. *The Caged Man.*

Whitin, E. S., and Lichtenberger, J. P. *Prison Labor.*

CHAPTER VI

The Evolution of American Criminal Jurisprudence As Illustrated by the Criminal Code and Penal Legislation of Pennsylvania

I. INTRODUCTION

The evolution of criminal jurisprudence in modern times is one of the most interesting aspects of the development of intellectual and social history. It illustrates the changing social attitudes with respect to the control of social and anti-social behavior, and well exemplifies the changing intellectual attitudes with respect to these types of behavior that are taken into cognizance by criminal jurisprudence. In general, the evolution of criminal jurisprudence has shown a general tendency away from the close interrelation of religion and criminal jurisprudence toward a gradual secularization, the attitude toward the criminal and his treatment coming gradually to be viewed in the light of its relation to social protection and well-being.

In choosing a state whose criminal code will perhaps illustrate as well as any the evolution of American jurisprudence, Pennsylvania has been taken because of its prominence in American criminal jurisprudence and prison reform, and because it admirably exemplifies well-nigh every stage through which the development of American criminal law has passed.

II. THE CRIMINAL CODES OF COLONIAL PENNSYLVANIA

It will be unnecessary in this place to deal in detail with the criminal code of colonial Pennsylvania before 1776, as this has been made the subject of a special study in another chapter.[1] We will here briefly summarize the essential facts with respect to the colonial jurisprudence of Pennsylvania. The first criminal code of Pennsylvania was that introduced in 1676, which embodied the contemporary severe English and Puritan theories and practices with respect to the treatment of crime. It provided for some eleven capital crimes, and prescribed either fines or corporal punishment for the lesser crimes and misdemeanors. In 1682, this original severe criminal code was replaced by a far different body of law, namely, the Quaker Code, which was introduced by William Penn, embodying the same unique liberality that had just previously been introduced in the Quaker criminal code of West Jersey. The Quakers were very much opposed to the shedding of blood, and, hence, there was but one capital crime provided for in the Quaker code of 1682, namely, premeditated murder. Another unique aspect of this Quaker criminal code of the colony of Pennsylvania was the fact that for crimes other than capital the prevailing procedure of prescribing corporal punishment or fines was replaced by the practice of imprisonment at hard labor. This Quaker innovation of the 17th century is usually regarded by historians of criminology and penology as the first general appearance of imprisonment as a method of treating the criminal.

The Quaker criminal code of Pennsylvania was, unfortunately, short-lived. The Quakers refused to take an oath, and the British government refused, in turn, to accept the criminal code of the Quakers in Pennsylvania. Finally, in 1718 the Quakers, in order to secure the right

[1] See Chapter II above.

of affirmation, instead of oath-taking, surrendered their criminal code and agreed to accept a criminal code similar in attitude and content to that of the earlier code of 1676, and based, like this earlier code, upon English attitudes and precedents. In this code of 1718 the following crimes were declared to be capital: treason, murder, manslaughter by stabbing, serious maiming, highway robbery, burglary, arson, sodomy, buggery, rape, concealing the death of a bastard child, advising the killing of such a child, and witchcraft. Larceny was the only felony which was not made a capital crime. A generation later counterfeiting was made a capital crime, there thus being some fourteen capital crimes in the criminal code with which Pennsylvania finished the colonial period. It was this situation which confronted the Pennsylvania legislators when the colony separated from Great Britain and set up an independent government in 1776.

III. THE REFORM OF THE CRIMINAL CODE, 1776-1829

There were two main causes for the reform of the barbarous provincial criminal code when Pennsylvania obtained its independence. The first was the feeling that the code of 1718 was not a native colonial and national product, but that it was the work of a foreign country, forced upon the province by taking advantage of its early religious scruples and divisions. Especially was this the view taken by the Quaker element in Philadelphia and eastern Pennsylvania. Therefore, it was natural that a reaction against the English criminal jurisprudence should be one of the first manifestations of national spirit after 1776. The second chief cause of reform was the growth of enlightenment and criticism abroad. The movement represented by Montesquieu, Voltaire, Diderot, Beccaria, Paine, Bentham and others had affected the leaders of colonial thought in Pennsylvania to such an extent that reform would probably have been inevitable without the strong local impulses which existed at home. This background of the reform of criminal jurisprudence in Pennsylvania has been well summarized by one of the ablest contemporaries of, and participants in, the movement, William Bradford, justice of the supreme court of Pennsylvania, attorney-general of the United States and designer of the reformed Pennsylvania penal codes of 1790 to 1794. Writing in 1793, he thus explained the transformation of the criminal codes of Pennsylvania:

> We perceive, by this detail,[2] that the severity of our criminal law is an exotic plant, and not the native growth of Pennsylvania. It has been endured, but, I believe, has never been a favorite. The religious opinions of many of our citizens were in opposition to it: and, as soon as the principles of Beccaria were disseminated, they found a soil that was prepared to receive them. During our connection with Great Britain no reform was attempted; but, as soon as we separated from her, the public sentiment disclosed itself and this benevolent undertaking was enjoined by the constitution. This was one of the first fruits of liberty and confirms the remark of Montesquieu, "That, as freedom advances, the severity of the penal law decreases."[3]

It was natural that when the American reaction against English jurisprudence took place in Pennsylvania, it should take the form of a return to the doctrines and practices of Penn. The new state constitution of September 28, 1776, directed a speedy reform of the criminal code along the line of substituting imprisonment for the various types of corporal punishment. It was stated that:

2 This passage follows immediately after a sketch of criminal jurisprudence in provincial Pennsylvania. Bradford's death in 1795, at the age of forty, was a great blow to American jurisprudence. His achievements up to that point incline one to surmise that with a normal life he would have quite displaced Edward Livingston as the greatest of early American legalists.

3 William Bradford, *An Enquiry How Far the Punishment of Death Is Necessary in Pennsylvania, With Notes and Illustrations*, Philadelphia, 1793, p. 20. References are to the London reprint of 1795.

The penal laws as heretofore used, shall be reformed by the future legislature of the State, as soon as may be, and punishments made in some cases less sanguinary, and in general more proportionate to the crimes.

To deter more effectually from the commission of crimes, by continued visible punishment of long duration, and to make sanguinary punishments less necessary; houses ought to be provided for punishing by hard labor, those who shall be convicted of crimes not capital; wherein the criminals shall be employed for the benefit of the public, or for reparation of injuries done to private persons. And all persons at proper times shall be admitted to see the prisoners at their labor.[4]

The absorption of attention and energy by the military struggle with England prevented any immediate reform of the criminal code, but on September 15, 1786, an act was passed which aimed to carry out the provisions of the constitution of 1776.[5] The juristic conceptions of the framers of the act were expressed in the following paragraph:

Whereas, it is the wish of every good government to reclaim rather than to destroy, and it being apprehended that the cause of human corruptions proceed more from the impunity of crimes than from the moderation of punishments, and it having been found by experience that the punishments directed by the laws now in force, as well for capital as for other inferior offences do not answer the principal ends of society in inflicting them, to wit, to correct and reform the offenders, and to produce such strong impression on the minds of others as to deter them from committing the like offences, which it is conceived may be better effected by continued hard labor, publicly and disgracefully imposed on persons convicted of them, not only in the manner pointed out by the convention, but in streets of cities

[4] *Constitution of 1776*, Chapter II, Sections 38-9.
[5] *The Statutes at Large of Pennsylvania*, Vol. XII, p. 280.

and towns, and upon the highways of the open country and other public works. . . .[6]

It was enacted, accordingly, that every person henceforth convicted of robbery, burglary, sodomy or buggery, instead of suffering the death penalty, should forfeit all property to the state and serve a sentence of not to exceed ten years at hard labor in the jail or house of correction in the county or city where the crime was committed.[7] Horse stealing was penalized by full restitution to the owner, the forfeiture of an equal amount to the state and imprisonment at hard labor for a term not to exceed seven years.[8] Simple larceny, over twenty shillings, was to be punished by full restitution, forfeiture of like amount to the state and imprisonment at hard labor for not over three years.[9] Petty larceny, under twenty shillings, was to receive a like punishment, except that the maximum term of imprisonment was limited to one year.[10] It was further decreed that a mother could not be convicted of the murder of a bastard child unless it could be shown that the child was born alive.[11] Finally, any other crimes not capital, in the earlier code, but punishable by "burning in the hand, cutting off the ears, nailing the ear or ears to the pillory, placing in or upon the pillory, whipping or imprisonment for life," should thereafter be punished by imprisonment at hard labor for not more than two years.[12] In this manner there disappeared from the statute books the most brutal and revolting phases of the criminal jurisprudence and procedure of the colonial period, although the death penalty was still retained for some ten crimes.

The important act of April 5, 1790, establishing the

6 *The Statutes at Large of Pennsylvania,* Vol. XII, pp. 280-81.
7 Ibid., p. 281.
8 Ibid., pp. 281-2.
9 Ibid., p. 282.
10 Ibid.
11 Ibid., p. 283.
12 Ibid., p. 283.

Pennsylvania system of imprisonment in solitary confinement, while primarily a law concerned with penal administration, specified the penalties for crimes committed, but this part of the act simply repeated the specifications of the law of September 15, 1786.[13] The act of September 23, 1791, while chiefly devoted to the details of criminal procedure,[14] made some advances with respect to ameliorating the severity of the criminal code. It repealed the death penalty for witchcraft,[15] and ordered that there should be no more branding, whipping or imprisonment at hard labor imposed for adultery or fornication. These crimes were to be punished by a fine of not more than fifty pounds and imprisonment for three to twelve months.[16]

The next great step in the progressive reform of the criminal code of Pennsylvania came in an act of April 22, 1794,[17] but before analyzing the contents of this act it will be useful and interesting to examine the chief doctrines of the able and influential pamphlet, published by William Bradford in 1793, on the desirability of reducing the number of capital crimes in Pennsylvania.[18] This work is most important in a number of ways. In the first place, it summarizes and indicates the sources of the doctrines of the jurist who drafted the revised penal code of Pennsylvania, as passed by the legislature during the years 1786 to 1794.[19] In the second place, it was very influential in bringing about the acceptance by the legislature of the law of 1794 reducing the category of capital crimes in Pennsylvania to that of murder in the first de-

13 *Statutes at Large,* Vol. XIII, pp. 511-15.
14 Ibid., Vol. XIV, pp. 128-31.
15 Ibid., p. 132.
16 Ibid., pp. 133-4.
17 Ibid., Vol. XV, pp. 174-181.
18 Bradford, op. cit. References, as above, to London edition of 1795.
19 The total abolition of the death penalty had been urged by Dr. Benjamin Rush in 1786-7. Roberts Vaux, *Notices,* p. 33. *A Statistical View of the Operation of the Penal Code of Pennsylvania,* 1817, pp. 3-4. *The Pennsylvania Journal of Prison Discipline and Philanthropy,* Vol. II, Number 3, pp. 205-10.

gree alone. Finally, as the product of the ablest legal mind in America at the time, it attracted wide attention at home and in Europe, and furnished the reformers with a valuable instrument for aiding in their assaults upon the old order in criminal jurisprudence.

Throughout the work, Mr. Bradford gave evidence of the fact that the works of Montesquieu, Beccaria and Blackstone were not only the chief source of his own conviction that the mitigation of the criminal laws was an indispensable and immediate necessity, but that he regarded them as the main inspiration which had produced the newer and more humane conceptions in criminal jurisprudence.[20] At the outset Mr. Bradford laid down the dictum that the only object of punishment is the prevention of crime.[21] The purpose of the death penalty, then, must be solely to prevent the person executed from the commission of another crime and to deter others from committing crime through fear of death. If these ends can be accomplished by other modes of punishment, then the death penalty is unjustifiable.[22] Mr. Bradford contended that solitary confinement at hard labor would accomplish all that had been claimed for the death penalty.[23] He showed that history proves that mild penalties do not encourage the commission of crime nor severe penalties deter from criminal action. The example of Rome and England demonstrates this conclusively. Rome never imposed the death penalty except upon slaves, and yet it was much more orderly than England with its unprecedentedly long list of capital crimes.[24] The experience of America has been similar to that of Rome and England.[25]

Mr. Bradford then turned to a scientific examination of the effect of the ameliorating law of September 15,

20 Bradford, op. cit., pp. 3, 49-80.
21 Ibid., p. 6
22 Ibid., pp. 6-7.
23 Ibid., pp. 7-8.
24 Ibid., p. 9.
25 Ibid., pp. 10 ff.

1786, in Pennsylvania, upon the commission of those crimes which were removed from the list of capital offences. He concluded that, when all disturbing influences were eliminated, the results revealed the fact that the number of commissions of these crimes was less in the six years after 1786 than in the six years previous to that time.[26] Mr. Bradford stated that he believed that society might safely dispense with the death penalty in the case of all crimes except premeditated murder and high treason, and it might be that, sooner or later, the progress of intelligence would be sufficient, so that capital punishment might be wholly abolished.[27] His conclusion is significant:

> The conclusion to which we are led by this enquiry seems to be, that in all cases, except those of high treason and murder, the punishment of death may be safely abolished, and milder penalties advantageously introduced. Such a system of punishments, aided and enforced in the manner I have mentioned, will not only have an auspicious influence on the character, morals, and happiness of the people, but may hasten the period, when, in the progress of civilization, the punishment of death shall cease to be necessary; and the legislature of Pennsylvania, putting the keystone to the arch, may triumph in the completion of their benevolent work.[28]

Mr. Bradford had the satisfaction of seeing his theories enacted into law in the act of April 22, 1794, "for the better preventing of crimes, and for abolishing the punishment of death in certain cases." It was declared that,

> It is the duty of every government to endeavor to reform, rather than to exterminate, offenders, and the punishment of death ought never to be inflicted where it is not absolutely necessary to the public safety.[29]

26 Ibid., pp. 20 ff.
27 Ibid., pp. 35 ff.
28 Bradford, op. cit., p. 46.
29 *The Statutes at Large of Pennsylvania,* Vol. XV, p. 174.

Accordingly, it was enacted,

> That no crime whatsoever, hereafter committed, except murder in the first degree, shall be punished with death in the State of Pennsylvania.[30]

It was specified that murder in the first degree would be constituted by all premeditated murder and by all murder committed in attempting rape, arson, robbery or burglary. All other types of murder were to constitute murder in the second degree.[31] The death penalty for murder in the first degree was to be inflicted "by hanging by the neck." [32]

In addition to this remarkable reduction of capital crimes, the act provided reduced penalties for the crimes which were eliminated from the list of those punishable by death. The following were the penalties prescribed: *murder in the second degree,* imprisonment of from five to eighteen years; *manslaughter,* imprisonment for from two to ten years, with from six to fourteen years for a second offence; *murder or concealment of the death of a bastard child,* imprisonment up to five years or a fine at the discretion of the court; *high treason,* imprisonment for from six to twelve years; [33] *arson,* imprisonment from five to twelve years; *rape,* imprisonment for from ten to twenty-one years; *malicious maiming,* imprisonment for from two to ten years and a fine up to one thousand dollars, three-fourths of which was to go to the party injured; *counterfeiting,* imprisonment from four to fifteen years and a fine up to one thousand dollars.[34] "Benefit of clergy" was "forever abolished." [35]

It was provided that if a person be convicted a second

[30] *The Statutes at Large of Pennsylvania,* Vol. XV, p. 174.
[31] Ibid., p. 175.
[32] Ibid., p. 180.
[33] The fact that high treason was not made a capital crime may in some degree be explained by the fact that the "Whisky Rebellion" in Pennsylvania was at its height in 1794.
[34] *The Statutes at Large of Pennsylvania,* Vol. XV, pp. 175-181.
[35] Ibid., p. 177.

time of a crime which was capital on September 15, 1786, he should be confined for life in the solitary cells of the Walnut street jail, unless the inspectors saw fit to remove him from these cells.[36] The only exception to this rule was in case the second offence was committed after escaping or being pardoned; in such instances the penalty for a second commission of the crime was to be imprisonment for twenty-five years.[37] With some minor revisions, especially in the Act of April 23, 1829, this law of 1794 remained the basis of the criminal code of Pennsylvania until the systematic revision of the code in 1860.

A slight increase in the severity of the penal code was produced by an act of April 4, 1807. The act of September 15, 1786, had decreed a punishment of not to exceed two years' imprisonment for those crimes, not capital in 1786, but which had been punished by the brutal forms of corporal punishment and by imprisonment for life. This act of April 4, 1807, raised the maximum limit for these crimes to seven years imprisonment, though it specified that this increase should not apply to bigamy, accessory after the fact in a felony, or the reception of stolen goods.[38] From this time until the act of April 23, 1829, there were no important alterations in the criminal code of Pennsylvania.[39]

IV. THE REVISION OF THE CRIMINAL CODE IN 1829

A resolution of the legislature, passed March 23, 1826, directed the appointment of three commissioners to revise the criminal code of the state.[40] Charles Shaler, Edward King and T. J. Wharton were appointed to perform this

36 Ibid., pp. 178-9.
37 Ibid., p. 179.
38 *Acts of the General Assembly of Pennsylvania*, 1806-7, p. 134.
39 For a list of the penal laws of Pennsylvania from 1700 to 1812, see Bioren's edition of the *Laws of the Commonwealth of Pennsylvania*, Vol. V, 1812, Index, pp. 270-72. An able revision of the penal code by Jared Ingersoll, in 1813, was rejected by the legislature.
40 *Acts of the General Assembly*, 1825-6, p. 413.

important task. They laid their report before the legislature on December 20, 1827.[41] The commission made no attempt at a complete new codification of the criminal law of the state, as they felt that their authorization did not extend to this limit and the time allotted was not sufficient for the completion of so extensive a task.[42] Rather they aimed at "lopping off relics of barbarism," giving a better definition of crimes and eliminating obsolete statutes.[43] One of the most original and valuable innovations introduced was the practice of specifying only the maximum sentence and leaving the minimum to the discretion of the court.[44] This procedure was defended with ingenuity and convinciveness.[45] In some cases, the commissioners thought it wise to extend the maximum, and their defence of this step is interesting as indicating that the struggle between prison reformers and the conservatism of the judiciary is not merely an incident of the present day. They stated that,

> In some instances, the punishment allotted to offences, appears hardly commensurate with the specified crimes, and this, whether we consider these punishments with practical men, as a means of prevention, or consider penitentiaries with some modern theorists, as mere schools of reform.[46]

On the whole, however, the revision was a work of great skill and ability and the failure of the legislature to adopt it was a severe blow to the progress of criminal jurisprudence in Pennsylvania. Not until 1860 was a criminal code provided which attained the level of excellence and modernity reached in the report of 1827. The reason for the failure to adopt the code is a part of the story of the struggle over penitentiary systems. The

41 *Report of the Commissioners on the Penal Code,* 1828, p. 105.
42 Ibid., pp. 93-4.
43 Ibid., pp. 94-5.
44 Ibid., pp. 98-100.
45 Ibid.
46 Ibid., pp. 96-7.

same commissioners had been directed to draw up rules for the regulation of the new state penitentiaries and they had reported in favor of the Auburn system.[47] This led to the opposition of the Philadelphia Society for Alleviating the Miseries of Public Prisons, and in the three-cornered conflict which ensued between the penal code commissioners, the commissioners charged with building the Eastern Penitentiary, and the prison society, the legislature ended by rejecting the revised penal code as well as the recommendation of the Auburn system.[48]

Instead of the code recommended by the commissioners, the legislature, by an act of April 23, 1829, adopted a revision which was much less thorough and systematic than the commissioners had suggested.[49] It followed the precedent of the code of 1794 in prescribing maximum and minimum penalties for the first offence of the specified crimes, and the recommendation of the commissioners of 1827 in usually prescribing only the maximum penalty for the second conviction. On the whole, the revision, while constituting no departure in juristic doctrine from the code of 1794, did produce a considerable reduction in the length of the term of imprisonment specified for the various crimes. This was, no doubt, due to the optimism at the time with respect to the remarkable reformative virtues of the Pennsylvania system of solitary confinement at hard labor.

In the first place, it was ordered that in all cases where imprisonment was the penalty imposed this should be carried out in solitary confinement at hard labor.[50] The following penalties were imposed for the crimes enumerated: *high treason,* for the first offence, imprisonment of

47 Ibid., pp. 77-82.

48 *The Pennsylvania Journal of Prison Discipline and Philanthropy,* Vol. I, Number 1, 1845, pp. 8-12.

49 *Laws of the General Assembly,* 1828-9, pp. 341-54. This code is also reproduced in Richard Vaux's *Brief Sketch of the Eastern Penitentiary,* pp. 36-42.

50 *Laws,* 1828-9, pp. 341-2.

from three to six years, and for the second offence, imprisonment for not to exceed ten years; *murder in the second degree,* for the first offence, imprisonment of from four to twelve years, and for the second offence, imprisonment for life; *manslaughter,* for the first offence, imprisonment of from two to six years, and for the second offence, imprisonment for from six to twelve years; *mayhem,* for the first offence, imprisonment of from one to seven years, and for the second offence, imprisonment for not to exceed fourteen years; *rape,* for the first offence, imprisonment of from two to twelve years, and for the second offence, imprisonment for life; *sodomy* and *buggery,* for the first offence, imprisonment of from one to five years, and for the second offence, imprisonment for not to exceed ten years; *kidnapping,* for the first offence, imprisonment of from five to twelve years, and for the second offence, imprisonment for twenty-one years; *arson,* for the first offence, imprisonment of from one to ten years, and for the second offence, imprisonment for not to exceed fifteen years; *burglary,* for the first offence, imprisonment of from two to ten years, and for the second offence, imprisonment for not to exceed fifteen years; *robbery,* for the first offence, imprisonment of from one to seven years, and for the second offence, imprisonment for not to exceed twelve years; *horse-stealing,* for the first offence, imprisonment of from one to four years, and for the second offence, imprisonment for not to exceed seven years; *forgery,* for the first offence, imprisonment of from one to seven years, and for the second offence, imprisonment for not to exceed ten years; *perjury,* for the first offence, imprisonment of from one to five years, and for the second offence, imprisonment for not to exceed eight years.[51] It was further specified that for all crimes not enumerated the penalties should remain as prescribed in earlier laws.[52] Such was the relatively

51 *Laws of the General Assembly,* 1828-9, pp. 342-4.
52 Ibid., p. 345.

mild penal code under which the Pennsylvania system began its complete operation, as it had made its beginnings under the codes of 1786, 1790, and 1794.[53]

V. THE ABOLITION OF IMPRISONMENT FOR DEBT

The failure of the penal code commissioners of 1828 to provide Pennsylvania with a relatively systematic and enlightened code of criminal jurisprudence has already been discussed. It has been shown that the recommendations of the commissioners were rejected primarily because they insisted on attaching to the revised criminal code, as a sort of a "rider," a set of provisions directing the adoption of the Auburn system of prison administration. The friends of the Pennsylvania system considered the sacrifice of the newly proposed criminal code less of an evil than the loss of their cherished penological principles and defeated the bill through lobbying with the judiciary committee of the state legislature. Not until 1860 was the ambition of the commissioners realized in the enactment of a new criminal code. In the interval between 1828 and 1860, however, one important advance was made in the modernizing and humanizing of one phase of jurisprudence which was until relatively recent times divided between civil and criminal law, namely, imprisonment for debt.

Throughout the colonial period many successive attempts had been made to relieve the condition of "distressed debtors," but the courts never adopted a liberal interpretation of the laws, and imprisonment for debt persisted far down into the period of the commonwealth. One of the most grievous sources of evil revealed in the Walnut street jail by the Philadelphia Society for Alleviating the Miseries of Public Prisons was the mode of

[53] As the basis of a comparison, see the admirable summary of the criminal codes of the period in the *Fourth Annual Report of the Prison Discipline Society of Boston*, 1829, pp. 31-54.

treating debtors in 1787-1790, and from 1818 to 1835 a separate prison on Arch street had been set aside for the incarceration of debtors and witnesses. The first important progressive legislation in this sphere was contained in an act of April 4, 1792, which was designed to do away with the evils of the extortionate fee system which had been in vogue down to that time. This act provided that the keeper of the debtors' apartment in the Philadelphia jail was to be granted a fixed salary of five hundred dollars, which was to supersede all fees hitherto allowed to him or his subordinates.[54] The basis of a general bankruptcy act was laid by a law of April 4, 1798, which provided, "That the person of a debtor shall not be liable to imprisonment for debt, after delivering up his estate for the benefit of his creditors, unless he has been guilty of fraud or embezzlement." [55] This liberal act met the fate of its predecessors and imprisonment for debt continued with little change. The first decisive step was taken in an act of February 8, 1819, which command that, "No female shall be arrested or imprisoned for, or by reason of, any debt contracted after the passing of this act." [56] The degree to which imprisonment for debt persisted may be seen from the fact that on June 16, 1836, a long and elaborate act was passed defining and prescribing the civil and criminal procedure in debtors' cases.[57] The final act abolishing imprisonment for debt in Pennsylvania was passed on July 12, 1842. In a most fundamental sense, this act and the many similar ones which were passed throughout the country in this same general period were, as Professor Carleton has so well shown, the product of the wave of indignation that swept over the country and demanded the abolition of this along with the many other undemocratic features of American

[54] *The Statutes at Large of Pennsylvania,* Vol. XIV, pp. 267-9.
[55] Ibid., Vol. XVI, pp. 98-106.
[56] *Acts of the General Assembly,* 1818-19, p. 57.
[57] *Laws of the General Assembly,* 1835-6, pp. 729-41.

society and politics. The movement was an incident of the development of the Jacksonian democracy and of the rise of the organization of the industrial proletariat.[58]

In a more immediate sense, it was the outgrowth of a vigorous campaign of invective directed against the antiquated laws on this point by Louis Dwight in the annual reports of the Boston Prison Discipline Society, from 1830 to 1845. In no phase of prison reform was Dwight more active than in agitating for the abolition of imprisonment for debt. In Pennsylvania, his efforts were ably seconded by the Philadelphia Society for Alleviating the Miseries of Public Prisons, this being about the only field in which they could work in harmony and agreement with the leader of the Boston society. The act of 1842, which was entitled, "An Act to Abolish Imprisonment for Debt and to Punish Fraudulent Debtors," provided that:

> From and after the passage of this act, no person shall be arrested or imprisoned on any civil process issuing out of any court of this commonwealth, in any suit or proceeding instituted for the recovery of any money due upon any judgment or decree founded upon contract, or due upon any contract, express or implied, or for the recovery of any damages for the non-performance of any contract, excepting in cases for contempt; to enforce civil remedies, action for fines or penalties, or on promises to marry, or moneys collected by any public officer, or for any misconduct or neglect in office, or in any professional employment, in which cases the remedies shall remain as heretofore."[59]

[58] Frank Carleton, "The Abolition of Imprisonment for Debt in the United States," in *The Yale Review*, Vol. XVII, pp. 338-44. Cf. J. R. Commons (ed.), *A History of Labor in the United States*, Vol. I, pp. 296 ff.

[59] *Laws of the General Assembly*, 1842, pp. 339 ff. For complete or nearly complete lists of laws dealing with imprisonment for debt in Pennsylvania, see *The Statutes at Large*, Vol. IV, pp. 183-4, note, and G. W. Pepper and W. D. Lewis, *Digest of the Laws of Pennsylvania*, 1896, Vol. I, p. 231-3. For a discussion of the abolition of debt in Pennsylvania, see W. C. Heffner, *The History of Poor Relief Legislation in Pennsylvania*, 1682-1913, pp. 202-4.

VI. THE CRIMINAL CODE OF 1860

By 1858, the anachronisms in the existing penal code and the confusion resulting from the successive additions to the act of 1829, which had itself been little more than an amendment of the codes of 1790-94, made further acquiescence in the existing penal code no longer possible, and on April 19th of that year the legislature resolved:

> That the Governor of this Commonwealth be and he is hereby authorized and required to appoint, by and with the advice and consent of the Senate, three competent citizens, learned in the laws of this commonwealth, as commissioners to revise, collate and digest all the acts and statutes relating to or touching the penal laws of the commonwealth.[60]

The commissioners appointed by Governor W. F. Packer to carry out this revision of the penal code were John C. Knox, David Webster and Edward King.[61] Judge King (1794-1873) had been one of three commissioners on the revision of the penal code in 1828, and he had the opportunity to put his juristic ideas and principles into practice after an interval of thirty-two years. It is generally agreed that the code of 1860 was mainly the work of Judge King, the most eminent of Pennsylvania authorities on the law of equity and for years President Judge of the criminal court of Philadelphia county.[62]

Apart from the specific penalties imposed by the code some of its outstanding features were the following: It

60 "The Revised Penal Code of Pennsylvania," reprinted from *The American Law Register,* August, 1860, pp. 1-2.

61 "The Revised Penal Code of Pennsylvania," loc. cit., pp. 2-3.

62 Ibid. It is significant that down to the present time all the great revisions of Pennsylvania criminal law have been primarily the work of some one man in each epoch. The enlightened Quaker codes of the late seventeenth century were prepared by William Penn; the notorious code of 1718 was compiled by David Lloyd, though he cannot be entirely blamed for its contents; the notable revisions of 1786 to 1794 were the work of William Bradford, Jr., inspired by the spirit of Benjamin Rush; the slightly revised code of 1829 was drawn up by Thomas Bradford, Jr., with the aid and advice of Roberts Vaux and S. R. Wood.

was drawn up in an admirably systematic manner, even if some of the divisions may have been too logical and artificial, a fault inherent in all attempts to classify criminal acts. The two most novel and progressive features of the code were the consistent practice of prescribing only the maximum penalty for the several offences and leaving the minimum to be fixed at the discretion of the sentencing court, and the courageous abolition of the monstrous and barbarous distinction between grand and petit larceny, which still remains embalmed in the statute books of many American commonwealths—a curious but oppressive relic of medieval juristic conceptions. The only reactionary anachronism introduced was that contained in the law imposing a penalty for blasphemy. This stipulated that,

> If a person shall wilfully, premeditately and despitefully blaspheme, or speak loosely and profanely of Almighty God, Christ Jesus, the Holy Spirit, or the Scriptures of Truth, such person, on conviction thereof, shall be sentenced to pay a fine not exceeding one hundred dollars, and undergo an imprisonment not exceeding three months, or either, at the discretion of the court.[63]

The following were the penalties imposed for the more important crimes. In the field of crimes against the state, *treason* was punished by a fine not exceeding two thousand dollars and imprisonment for a period not to exceed twelve years. *Misprison of treason* was penalized by a fine of not to exceed one thousand dollars and imprisonment for not more than six years.[64]

The following penalties were prescribed for crimes against public morals and decency: *blasphemy,* as above; *sodomy* and *buggery,* a fine not to exceed one thousand dollars and imprisonment for not more than ten years; *bigamy,* a fine of not more than one thousand dollars and

[63] *Laws of the General Assembly,* 1860, p. 392.
[64] Ibid., p. 385.

imprisonment for not more than two years; *adultery,* a fine of not more than five hundred dollars and imprisonment for not more than one year; *fornication,* a fine of not more than one hundred dollars; *incest,* a fine up to five hundred dollars and imprisonment for not more than three years.[65]

Crimes against persons were dealt with in the following manner: *murder in the first degree,* "death by hanging by the neck"; *murder in the second degree,* imprisonment for not more than twelve years for the first offence and life imprisonment for the second offence; *voluntary manslaughter,* a fine of not more than one thousand dollars and imprisonment for not more than twelve years; *mayhem,* a fine of not more than one thousand dollars and imprisonment for not more than five years; *rape,* a fine of not more than one thousand dollars and imprisonment for not more than fifteen years; *kidnapping,* a fine of not more than two thousand dollars and imprisonment for not more than twelve years; *assault and battery,* a fine of not more than one thousand dollars and imprisonment for not more than one year, both or either at the discretion of the court.[66]

The punishments decreed for offences against personal property were as follows: *robbery,* a fine of not more than one thousand dollars and imprisonment for not more than ten years; *assault to rob,* a fine of not more than one thousand dollars and imprisonment for not more than five years; *larceny,* a fine of not more than five hundred dollars and imprisonment for not more than three years.[67]

The punishment prescribed for offences against real property follow: *burglary,* a fine of not more than one thousand dollars and imprisonment for not more than ten years; *arson,* without a person in the dwelling house, a fine of not more than two thousand dollars and impris-

65 *Laws of the General Assembly,* 1860, pp. 392-5.
66 Ibid., pp. 402-8.
67 Ibid., pp. 408-15.

onment for not more than five years, and with a person in the dwelling house, a fine of not more than four thousand dollars and imprisonment for not more than twenty years.[68]

Finally, with respect to offences against the coin and forgery, the following penalties were prescribed: *counterfeiting,* a fine of not more than one thousand dollars and imprisonment for not more than five years; *forgery,* the same as for counterfeiting.[69]

The only capital crime, then, in the code of 1860 was murder in the first degree, as in all codes from 1794 to 1860. A revised code of criminal procedure was also prepared by the commissioners and accepted by the legislature.[70] In their long and able report the commissioners presented an elaborate exposition, explanation and defence of their work which was of great assistance in securing its enactment into law.[71]

That the report and the codes were considered of a high order by authoritative contemporary critics is evident from the following comment in one of the leading law reviews of the time:

> The report, as a whole, is a most masterly production, and reflects infinite credit upon the ability, learning, industry, and faithfulness of the Commissioners, and will prove an enduring monument to their fame. It is deserving of careful study in all its details, not only by those who are engaged in the practice of criminal law, but by the legislator, and by all who are interested in penal legislation and the entire subject of crimes and punishments. Pennsylvania may now congratulate herself upon possessing a system of

[68] Ibid., pp. 415-20.
[69] Ibid., pp. 420-25.
[70] Ibid., pp. 427-58.
[71] "The Revised Penal Code of Pennsylvania," loc. cit., pp. 4 ff. The complete documentary sources for this revision are contained in the following: *Report of the Commissioners Appointed to Revise the Penal Code of the Commonwealth of Pennsylvania,* Harrisburg, 1860, pp. 129, and *The Penal Laws of Pennsylvania, Passed March* 31, 1860, Harrisburg, 1860, p. 72.

penal laws worthy of her advanced civilization, and adapted to the wants of her extended and varied population.[72]

VII. THE CONTEMPORARY MOVEMENT FOR A SYSTEMATIC REVISION OF THE CRIMINAL CODE

While there is little doubt that the laudatory strain in the above quotation was justified, in view of the relative condition and level of criminal jurisprudence at that time, the progress in the concepts of criminal law in the last half century is evident from the following incisive criticism passed upon this code of 1860 by Professor William E. Mikell, Dean of the Law School of the University of Pennsylvania, one of the most eminent of American authorities on criminal jurisprudence, in general, and on the criminal law of Pennsylvania, in particular:

> Perhaps, in the true sense of the term, there is no criminal "code" in Pennsylvania. The whole body of criminal law has never been reduced to a written code in this state in the sense in which this has been done in some of the States of the Union in which jurisdictions there are no crimes except those specifically prescribed. . . .
>
> Viewing the code, however, as a whole, there is an utter lack of principle in the grading of crimes as felonies or misdemeanors, either according to the moral heinousness of the offence or the severity of the punishment. . . .
>
> The work of the commissioners who framed the Code of 1860 shows an utter lack of consistent theory not only of grading the crimes as felonies and misdemeanors, but also in grading the punishment fixed for the various crimes. . . .
>
> In the case of almost every crime denounced by the code fine and imprisonment are associated. In most cases the penalty provided is fine and imprisonment, in some it is fine or imprisonment. In a few cases imprisonment alone with-

72 "The Revised Penal Code of Pennsylvania," loc. cit., p. 26. For a list of the criminal laws repealed by the code of 1860, which constitutes a fair index to the previous criminal law of Pennsylvania, see *Laws of the General Assembly*, 1860, pp. 451-8.

out a fine is prescribed, and in a few others, it is a fine alone without imprisonment. We seek in vain for any principle on which the fine is omitted, where it is omitted; or for a principle on which it is inflicted in addition to imprisonment in some cases, and as an alternative to imprisonment in others. . . .

The Pennsylvania code has no general section on attempts, but in a haphazard manner, in providing for some crimes, provides for the attempt to commit the same, and in some cases has no provision for such attempts. A study of those cases in which provision for punishing the attempt is made, shows an entire absence of any theory or principle in assessing the punishment. . . .[73]

The criminal code of 1860 has never been systematically revised and remains to the present day the basis of Pennsylvania's criminal jurisprudence. It has been modified by many additions and amendments, but these alterations have contributed rather to greater confusion than to clarity and modernity. Dean Mikell also calls attention to this point:

The writer has attempted to point out in this paper some of the more glaring and interesting defects in the code. He has by no means exhausted them. There is a great need for a complete revision of the code. It is a jumble of inconsistent theories; a great many sections are badly drawn, others are obsolete; many are inconsistent, many are in conflict; there is much overlapping due to different acts having been passed at different times covering in part the same subject matter, so that it cannot be told whether a given crime should be punished under one section or another prescribing a different punishment.[74]

By 1917 the condition of the penal code of Pennsylvania as regards anachronisms, conflicts and points of con-

[73] *The Journal of Prison Discipline and Philanthropy*, March, 1918, pp. 89-91.
[74] Ibid., p. 92.

fusion had become much like that which existed in 1860, and an act of July 25, 1917, directed the governor to appoint five commissioners to

> . . . revise, collate, and digest all the acts and statutes relating to or touching the penal laws of the Commonwealth in such a manner as to render the penal code of Pennsylvania more efficient, clear, and perfect, and the punishments inflicted on crimes more uniform and better adapted to the suppression of crime and the reformation of the offender.[75]

Governor Brumbaugh, accordingly, appointed the commissioners and they are now engaged upon the task of revision which presents an opportunity for constructive and progressive juristic reform unequalled since the days of William Bradford, Jr., as the scientific background of criminal jurisprudence has made more progress since 1860 than it had between the time of Draco and 1860. As a member of the commission charged with the revision, Dean Mikell has given above some notion of the task and at least a slight indication of the promising spirit in which it will be attacked.[76] The commissioners appointed drafted a revised code, but the Legislature thus far (July, 1925) refused to accept their work and bring Pennsylvania criminal jurisprudence up to the level of modern juristic science and penal practice.

In any survey of the history of criminal law it is, however, necessary to emphasize the fact that even the progressive and scientific juristic measures advocated by Dean Mikell and by the members of the American Bar Association who are concerned with the revision of the criminal codes of the country are as much out of harmony with the self-evident and thoroughly established principles of psychology, social science and criminology as the duck-

[75] *Laws of the General Assembly*, 1917, pp. 1188-9.

[76] The following commissioners were appointed by Governor Brumbaugh to revise the criminal code, Edwin M. Abbott, William E. Mikell, George C. Bradshaw, Clarence E. Coughlin and Rex N. Mitchell.

ing-stool and the pillory. The most advanced criminal code ever proposed by a professional lawyer with any serious hope of its adoption has rested upon assumptions which have been completely repudiated by modern psychological, social and criminal science. Such advanced codes still accept as their fundamental postulate the doctrine that the criminal is a physically and mentally normal individual, and a free moral agent capable at all times of choosing his actions and determining whether he will be a law-abiding citizen or a heinous criminal. All criminals are assumed to be equal before the law, not only with respect to their legal rights but also, with a few exceptions, with regard to their physical and mental capacities and responsibilities.

The law, lawyers and courts are held to be the legitimate agencies for determining and controlling society's methods of dealing with the delinquent classes. It is maintained that it is possible to adjust the penalty to the crime on the basis of the relative assumed damage or challenge to society inherent in the particular act. The major interest and concern of the law and the court remains in the crime rather than in the criminal, and the reaction of society in the circumstances is adjusted to the nature of the crime rather than to the characteristics and personality of the individual who has committed it. Penalties are held to be adequate to deter from the commission of crime in direct proportion to their severity, irrespective of the personality of the individual punished. Punishment is regarded as actually and potently reformative in its operation, and, after the term of its imposition has expired, the individual criminal is viewed as a fit and proper person to resume his position as a free citizen in society, irrespective of the fact that the physical or mental causes of his original criminal behavior may in reality have been greatly accentuated by the conditions of life during his term in prison.

As archaic as the postulates of the most advanced proposed criminal codes are the methods of criminal procedure approved by even the most progressive jurists. The police, district-attorney, judge and jury are held to be competent and adequate to the task of determining the guilt of the accused and the treatment to be meted out to him. Likewise, the guilt or innocence of the particular crime with which the defendant is charged is regarded as a much more vital matter than the potential menace of a pathological personality to the community at large. In fact, the question of the commission of the specific crime charged is the only matter with which the court directly concerns itself. And the procedure followed in court is a combination of magic, rhetoric and contradictory and absurd rules of evidence which would bring forth a roar of ribald and contemptuous laughter if they were proposed as the methods to be followed in the science laboratories of even a southern Fundamentalist college.

It is necessary for us to come to realize the fact that every dictate of medical and social science unquestionably indicates that lawyers and courts have no more proper function in dealing with criminals (using this term in a scientific sense) than they have in taking full charge of the treatment of mentally defective and insane types—types which were once as much under the sole jurisdiction of lawyers and judges as are the criminals at the present time. As soon as science, natural, biological, medical, psychological and social, comes to be applied to our methods of handling the delinquent classes it will be seen that the function of criminal law ends with the legal or judicial supervision of the mere forms of procedure involved in turning over the accused individual to the properly equipped authorities. Such a procedure would be comparable to the judicial supervision at present of the processes of committing an alleged insane person to a hospital for the insane and approving his discharge after a cure has been effected.

Hence, even the improvements in the Pennsylvania penal code recommended by Dean Mikell and his associates appear in the light of modern criminal science to be as little founded upon the scientific facts in the circumstances as the ordeal, torture and the doctrine of demoniacal possession. But the day of the operation of scientific criminology is far off, and for the time being the advocates of reform must content themselves with such temporizing patch-work on an obsolete structure as Dean Mikell recommends, and upon the hope of undoing the unfortunate effects of unwise criminal procedure prior to sentence by such quasi-juristic advances as the commutation of sentence, the indeterminate sentence, parole and probation. By a sane procedure after conviction we may even now do much to offset the evil operation of contemporary criminal jurisprudence and court procedure, though efforts in that direction will be hampered as long as we do not have general facilities for applying probation methods universally to those classes who never should be subjected to the demoralizing influence of penal institutions, and as long as we do not have a real indeterminate sentence law which will enable properly guided prison authorities to retain indefinitely in segregation those delinquent types whose reformation and safe existence in society is impossible or manifestly unlikely. We may now turn to a consideration of what has been achieved in Pennsylvania to date with respect to the indeterminate sentence, parole and probation.

VIII. THE COMMUTATION OF SENTENCE FOR GOOD BEHAVIOR

What is probably the earliest instance of the application of the principle of the commutation of the sentence of a prisoner for good behavior appears in a law passed in 1817 in the state of New York and put into operation in the state prison at Auburn. It provided that all prisoners sentenced for five years or less might earn a reduction of one-fourth of their sentence by good behavior and the performance of a stipulated amount of "overwork." This appears, however, to have been regarded quite as much an economic measure as a disciplinary feature, and it remained purely a local enactment.[77] It is to the broader development of the principle as an integral factor in the improvement of prison discipline that one must look for the sources from which it came into the practice of the state of Pennsylvania. It is generally held that the first writer to enunciate the doctrine of the commutation of sentence for good behavior as a basic principle in the improvement of prison discipline was Archbishop Whatley of Dublin. In 1829 he published a letter in the *London Review* in which he set forth his belief that the definite time sentence should be replaced by one which represented a certain amount of labor to be performed before release and would allow a convict to reduce his sentence by industrious application to assigned tasks. This suggestion was given a practical application with great success by Captain Alexander Maconochie in his reconstruction of the penal discipline at Norfolk Island, an Australian penal colony, in the years following 1842. When Walter Crofton began his epoch-making work in reorganizing the Irish prisons in 1853 he adopted as a component part of his celebrated "Irish" system of prison administration the so-called "mark" or commutation system of Maconochie. From Ireland it was introduced into America by the enthusiastic admirers of Crofton's methods, among whom were E. C. Wines, Theodore Dwight, Frank Sanborn, Gaylord B. Hubbell and Z. R. Brockway. Though all of the principles of the "Irish" system have since been

[77] P. Klein, *Prison Methods in New York State,* pp. 406-7.

in differing degree adopted in this country, the principle of commutation was the first element of this system to be introduced, primarily, no doubt, because it necessitated the least violent and extensive break with traditional administrative methods.

The introduction of the commutation system into the administrative procedure of Pennsylvania was primarily the result of the work of the *Philadelphia Society for the Alleviation of the Miseries of Public Prisons.*[78] By their agitation and campaign of education the legislature was induced to pass the act of May 1, 1861, which first established the principle of commutation in Pennsylvania.[79] This act directed the wardens of the two state penitentiaries to keep an accurate record of all infractions of the disciplinary rules of the institution. In case of no violation of these rules a prisoner was to be entitled to the following reduction of his sentence: one day for the first month; three days for the second month; six days for the third month, and the remainder of the first year; four days for each month in the second year; an additional day for each month from two to ten years; and two additional days above ten years. The wardens were directed to discharge convicts with a certificate of good conduct as soon as they had served out their sentences less the prescribed deductions.[80]

The inspectors of both state penitentiaries violently opposed this commutation act, in part, no doubt, because its peculiarly complicated schedule of reductions would require a large amount of additional administrative labor. In their report for 1861 the inspectors of the Eastern Penitentiary sharply condemned the law, their main objection apparently being the additional labor of compil-

[78] The name of this society was changed to *The Pennsylvania Prison Society* on its hundredth anniversary in 1887.

[79] *The Journal of Prison Discipline and Philanthropy,* Vol. XVI, October, 1861, Number 4, pp. 170-200. (This reference includes an argument against the system.)

[80] *The Laws of the General Assembly,* 1861, pp. 462-3.

ing the individual records, though it is difficult to see how this could have been a serious objection if the Pennsylvania system was, as its exponents claimed, founded primarily upon a careful attention to individual conduct on the part of the prisoners.[81] Even more outspoken was the criticism of the inspectors of the Western Penitentiary. They maintained that it would make so much extra work that more officials would be required; that it was unconstitutional to take the pardoning power from the governor in such a manner; and that the inspectors would not execute the law in their institution. They further commended the inspectors of the Eastern Penitentiary for their stand with respect to the law.[82] The opposition of the prison authorities and the ruffled pride of the courts were sufficient to procure the declaration by the courts that the commutation law of 1861 was unconstitutional. In their report for 1862 the inspectors of the Western Penitentiary proclaimed their great satisfaction that "the constitution of the Commonwealth had been thus preserved," though their satisfaction could not have been less over the reduction of administrative duties.[83]

The friends of prison reform were not discouraged, however, and persisted in their demand for a commutation law until the act of May 21, 1869, was passed. This directed that the wardens of the penitentiaries keep a record of the conduct of all prisoners and stated that if no charges of misconduct stood against the prisoner he was entitled to a reduction of one month for each of the first two years; two months for the third and fourth year; three months for the fifth to the tenth years; and four months for the period from the tenth year to the time of discharge.[84] As this law was much more liberal than

81 *Report of the Inspectors of the Eastern Penitentiary*, 1861, pp. 36 ff., and Appendix, passim.

82 *Legislative Documents*, 1862, pp. 847-8.

83 *Report of the Inspectors of the Western Penitentiary*, 1862, p. 7.

84 *Laws of the General Assembly*, 1869, p. 1268.

that of 1869, the delay was not entirely fruitless. By this time the new board of inspectors had come into power in the Western Penitentiary and were from the first advocates and supporters of the second commutation law.[85] The inspectors of the Eastern Penitentiary, while no longer violent in their criticism of the commutation law, belittled its significance. They maintained that it was but an expedient devised by administrators of congregate prisons to lessen the difficulty of maintaining discipline in so defective a system. It was entirely superfluous in so perfect a system as that in operation in the Eastern Penitentiary.[86]

The act of 1869 remained in force as the basis of the commutation system until the passage of the act of May 11, 1901, which provided—

> That every convict confined in any state prison, penitentiary, work house, or county jail in this state, on a conviction of felony or misdemeanor, whether male or female, where the term or terms equal or equals or exceeds one year, exclusive of any term which may be imposed by the court or by the statute as an alternative to the payment of a fine, or term of life imprisonment, may, if the Governor shall so direct, and with the approval of the board of managers, earn for himself or herself a commutation or diminution of his or her sentence, as follows, namely: Two months for the first year, three months for the second year, four months for the third and fourth years, and five months for each subsequent year. And for each fractional part of a year the said convict may earn the same rate of commutation as is provided for in the year in which the said fractional part occurs.[87]

This act was, thus, considerably more generous in its prescribed reductions than that of 1869. This remained in

[85] *Report of the Inspectors of the Western Penitentiary*, 1869, pp. 5-6.
[86] *Report of the Inspectors of the Eastern Penitentiary*, 1870, p. 25.
[87] *Laws of the General Assembly*, 1901, p. 166.

operation in the state penitentiaries until the acts of May 10, 1909, and June 19, 1911, provided for the introduction of the principle of the indeterminate sentence.[88]

IX. THE INDETERMINATE SENTENCE AND PAROLE

1. *The Indeterminate Sentence*

The principle of commutation discussed above was in one sense a type of indeterminate sentence. It was, however, much too rigid and definite in its provisions to constitute a true indeterminate principle. The first application of the principle of an indeterminate sentence in America, if not in the world, seems to have been in the New York House of Refuge provided by a law of 1824.[89] A very similar condition was introduced into the government of the Philadelphia House of Refuge which was created in 1826. Here the board of managers was given large discretion in the matter of discharging or indenturing inmates.[90] This application of the indeterminate principle was, however, wholly limited to juvenile institutions, and few, if any, reformers possessed any idea that the principle might be beneficially extended to institutions for adult delinquents. As with the practice of commutation, one has to turn to Europe for the origins of the principle of the indeterminate sentence as applied to adult convicts. Archbishop Whatley had certainly anticipated the principle in his letter of 1829. It has been held upon reputable authority that the first comprehensive statement and defense of the theory of the indeterminate sentence was contained in the *Moral Philosophy* of the brilliant if eccentric Scot, George Combe, written about 1835.[91] In 1839

88 *Laws of the General Assembly,* 1909, pp. 495 ff.; 1911, pp. 1055-9.
89 *Laws of the State of New York,* 1824, pp. 110-12.
90 *Acts of the General Assembly of Pennsylvania,* 1825-6, pp. 133 ff.
91 A brief summary of the penal philosophy of Combe is contained in an article on "Early Anticipations of Prison Reform," by O. F. Lewis, in the *Unpartizan Review,* Jan.-March, 1921.

Frederick Hill, inspector of prisons for Scotland, in his report to the secretary of state for home affairs, definitely recommended the introduction of the indeterminate sentence into the prisons of England and Scotland. As far as the writer is aware, it has never been fully determined whether or not Hill obtained the idea of the indeterminate sentence from Combe or as the result of his own experience. But whoever may claim the honor of having first presented the principle, it is doubted by no one that its most effective exponent was Matthew Davenport Hill, the brother of Frederick Hill.

Almost from the first it has been agreed that the indeterminate sentence must have as a supplementary principle and practice the system of parole or "ticket-of-leave," as it is known in England. The fundamental value of the parole system in the discharge of prisoners was noted by Jeremy Bentham as early as the close of the eighteenth century. The elaboration of the principle was left, however, to Bonneville De Marsangy of France, who became its great and untiring exponent. The "twin principles" of the indeterminate sentence and parole were combined by Crofton in his Irish prison system and were introduced into American practice in the famous "Elmira system," where they were first applied in the treatment of young and relatively petty offenders, though the Cincinnati Prison Congress of 1870 recommended their immediate application in all state penitentiaries. Though it is generally held that the parole and the indeterminate sentence are a fundamental unity in principle and successful practice, their progress and acceptance in America was more or less uneven. The parole system, being less radical in appearance, as a rule, came earlier, entering the state prisons of this country rather generally in the decade of the "nineties." The indeterminate sentence found no widespread welcome until about 1910, when a campaign for its introduction was waged by the enlightened jurists of the country and by the *American Institute of Criminal Law and Criminology.* At the present time over half of the states have adopted some form of the indeterminate sentence and still more the parole system.

Before taking up the subject of the formal adoption of an indeterminate sentence law in Pennsylvania, it will be interesting briefly to refer to a type of extra-legal indeterminate sentence which prevailed in the state penitentiaries during the middle of the last century, namely, the practice of wholesale pardoning. As early as 1835 the inspectors of the Eastern Penitentiary complained of the excessive use of the pardoning power by the governor and urged that this right should be used only in cases of clearly established innocence.[92] In their report for 1864 the inspectors of the Western Penitentiary presented the summary statistics for the use of the pardoning power in that institution. Since the opening of the institution two thousand and eighty-two convicts had been admitted and no less than four hundred and sixty-three had been pardoned by the governor.[93] In 1867 the inspectors of the same institution stated that this abuse of the pardoning power constituted the most serious obstacle to an effective system of discipline.[94] To how great an extent the inordinate amount of pardoning revealed by these statistics was a result of the importuning of the prisoner and his friends and how far it was the result of the recommendations of the inspectors to prevent physical or mental breakdown in prison, as was charged by Governor Johnston, is a subject for future special investigation. It would seem, then, that a very real, if extra-legal, form of indeterminate sentence existed in Pennsylvania at a very early date, or to put it in another

[92] *Report of the Inspectors of the Eastern Penitentiary,* 1835, *Senate Journal,* 1835-6, Vol. II, p. 323.

[93] *Report of the Inspectors of the Western Penitentiary,* 1864, p. 7.

[94] Ibid., 1867, pp. 5, 37.

way, that the portion of the sentence actually served was determined, as the inspectors of the Western Penitentiary expressed it, "by the amount of money and the number of friends available to press the suit for a pardon." [95]

Aside from the above-mentioned use of an approximately indeterminate sentence in the House of Refuge following 1826, the first introduction of the principle of the indeterminate sentence in Pennsylvania was contained in the act of April 28, 1887, organizing the government of the Huntingdon Reformatory. This provided a very close approach to the true indeterminate sentence; the only time specification allowed in the sentence was that it could not exceed the maximum prescribed for the crime in the penal code of the state.[96] More than twenty years passed before this principle was extended to the state penitentiaries, in even a temporary and imperfect manner. The interesting steps which led up to the passage of the law of 1909 introducing the indeterminate sentence in the Pennsylvania penitentiaries, as well as an enumeration of the different individuals and societies instrumental in securing this important reform measure, are well set forth in the following memorandum furnished the writer by Dr. J. F. Ohl, who has for the last fifteen years been an indefatigable worker in the cause of prison reform in Pennsylvania:

In 1904 the *Pennsylvania Prison Society* appointed a standing committee on legislation of which the Rev. Dr. J. F. Ohl has from the beginning been the chairman. Some time between 1904 and 1907 Judge William H. Staake called the attention of Dr. Ohl to the desirability of making the acquaintance of General St. Clair A. Mulholland, then an inspector of the Philadelphia County prisons, with advanced ideas on penal subjects, and gave him a letter of introduction to the general. Dr. Ohl and General Mulholland at

[95] *Report of the Inspectors of the Western Penitentiary*, 1867, pp. 5, 37.
[96] *Laws of the General Assembly*, 1887, p. 65.

once found that their views on the necessity of many reforms were identical and began to gather information as to methods, experiences and results from every possible source. They carried on an extensive correspondence with governors, attorney generals, penitentiary wardens, and other persons interested in prison reform in all the states in which progressive legislation had been enacted and tried. Further, until the general's death in February, 1910, they made a number of trips to Harrisburg to argue bills before the proper committees. The material gathered through correspondence served as a basis for the legislation subsequently proposed, and for a widespread propaganda throughout the state by means of circulars, letters, pamphlets, and leading newspapers.

In 1907, authorized by the *Pennsylvania Prison Society,* Dr. Ohl and General Mulholland succeeded in having a joint resolution introduced in the legislature at Harrisburg providing for the creation of a commission to investigate the condition of the penal, reformatory and correctional institutions of Pennsylvania and to suggest necessary steps in reorganizing the penological concepts and practices of Pennsylvania. This resolution was passed, but was vetoed by Governor Stuart on the ground that there were already too many commissions, that he did not think it wise to add another, and that he deemed it better if those interested in matters of prison reform would come to the legislature with bills of a more specific nature. Thus it came about that members of the *Pennsylvania Prison Society,* the *Protestant Episcopal City Mission,* and the *American Society for Visiting Catholic Prisoners,* together with State Senator Ernest L. Tustin, met at the residence of Mr. John E. Baird, on the evening of April 24, 1908, to discuss what might be done to start penal reform in this state. The meeting was organized by the election of the Rev. J. F. Ohl as chairman, and General Mulholland as secretary. At this meeting it was unanimously resolved to secure, if possible, at the next meeting of the legislature (1909) the enactment of a law providing for adult probation, the indeterminate sentence and parole. At the second meeting of this self-constituted committee, held September 14, 1908, at the residence of James E. Gorman, Esqr., the committee resolved to call itself "The Pennsylvania Society for the Promotion of Improved Penal Legislation," with the officers of the committee respectively as president and secretary. At a subsequent meeting Mr. John E. Baird was made treasurer, who, not wishing to serve, was succeeded by the Rev. R. Heber Barnes. Meanwhile the president and secretary, utilizing to the fullest extent the material they had assembled, prepared the draft of a bill providing for adult probation, the indeterminate sentence and parole, and had the same printed. At a meeting at Mr. Gorman's residence on December 19, 1908, a subcommittee was appointed with B. Frank Clapp, Esqr., as chairman, to take the draft of this bill into consideration and "to perfect it so as to embody these ideas." At this meeting it was also announced that the *Pennsylvania Prison Society* and the *American Society for Visiting Catholic Prisòners* would each contribute fifty dollars toward expenses. The bill as finally perfected, chiefly by Mr. Clapp, was introduced at Harrisburg by Senator Tustin, and became known as the Tustin bill. It was passed, received the Governor's signature May 10, 1909, and went into effect June 30, 1909. This act was pronounced "admirable" by the Committee on Criminal Law Reform in its report at the Prison Congress of 1910.[97]

The following provisions constitute the essentials of the "Tustin Bill" which refer to the matter of the indeterminate sentence.[98] The general policy and procedure of the new law was set forth in the following paragraph:

Whenever any person, convicted in any court of this commonwealth of any crime, shall be sentenced to imprisonment in either the Eastern or Western Penitentiary, the court, instead of pronouncing upon such convict a definite or fixed term of imprisonment, shall pronounce upon such

[97] Adapted and condensed from a manuscript memorandum furnished to the writer by the Rev. Dr. J. F. Ohl.

[98] *Laws of the General Assembly*, 1909, pp. 495 ff. The provisions of this act relating to probation will be dealt with in another place.

convict a sentence of imprisonment for an indefinite term; stating in such sentence the maximum and minimum limits thereof; fixing as the minimum time of such imprisonment, the term now or hereafter prescribed as the minimum imprisonment for the punishment of such offense; but if there be no minimum time so prescribed, the court shall determine the same, but it shall not exceed one-fourth of the maximum time, and the maximum limit shall be the maximum time now or hereafter prescribed as a penalty for such offense.[99]

Certain exceptions were made to the universal application of this law. It was stipulated that in cases of third convictions of crimes receiving a penitentiary sentence the maximum penalty imposed in every case should be thirty years. Further, it was stated that the benefits of the commutation law of 1901 should not apply to those sentenced under the new indeterminate sentence law. The necessity of creating a parole system as the indispensable accompaniment of the indeterminate sentence was recognized. It was provided that the boards of inspectors of the two state penitentiaries should meet monthly and examine the records of prisoners who had served their minimum sentence, and, after reviewing their cases, should recommend to the governor of the state that he release on parole such of these prisoners as the inspectors believed would "live and remain at liberty without violating the law." If the inspectors felt that they could not justly recommend the paroling of any prisoner who had served his minimum sentence, they were directed to forward to the governor in writing their reasons for their action. Before the governor could parole [100] any prisoner recommended to him by the inspectors as eligible for parole, it was necessary that the case should previously be examined by the board of pardons, composed of the lieutenant-governor, the secretary of the commonwealth,

99 *Laws of the General Assembly*, 1909, p. 496.

100 Ibid., p. 498. The same limitations are placed upon the governor's power to exercise the pardoning power in Pennsylvania.

the attorney-general and the secretary of internal affairs. If they recommended parole the governor was authorized to order such action.[101] It was stipulated that the convict should legally be regarded as on parole to the expiration of the maximum sentence unless earlier pardoned. In case of a violation of the conditions of the parole the convict was to be required to serve out the unexpired maximum sentence unless sooner pardoned or paroled. If a paroled prisoner should be convicted of crime while on parole, it was decreed that he should serve both the new sentence and the remainder of the old maximum without enjoying any privileges of commutation. If, on the other hand, the paroled prisoner gave evidence by his conduct on parole that he had been cured of his criminal propensities, the inspectors might recommend to the governor that the prisoner receive a full pardon. To insure some effective control and supervision of the parole system of each institution the inspectors were directed to appoint one or more parole officers to take charge of the parole machinery of each state penitentiary.

While not a pure indeterminate sentence law, the above statute was one of the most liberal in the history of criminal jurisprudence as applied to a state prison. With its limitation of the minimum to one-fourth of the maximum it made possible the relatively speedy release of the less serious type of convicts or of those who gave evidence of having been reformed by their term of incarceration, while the provision of a maximum of thirty years for all types of recidivists enabled the authorities to retain in confinement for practically a life term that most serious and clearly marked criminal class. Had it been possible to preserve this act for permanent enforcement Pennsylvania might have again attained to something like the preeminence she enjoyed in liberal criminal jurisprudence in the latter part of the eighteenth century. The new law,

101 This board rarely or never reverses the judgment of the inspectors.

however, was bitterly opposed by the more conservative members of the judiciary of the state [102] and was soon emasculated in a way to make its operation much less liberal and effective in all cases, while in some instances it was much more oppressive than the conditions which had existed before the passage of the 1909 act. In 1911 Mr. Edwin M. Abbott, a Philadelphia criminal lawyer and then a member of the legislature, introduced an amendment to this act which removed the limitation of the minimum sentence to one-fourth of the maximum and made it possible for the judges to fix the minimum at any point up to one day less than the maximum. The thirty-year maximum for recidivists was also abolished, as well as the provision that the maximum sentence must be the maximum provided in the penal code of the state. The amended bill was passed on June 19 [103] and its application has caused the practical destruction of the principle of the indeterminate sentence in Pennsylvania until the passage of the act of June 29, 1923. In commenting on the effect of the new law in the *Journal of Prison Discipline,* Dr. J. F. Ohl made the following pertinent observations upon the fatal significance of the amendments:

The act of 1909 was based upon a very careful study of the writings of the most advanced penologists and of the statutes of those progressive states that have introduced the indeterminate sentence and parole with the greatest amount of success. Its viewpoint was that of those who seek the reformation of the wrongdoer, and not of those who still have in their minds the old idea of retributive justice only; it made a break with the old codes, aimed to deal with the man and not with his crime, and had regard to his future rather than to his past. This bill was so amended (in 1911) as virtually to eliminate from it the vital principle underlying

102 A number of the more progressive judges, on the other hand, have expressed their emphatic approval of a real indeterminate sentence. See the *Journal of Prison Discipline,* March, 1914, pp. 27-8.

103 *The Laws of the General Assembly,* 1911, p. 1055 ff.

the indeterminate sentence and parole. This amendment puts it into the power of the court to fix any minimum below the maximum, instead of a minimum not exceeding one-fourth of the maximum; it permits the court to name a lower maximum than the one now prescribed by law for any given offense; and it strikes out the thirty-year clause altogether. The practical effect of these changes is to destroy in great measure the value and efficiency of the indeterminate sentence as a remedial and reformatory measure. In other words, the amendment restores the vicious inequality of sentences, which is always so apt to breed a feeling of injustice and resentment in the one convicted, and which therefore greatly unfits him as a subject for reformatory treatment. It proceeds upon the long-accepted but false assumption that the court can in every case determine the exact degree of culpability and then adjust the punishment accurately to the crime. This is not only absurd, but it is impossible. As the law now stands, we shall again find, as is indeed already the case, that the same court or adjoining courts may, even under practically identical conditions, impose greatly varying sentences, instead of putting all upon whom sentence is passed on an equality and giving all, under identical conditions, an equal chance, as the law originally contemplated. Again, under the amended law the *court* virtually determines when a prisoner shall be eligible to parole. This is, however, utterly subversive of the theory upon which the indeterminate sentence is based, namely, *that parole is to be granted when a prisoner is believed to be fit to be restored to society as a law-abiding citizen.* The time when this may be done no court under the sun can fix, but only those who have the prisoner in charge and under observation, and even they may make mistakes.[104]

The operation of the amended act has not been less vicious than Dr. Ohl predicted. The grossest inequality of sentences for the same crime exist, and in many cases

104 *The Journal of Prison Discipline and Philanthropy,* November, 1911, pp. 21-23. His complete remarks have been somewhat condensed.

the minimum sentences have been so high that they have compelled a longer term of imprisonment than would have been necessary under the older commutation system. To be sure, some of the more progressive judges have made a wise use of the almost complete discretionary power which was conferred upon them by the act of 1911 and have been most intelligent and liberal in the use of their sentencing powers, and in their case the amendment has operated to improve the penal practice of the state, but with the vast majority of the judges the amendment has led to a gross abuse of this extensive power bestowed upon the judiciary.[105] Mr. Albert H. Votaw calls attention to the following examples of the severity of the operation of the "indeterminate sentence" law of 1911:

The court has the power by this law to make the minimum sentence any time at all to within one day of the maximum. A convict whose offense by statute may be punished by an imprisonment of twenty years could have a minimum sentence fixed at any time from one day to nineteen years, eleven months and twenty-nine days. There were four prisoners at the Eastern Penitentiary at the time the last report was made whose maximum was twenty years and whose minimum was the same lacking one day. There were thirty-eight prisoners sentenced to a maximum of twenty years whose minimum was eighteen years or more. According to the old law of commutation for good behavior, every one of these prisoners would have been entitled to freedom on good behavior at the end of twelve years and three months. This law of commutation for satisfactory conduct has been in vogue for fifty years and we have not learned that the judiciary of the state has issued any remonstrance. The number according to the last report whose maximum was twenty years was 86. These under the old law of commutation might be released in 12 years, 3 months. Of these 88, under present law, 55 will remain longer than under com-

[105] A study of the sentences imposed between 1911 and 1918 seems to indicate that the judges in the western part of the state have exhibited the greatest degree of liberality in applying the law of 1911.

mutation. And under present law, 31 may be released earlier than under commutation. It is the inequality of sentences which has produced dissatisfaction.[106]

These instances can be supplemented by many others. Among those received in the Western Penitentiary in 1916, five were given a minimum of six and a maximum of eight years; five a minimum of seven and a maximum of ten; three a minimum of ten and a maximum of twelve; five a minimum of ten and a maximum of thirteen; six a minimum of ten and a maximum of fifteen; four a minimum of sixteen and a maximum of twenty; five a minimum of eighteen and a maximum of twenty; and one a minimum of nineteen and a maximum of twenty.[107] Even worse abuses of the sentencing power are revealed by the records of the Eastern Penitentiary. In 1917 there were in that institution thirty-one prisoners with a minimum sentence of four years and a maximum of five years; twenty-five with a minimum of five and a maximum of six; forty-two with a minimum of five and a maximum of seven; fifteen with a minimum of six and a maximum of seven; eleven with a minimum of nine and a maximum of ten; fifteen with a minimum of ten years and a maximum of twelve; twenty with a minimum of ten and a maximum of fifteen; fifteen with a minimum of twelve and a maximum of fifteen; fourteen with a minimum of fifteen and a maximum of twenty; thirteen with a minimum of eighteen and a maximum of twenty; thirteen with a minimum of nineteen and a maximum of twenty; eight with a minimum of nineteen years and eleven months and a maximum of twenty years; and one with a minimum of twenty-seven years and a maximum of twenty-eight.[108] Of course, it must be granted that in

106 Albert H. Votaw, *Penal Legislation of 1917 in the Commonwealth of Pennsylvania*, p. 18.
107 *Biennial Report of the Western Penitentiary*, 1916, pp. 49-50.
108 *Annual Report of the Eastern Penitentiary*, 1917, pp. 54 ff.

many cases the minimum should be made as near the maximum sentence as is possible in order to restrain and keep in custody during the longest possible period those dangerous recidivists and degenerate criminals who require and should receive permanent and effective segregation from society during their entire lifetime, but there is little evidence that the cases of extreme minimum sentences were scientifically and systematically applied for this purpose. No machinery as yet exists in Pennsylvania which will enable a sentencing judge to learn with certainty the identity of the habitual criminals. In most cases the extreme minimum sentences seem to have been arbitrarily imposed on account of the heinous nature of the crime itself, or from unusually revolting conditions under which it was committed, or because of the unfavorable impression created by the prisoner in the courtroom.

Realizing that the 1911 amendments had defeated the real purpose and methods of the indeterminate sentence, the advocates of the more progressive penology in Pennsylvania, especially the committee on legislation of the Pennsylvania Prison Society, kept up an enlightened agitation for the restoration of the 1909 law, and in 1917 was able to secure the passage of an act achieving this desirable end, but this promising accomplishment was destroyed by Governor Brumbaugh, who, with typical opaqueness to modern thought and practice and want of sympathy with the penological progress of the last half century, vetoed the bill.[109]

Some relief from the intolerable situation created by the 1911 amendment was secured by the passage of the so-called "Ludlow Bill" of June 29, 1923. This was not as liberal as the 1909 law, as the 1909 bill limited the minimum sentence to one-fourth of the maximum, while the limit imposed by the 1923 act was only one-half of

109 Albert H. Votaw, *Penal Legislation of* 1917 *in the Commonwealth of Pennsylvania,* pp. 18-19.

the maximum. Even in this form the "Ludlow Bill" has been vigorously attacked by the more antiquated and illiterate judges in the State. The relevant section of the "Ludlow Bill" follows:

Whenever any person, convicted in any court of this Commonwealth of any crime punishable by imprisonment in a State penitentiary, shall be sentenced to imprisonment therefor in any penitentiary or other institution of (the) this State, or in any county or municipal institution, the court, instead of pronouncing upon such convict a definite or fixed term of imprisonment, shall pronounce upon such convict a sentence of imprisonment for an indefinite term: Stating in such sentence the minimum and maximum limits thereof; and the maximum limit shall never exceed the maximum time now or hereafter prescribed as a penalty for such offense; and the minimum limit shall never exceed one-half of the maximum sentence prescribed by any court.

Though the principle of the indeterminate sentence has been partially defeated in the state penitentiaries since 1911, it won a victory in another field in 1913. The act of July 25, 1913, providing for the creation of the State Industrial Home for Women, which has since been erected at Muncy, embodied the application of the principle of the indeterminate sentence and parole for all sentenced to the institution. The institution was to receive "any female between sixteen and thirty years of age, upon conviction for, or upon pleading guilty of, the commission of any criminal offense punishable under the laws of the state." The sentence imposed upon such women convicts was to be indeterminate. No minimum was allowed to be specified, while the maximum was to be three years, unless the legal maximum for that crime was more than three years, in which case the legal maximum was to be given. The controlling board was empowered to parole inmates at their discretion and to recommend permanent discharge of inmates to the convicting judges when such action was deemed desirable.[110] The principle of the indeterminate sentence, then, in Pennsylvania is fully recognized and applied in the two reformatory institutions and in the two correctional institutions.

2. *Conditional Release and the Parole System*

Though the 1911 amendments to the indeterminate sentence law greatly lessened its usefulness and thwarted some of its chief principles and aims, the system of parole was at least partially saved from the wreckage. Even the parole system was handicapped by the amendment of 1911, which allowed the sentencing judge to fix the minimum sentence. This, as Dr. Ohl pointed out in the preceding passage, has made it possible for the judge rather than the paroling board to determine when the prisoner shall be paroled. The minimum sentence, which must expire in all cases before paroling is legally possible, is normally too long for those who deserve to be paroled at all, and too brief for that well-defined class who require life-long segregation and confinement. This arbitrary power given to the judges makes it impossible for the paroling board to release a prisoner on parole as soon as his conduct has justified such action; in other words, it abrogates the whole principle of the preparatory phases of the parole system. But within these irritating limitations the parole system has made notable progress in the two state penitentiaries. The following analysis of the parole system in the state penitentiaries will be based upon the practice of the Western Penitentiary, not with any desire to disparage the commendable administration of this department in the Eastern Penitentiary, but because the Western Penitentiary has given more specific attention to the development of this work and has special

[110] *Laws of the General Assembly*, 1913, pp. 1311-19.

advantages not possessed by the eastern institutions, in that the farm site in Center County makes it possible to give the convicts a transitional period of partial freedom before they receive total freedom on parole.

The parole system was introduced in the Western Penitentiary almost synchronously with the induction of Mr. John Francies as warden, and its development has been one significant aspect of his constructive administrative policy. He was peculiarly fortunate in securing as his chief parole officer, Mr. John M. Eagan, who has combined to an unusual degree real administrative capacity with a sympathetic insight into the aims of the newer penology. Preparatory to organizing their parole department, Mr. Francies traveled widely, advising with the leading prison officials and penological experts as to the desirable elements of a successful parole system, and Mr. Eagan made a personal inspection of the more important institutions which had parole systems in operation. After about a decade of developmental experience the parole system at the Western Penitentiary operates essentially as follows.[111] A prisoner is eligible for parole at the expiration of his minimum sentence if his conduct and other elements in his past record are such as to justify the parole officer and the inspectors in believing that the convict would live in freedom without violating the conditions of his parole or the laws of the commonwealth. Since the progress of the new institution at Rockview during the last few years has enabled the warden to send a large number of convicts to this site to labor on construction work and on the extensive farms, it has been the practice to send men to the new site some time in advance of the expiration of their minimum sentence, so that they may have a preliminary training in partial freedom. Three months before the expiration of

[111] This description is based upon the personal investigation of the writer.

his minimum sentence each convict is allowed to apply for release on parole, irrespective of his conduct or his mental and physical condition. Every convict who so applies must also be given a hearing by the parole board, which in both state penitentiaries consists of the board of inspectors of the institution. The action that the board will take on the granting of any particular application from a convict will depend upon his past criminal history, upon the record of the convict while incarcerated, and upon his mental and physical condition. This information is furnished to the board by the chief parole officer and by the warden. Unless there are evident reasons why the application for parole should not be granted the inspectors will normally recommend favorable action on the petition. The board does not, however, have power to parole directly, but can only make recommendation on this point to the above-mentioned board of pardons and the governor. If they deem that the application shall not be granted they must submit their reasons for this decision to the board of pardons and the governor, exactly as in the case of recommending positive action. In spite of this complicated formal process of securing action on parole, which requires that the parole board shall recommend action to the board of pardons, which, in turn, is required to advise the governor as to his decision, there has never yet been an instance where either the board of pardons or the governor has reversed the decision of the local parole board.

The duration of actual supervision of a paroled convict and the thoroughness of the inspection of his conduct depends entirely upon the individual convict. If his criminal record is not serious, if his conduct in prison has been commendable, and if his record while on parole has been wholly satisfactory, discharge from parole is likely to be speedy, coming after about eighteen months' time in the most favorable cases. On the other hand, if the convict has had a suspicious criminal past, has exhibited indifferent conduct while in the penitentiary and has given no conclusive demonstration of complete reformation on parole, he will be likely to be retained on parole under more or less active supervision until the expiration of his maximum sentence. In many cases the relatives of the prisoners request that the period of parole and supervision be extended as long as legally possible because it furnishes an additional incentive to good conduct on the part of the convict. While on parole the convict is required to submit reports monthly to the chief parole officer on blanks furnished each month by the institution. These reports are examined by the chief parole officer and by the head clerk of the prison, and if any personal inspection is deemed necessary they inform the field parole officer who will visit the convict in question. Final discharge comes automatically at the expiration of the maximum sentence, but may come sooner if the paroled convict applies for discharge and the officials deem his request reasonable and sustained by the facts in his case. Normally, however, the initiative in securing the discharge of a deserving paroled convict is taken by the parole officer, who makes such a recommendation to the parole board and the same steps are taken and the same administrative machinery is used as in obtaining the original grant of parole. Final discharge restores the convict to the enjoyment of his civil rights as an inhabitant of the state of Pennsylvania, except in cases where the conviction has been for treason or perjury.

The violation of the conditions of parole requires the return of the convict to the institution where he must serve the remainder of his maximum sentence unless sooner reparoled, discharged or pardoned. In case of the conviction of crime while on parole, the convict must serve out the remainder of the maximum sentence and then the sentence imposed for the crime committed while on parole. The period of partial freedom at the Rockview site is safeguarded by the rather oversevere Pennsylvania penalty for escapes or attempted escapes which condemns a prisoner who has been apprehended after escape to serve double his previous sentence after his apprehension. The office and recording phase of the parole department of the Western Penitentiary approaches perfection in the thoroughness, system and efficiency of its organization, but the parole work is badly handicapped by the lack of a sufficient field force. Only one field officer for visiting paroled prisoners has been provided by the state, though four such officers would find it difficult to care for this work as it should be attended to, there being in 1918 nearly nine hundred men under formal supervision on parole from that institution. This condemns the field supervision to hopeless superficiality and calls for an immediate remedying by the legislature. The need for added field supervisors is equally great in the Eastern Penitentiary, where over eight hundred paroled convicts were in 1918 left to the supervision of one man, aided by two office clerical assistants. With the provision of more field workers the parole system in the state penitentiaries would be on a very satisfactory level of working efficiency within the limitations imposed by the illogical and archaic indeterminate sentence law which governs their procedure.

The parole system was extended to the jails and workhouses by an act of June 19, 1911. By an act of May 14, 1925, a commission of five was created to make a thorough study of the parole system and submit recommendations.

X. THE SUSPENDED SENTENCE, PROBATION AND THE NON-INSTITUTIONAL CARE OF DELINQUENTS

The beginnings of the non-institutional care of delinquents may be traced to the ticket-of-leave or parole system, which originated in the middle of the nineteenth century and has come to be a cardinal feature of modern penological theory and practice. This, however, merely made possible the removal of the convict from imprisonment during the latter portion of his term and in no way attempted to do away with imprisonment altogether. With the gradual growth among careful students of penology of the conviction that in many if not most cases the convict issued from prison a worse character than he was upon entry, especially in the case of young first offenders, there has arisen a determined movement to secure the introduction of a system of suspended sentence and probation, to be applied to those first offenders and others, who, it seems reasonable to believe, can be most effectively treated outside of a penal institution. As has been the case with nearly all of the radical innovations in penology, this progressive practice was first applied to juvenile delinquents, especially in connection with the creation of a juvenile court system in the more advanced municipalities of the country, a movement in which Judge Benjamin B. Lindsey of Denver was a pioneer and the most picturesque figure.

While there were earlier approximations to a juvenile court system in Pennsylvania, the basis of the present system was laid by acts of 1903. That of March 26, 1903, directed that "no child under the age of sixteen years shall be committed by any Magistrate or Justice of the Peace to any institution for the purpose of correction or reformation, but all applications for such commitment shall be made to the Court of Quarter Sessions of the county." [112] The powers of the Court of Quarter Sessions in dealing with these cases of juvenile delinquents under sixteen years of age were defined in an act

[112] *A Comprehensive Review of the Work of the Juvenile Court of Philadelphia*, 1903-8, Philadelphia, 1908, p. 58. An earlier act, that of June 12, 1893, had provided for the separate and distinct trial of juvenile delinquents.

of April 23, 1903. The premises and purposes of this act were set forth as follows:

> The welfare of the state demands that children should be guarded from association and contact with crime and criminals, and the ordinary process of the criminal law does not provide such treatment and care and moral encouragement as are essential to all children in the formative period of life, but endangers the whole future of the child.
>
> Experience has shown that children, lacking proper parental care or guardianship, are led into courses of life which may render them liable to the pains and penalties of the criminal law of the state, although, in fact, the real interests of such child or children require that they be not incarcerated in penitentiaries and jails, as members of the criminal class, but be subjected to a wise care, treatment and control, that their evil tendencies may be checked and their better instincts may be strengthened.
>
> To that end, it is important that the powers of the courts, in respect to the care, treatment and control over dependent, neglected, delinquent and incorrigible children should be clearly distinguished from the powers exercised in the administration of the criminal law.[113]

It was also decreed that a judge of the Court of Quarter Sessions should hold a juvenile court for the purpose of carrying out the provisions of the act.[114] He was to exercise his powers when, in the opinion of a magistrate, justice of the peace, district attorney or judge involved in the case, the interests of both the child and the state could no longer be served by allowing the child his ordinary liberties or by committing him to an ordinary institution for juvenile delinquents.[115] In such cases the judge of the juvenile court was authorized to "commit such child to the care of its parents, subject to the supervision of a Probation Officer, or to some suitable institution, or to

113 *A Comprehensive Review of the Work of the Juvenile Court of Philadelphia*, pp. 53-4.

114 Ibid., p. 54.

115 Ibid., pp. 54-55.

the care of some reputable citizen of good moral character, or to the care of some training school, or to an industrial school, or to the care of some association willing to receive it.[116] The parents, institution, association or individual to which the child was committed became by that fact its guardian.[117] The commitment could not, however, extend beyond the age of twenty-one years.[118] It was further specifically ordered that no child under twelve years of age should be sent to a reformatory or correctional institution unless the suspended sentence and probation failed to operate successfully in such a case.[119] The court was authorized to appoint suitable probation officers to investigate the circumstances connected with the cases of all children brought before the court in accordance with the provision of the act. The possibility of readily obtaining competent probation officers was, however, made exceedingly remote by the stipulation that they should receive no salary.[120]

Since the passage of the act of 1903 several important additions have been made to the legal basis of the probation of juveniles in Pennsylvania. An act of July 12, 1913, established a Municipal Court for the city of Philadelphia and gave it the jurisdiction over cases involving juvenile delinquents and their probation.[121] The jurisdiction was confirmed and further defined in an act of June 17, 1915.[122] An act of March 15, 1915, gave the county court of Allegheny county jurisdiction over cases involving juveniles in that county.[123] It also provided for

[116] Ibid., p. 56.
[117] Ibid.
[118] Ibid., p. 57.
[119] Ibid.
[120] Ibid., pp. 55-56. The laws relating to juvenile courts, probation and juvenile institutions are conveniently brought together by John H. Fertig and S. Edward Hannestad in *A Compilation of the Laws Relating to the Juvenile Courts and Dependent, Neglected, Incorrigible and Delinquent Children*, Harrisburg, 1916.
[121] *Laws of the General Assembly*, 1913, pp. 711 ff.
[122] Ibid., 1915, pp. 1017 ff.
[123] Ibid., pp. 5 ff.

the securing of competent probation officers by making it possible to pay the chief probation officer three thousand dollars per year and his subordinates one-half of that sum.[124] The absurd provision in the act of 1903 that probation officers should receive no public salary in Pennsylvania was wiped out by an act of April 1, 1909, which allowed the court of quarter sessions to pay probation officers a salary of not to exceed one hundred dollars per month.[125] As the Municipal Court of Philadelphia contemplated a rather extensive application of the principle of probation to both juvenile and adult delinquents in accordance with the laws of April 23, 1903, May 10, 1909, and June 19, 1911, an act of June 15, 1915, made provision for a salary for probation officers in Philadelphia which would make it possible to secure officers of high capacity who might be expected to devote all of their time to their duties. The president judge of the municipal court was authorized to appoint a chief probation officer for the city who would receive a salary of not to exceed five thousand dollars and subordinates to receive not over half that amount.[126]

The actual mode of operation of the act of 1903 and its subsequent minor revisions is thus set forth by Judge William H. Staake, who has long been the leader among Philadelphia jurists in the cause of the reform of criminal procedure in cases dealing with juvenile delinquents:

> There are no classes specifically entitled to probation instead of "incarceration." What is meant by this is: The whole Juvenile Court idea is, that the offender is only a delinquent, and not an intentional violator of the law, or in fact a criminal. He is not incarcerated in the sense of imprisonment. He may be, and is, liable to detention in the care of an individual, or, in some cases, in the care of an institution.

124 *Laws of the General Assembly*, 1913, pp. 5 ff.
125 Ibid., 1909, pp. 89 ff.
126 Ibid., 1915, pp. 988 ff.

The person or official who is to decide what shall be the disposition made of the delinquent juvenile was formerly the judge of the Court of Quarter Sessions, now the judge of the Municipal Court, so far as Philadelphia is concerned; that court having as a statutory, and not as a constitutional court, taken over all matters incidental to the Juvenile Court, as well as matters affecting domestic relations, such as making orders for the maintenance of the wife by the husband or of the wife and children by the husband, or of the children alone by the husband.

It should be stated that the Municipal Court in Philadelphia and another analogous court in the County of Allegheny, are the only special courts which have charge of this work. In the counties other than Philadelphia and Allegheny the Court of Quarter Sessions for such individual county or judicial district would have the jurisdiction and the authority in connection with juvenile delinquents.

The judge, who under the calendar of the particular court, exercises the discretion, whether to detain the delinquent juvenile offender, or whether to place him on probation in his own family under the oversight or superintendency of a probation officer, or whether to place him in the care of some private person, who would be willing to undertake the responsibility for such supervision, or to place him in a suitable institution such as the institution at Glen Mills, or under the supervision of an officer of certain well-known charities, such as the Children's Aid Society and the Society for the Prevention of Cruelty to Children, or other recognized societies having the same object in view.

In Philadelphia and Allegheny, and in other counties, the probation officers appointed by the respective courts would investigate the conduct of juvenile delinquents, and then report regularly to the tribunal appointing him.

The results of violation of probationary conditions would be either a continuance of the probation by the court, instead of a discharge of the probationer, on the recommendation of the probation officers, or in some cases, where it was found the delinquent was a hopeless case, and was not controlled by the court's probation officers, there might be a commitment to an institution for juvenile delinquents, or even to the Huntingdon Reformatory, so far as male juvenile delinquents are concerned, when the seriousness of the offense of the delinquent was of a character to submit the case to a formal trial in the courts.[127]

As has been the case with almost every progressive prison reform practice in the past so with probation, its application to juvenile delinquents was soon followed by its introduction into the methods of treating adult delinquents not convicted of major crimes. At the present time some twenty-six states now have probation systems which are applied to adult delinquents with a greater or less degree of thoroughness. Probation on suspended sentence for all convicted persons except the more defective and degenerate types seems to be dictated by both science and common sense. Probation, linked up with proper guidance and psychiatric aid, presents a double advantage over the house of correction, jail and prison. It gives the individual a strong incentive to reform and provides intelligent guidance and encouragement. It also saves the person from the stigma, humiliation, degradation and demoralizing association which is everywhere to be found in our penal and correctional institutions. For the time being the extension of probation is one of the most promising immediate steps which can be taken in criminal science and jurisprudence.

Adult probation was first permitted in Pennsylvania according to the provisions of an act of May 10, 1909, and was continued practically unchanged by an act of June 19, 1911. As a part of the acts also establishing the parole and indeterminate sentence systems in Pennsylvania, it was the product of the agitation of the same group of reformers that has been described above in connection with the establishment of the indeterminate

[127] From a memorandum kindly furnished to the writer by Judge Staake at the request of Dr. J. F. Ohl.

sentence in that state.[128] That portion of the act of 1911 which deals with the subject of probation still governs that practice in Pennsylvania and is given in the following paragraphs:

Be it enacted, etc., That whenever any person shall be convicted in any court of this commonwealth of any crime, except murder, administering poison, kidnapping, incest, sodomy, buggery, rape, assault and battery with intent to ravish, arson, robbery or burglary, and it does not appear to the said court that the defendant has ever before been imprisoned for crime, either in this state or elsewhere (but detention in an institution for juvenile delinquents shall not be considered imprisonment), and where the said court believes that the character of the defendant and the circumstances of the case are such that he or she is not likely again to engage in an offensive course of conduct, and that the public good does not demand or require that the defendant should suffer the penalty imposed by law; said court shall have power to suspend the imposing of the sentence, and place the defendant on probation for a definite period, on such terms and conditions as it may deem right and proper, said terms and conditions to be duly entered on record as a part of the judgment of the court in such case.

In any case where a fine only is imposed, and the defendant might be imprisoned until such fine be paid, the court may direct, as one of the terms of the probation, that such fines shall be paid in certain instalments at certain times: Provided, however, that upon payment of the fine, judgment shall be satisfied and probation cease.

Whenever or wherever the court may deem it necessary and desirable, it may appoint a discreet person to serve as probation officer, for the performance of such duties as the court shall direct. The salary of such officer shall be determined by the court, and this, together with the necessary expenses incurred while in the actual performance of duty, shall be paid by the county, upon vouchers approved by the court and county commissioners. In no case, however, shall

128 See above, pp. 220 ff.

a defendant be committed in the custody of a probation officer of the opposite sex.

Whenever a person placed on probation, as aforesaid, shall violate the terms of his or her probation, he or she shall be subject to arrest in the same manner as in the case of an escaped convict; and shall be brought before the court which released him or her on probation, which court may thereupon pronounce upon such defendant such sentence as may be prescribed by law, to begin at such time as the court may direct.

Whenever it is the judgment of the court that a person on probation has satisfactorily met the conditions of his or her probation, the court shall discharge such defendant and cause record thereof to be made: Provided, That the length of such period of probation shall not be more than the maximum term for which the defendant might have been imprisoned.[129]

Though the provisions of this act make possible a very liberal use of the principle of adult probation and the suspended sentence in Pennsylvania, the fact that their application has been made optional rather than obligatory has made the operation of the law in this respect as variable and inconsistent as the application of the parole and indeterminate sentence law in that state. Just as educated and sensible judges make a wise and liberal use of their power to fix the minimum sentence, so they frequently apply their power to suspend sentence and admit the convicted person to probation; and in the same manner that reactionary and short-sighted judges make a vicious use of the minimum sentence provision, so they rarely or never admit a convict to probation. Without either the compulsory probation of certain classes of lesser offenders or a more universally intelligent judiciary the suspended sentence and probation can meet with only limited success in Pennsylvania, as elsewhere. Only in connection with the probation department of the Philadelphia

[129] *Laws of the General Assembly,* 1911, pp. 1055-6.

Municipal Court, under the direction of Chief Probation Officer Louis N. Robinson, has any notable progress been made, but here the prospects for a successful application of the principle of the suspended sentence and parole to delinquents are unexcelled in this country. Whatever the shortcomings in its use in Pennsylvania at the present time, there can be no doubt but that it will come to be one of the vital features of the penology of the future. Its value and its desirability have been admirably summarized in the recent report of the Committee to Investigate Penal Systems:

Conceived as a mere incident of the sentencing power, to be exercised only in exceptional cases, the suspended sentence and probation are beginning to disclose themselves as a momentous, not to say revolutionary, step in the progress of penology, not less important in its ultimate consequences than the substitution a century ago of imprisonment for the death penalty and other forms of physical punishment. Like the older forms of punishment which it superseded, imprisonment, too, has proved a failure so far, at least, as the newer aim of punishment, the reformation of the wrongdoer, is concerned. As we are coming to see, the protection which society enjoys through the imprisonment for a few months or years of a small portion of the criminal class is dearly purchased by a system which returns the offender to society less fitted than before to cope with the conditions of a life of freedom. More and more, as we develop a probation service worthy of the name, will the courts be reluctant to commit men, women and children to the demoralizing associations and discipline of institutional life and will give them their chance to redeem themselves under competent guidance and supervision among the associations and activities of everyday life.[130]

[130] *Report of the Commission to Investigate Penal Systems,* Philadelphia, 1919, p. 25.

XI. THE SEPARATION OF MENTALLY ABNORMAL CONVICTS AND THEIR PSYCHOLOGICAL ANALYSIS AND STUDY UNDER CLINICAL OBSERVATION

In Pennsylvania, as elsewhere, the only recognition of the differences between accused criminals permitted by the courts relates to the legal concept of "insanity," a loose general term no longer of medical significance. It is rendered even less useful in court procedure as it is still the general procedure to allow an ignorant and illiterate jury to decide as to the highly technical medical fact of psychopathology.

In no phase of penology has the progress been greater in the last century than in the growing recognition of the intimate correlation between mental abnormalities and criminal conduct.[131] This advance has, of course, been primarily a result of the unparalleled progress of psychiatry or medical psychology during this period. As long as insanity was regarded the product of demoniacal possession, and idiocy was believed to be a divine curse on the individual due to ancestral indiscretions, it was no more possible to entertain a rational conception of abnormal mental states than it was to hold a valid notion of criminality when all types of criminals were indiscriminately viewed as "perverse free moral agents"—the victims of their own self-willed folly. Two influences, which had a somewhat parallel development, tended to destroy this barbarous theological heritage and make possible the present-day attitude on these questions. Both sprang from the contributions of the English *Deists* and the French *Philosophes* of the seventeenth and eighteenth centuries, who shattered the theological epic that had restrained scientific progress for more than a thousand years, as-

[131] See the very authoritative and interesting treatment of this subject in William A. White's *Principles of Mental Hygiene,* Chapter V. The best treatments of the subject are S. S. Glueck, *Mental Disorder and the Criminal Law;* White, *Insanity and the Criminal Law;* and Hoag and Williams, *Crime, Abnormal Minds and the Law.*

serted the amenability of man to scientific study and investigation, and declared a healthy confidence in man's inherent decency and worth which was the indispensable preliminary to humanitarian efforts to improve the earthly lot of mankind.[132] The beginning of a really scientific insight into the nature and problems of insanity is usually associated with the work of the Frenchman, Pinel (1745-1826), and there is no more notable chapter in the history of medical and social science than the progress of psychiatry from Pinel to Charcot, Janet and Freud. The humanitarian current was continued in the work of reformers, such as John Howard and Elizabeth Fry, and in the multifarious activities of the Quakers in social and penal reform. In the introduction of the humanitarian impulse into the treatment of the insane the name of an American woman, Dorothea Lynde Dix (1802-1887), stands out beyond all others in this country or Europe. To her prodigious labors and untiring devotion to the cause of more rational and humane treatment of this class of unfortunates is mainly due the establishment of hospitals for the insane in the United States during the first half of the last century.

As early as 1835 the inspectors of the Eastern Penitentiary complained of the administrative difficulties caused by the presence of insane convicts. The warden stated that "a minute inspection of the character of the unhappy inmates of prisons has developed another interesting fact, that many more of them than was supposed are really irresponsible beings." He recommended the provision of a state institution for such individuals.[133] Nothing was done to remedy the situation, and a decade later another vigorous complaint was made regarding the

[132] A brilliant and sympathetic treatment of the origin of this type of thought is contained in Robinson and Beard's *Development of Modern Europe*, Vol. I, Chapter IX. See also W. E. H. Lecky's *Rise and Influence of Rationalism.*

[133] *Annual Report of the Eastern Penitentiary*, 1835, *Senate Journal*, 1835, II, p. 326.

same problem.[134] That the same conditions existed in the Western Penitentiary is apparent from a protest of its officers in 1845 against the necessity of having to house insane convicts in the institution.[135] In the year 1844 Miss Dix made a detailed investigation of the number of insane in the state penitentiaries, the county penal institutions and the almshouses, and set forth the amazing but deplorable conditions thereby revealed in a powerful *Memorial* to the state legislature requesting legislative sanction for the erection of a state hospital for the insane in Pennsylvania.[136] *The Philadelphia Society for Alleviating the Miseries of Public Prisons* ably seconded Miss Dix's plea in a supplementary *Memorial* to the legislature urging immediate action in establishing a state hospital for the insane.[137] Primarily as a result of these *Memorials,* the legislature passed the act of April 14, 1845, providing for the establishment of the Pennsylvania State Lunatic Hospital at Harrisburg.[138] This original act, however, made no adequate arrangements for the transfer of insane prisoners from the penitentiaries to the hospital for the insane. In 1850 and 1851 the inspectors of the Eastern Penitentiary complained once more of the difficulty of retaining insane prisoners in the institution.[139] By the provisions of an act of May 4, 1852, it was made possible for the authorities of the Eastern Penitentiary to transfer insane prisoners to the Harrisburg hospi-

[134] *Annual Report of the Eastern Penitentiary,* 1844, p. 23.

[135] *Annual Report of the Western Penitentiary,* 1845, *Senate Journal,* 1845, II, pp. 186-7.

[136] *Journal of Prison Discipline and Philanthropy,* Vol. I, Number 3, 1845, pp. 211-5. In January of the same year Miss Dix had submitted a similar "Memorial" to the legislature of New Jersey.

[137] Ibid., Vol. I, Number 2, 1845, pp. 190-99.

[138] *Laws of the General Assembly,* 1845, pp. 440 ff.; J. H. Fertig and Frank M. Hunter, *A Compilation of the Laws Relating to the Board of Public Charities with Important Provisions of the Laws Relating to the Several State Institutions and the Rules and Regulations of the Committee on Lunacy,* Harrisburg, 1916, pp. 115 ff. (This was compiled for the Legislative Reference Bureau.)

[139] *Annual Report of the Eastern Penitentiary,* 1850, p. 28; Ibid., 1851, p. 14. The warden complained in 1851 that the Harrisburg hospital was designed to accept only the curable insane criminals and asserted that he would have to retain the incurables.

tal, which had been opened in the previous October.[140] This privilege was, however, not extended to the Western Penitentiary at this time.[141] The acts of March 24, 1858, and March 31, 1860, made a partial attempt to remedy this defect, but not until the passage of an act of May 14, 1874, was systematic provision made for the transfer of insane prisoners from both state penitentiaries to the appropriate state hospitals. The significant section of this act reads as follows:

> Whenever any person is imprisoned within the commonwealth, convicted of any crime whatever, or charged with any crime and acquitted on the ground of insanity, application in writing may be made by the warden, superintendent, physician or any inspector of the penitentiary or prison in which such person is imprisoned, or by the general agent of the Board of Public Charities, to the court hereinafter named, or any law judge thereof, which application shall certify under oath or affirmation that such prisoner is believed to be insane, and shall request that such prisoner shall be removed to a hospital for the insane; whereupon it shall be lawful for any judge learned in the law of any court within this commonwealth having immediate cognizance of the crime with which such prisoner is charged, or of the court by which such prisoner has been convicted, to appoint a commission of three citizens of this commonwealth, one of whom shall be of the profession of medicine, and one of the profession of the law, whose duty it shall be to inquire into and report the mental condition of such prisoner; and

140 *Laws of the General Assembly,* 1852, pp. 524 ff.; Fertig and Hunter, p. 117.

141 The early provisions for the transfer of criminal insane from the Western Penitentiary were both crude and complicated. The Western Pennsylvania Hospital, a private institution, was incorporated by an act of March 18, 1848, and was allowed to establish an insane department which was opened on January 18, 1853. By an act of March 19, 1856, the institutions took on a semi-state character through a provision allowing the state to appoint three members of the board of managers. The new buildings were opened at Dixmont in Allegheny on November 13, 1862. An act of March 24, 1858, allowed the Western Penitentiary to send insane prisoners to this institution, but another act of April 22, 1863, permitted the hospital to return all incurable insane convicts to the penitentiary.

if in a report signed by a majority or all the members of such commission it shall appear that the prisoner inquired of is of unsound mind and unfit for penal discipline, it shall be lawful for the judge issuing such commission, or for any other judge of the same court learned in the law, to make an order under the seal of such court, directing the removal of such prisoner from the place of his or her imprisonment, and that he or she shall be received, maintained and cared for by the hospital for the insane, nearest to such place of imprisonment, and which shall or may receive aid or support from the treasury of the state, and that such patient shall be detained in such hospital, until an order, as hereinafter provided, shall be granted by the said court, or any judge thereof learned in the law, for the return of such prisoner to the penitentiary or prison from which he or she was removed, or for his or her discharge from such hospital: Provided always, That whenever any hospital shall be established especially for the care of insane patients who shall have been convicted of crime, or whenever separate accommodations shall be made for such patients, in any hospital aided from the treasury of the state, the order, as aforesaid, for the removal of any such person from his or her place of imprisonment, shall direct that he or she shall be received, maintained or cared for in such special hospital, or in the separate accommodations of any hospital prepared for such purpose.[142]

Elaborated to some extent by the act of May 8, 1883, this act of 1874 remains to the present day the law governing the transfer of insane convicts from the state penitentiaries to the state hospitals for the insane.[143]

Since the establishment of the original hospital for "lunatics" at Harrisburg, Pennsylvania has made provision for a number of similar institutions which can make at least a moderately decent pretention to housing the insane of the state. These additional state hospitals for

142 *Laws of the General Assembly,* 1874, pp. 160 ff.; Fertig and Hunter, op. cit., p. 41.

143 *Laws of the General Assembly,* 1883, pp. 21 ff.; Fertig and Hunter, p. 61.

the insane are: The State Hospital for the Insane at Danville in Montour County, established by an act of April 13, 1868, and opened on November 6, 1872;[144] the State Hospital for the Insane at Warren in Warren county, established by an act of August 14, 1873, and opened on October 6, 1880;[145] the State Hospital for the Insane at Norristown in Montgomery county, established by an act of May 5, 1876, and opened on July 12, 1880;[146] the State Asylum for the Chronic Insane at Wernersville in Berks county established by an act of June 22, 1891, and opened on June 28, 1893;[147] the Homeopathic State Hospital at Allentown in Lehigh county, established by an act of July 18, 1901, and opened on October 3, 1912;[148] and the Western State Hospital for the Insane established by an act of July 18, 1915, and now in the process of construction at Blairsville Intersection in Westmoreland county.[149] After a half century of delay there has at last been provided a distinct state hospital for the criminal insane; this was established by an act of May 11, 1905, and was opened in a partially completed condition at Farview in Wayne county on December 17, 1912.[150] To this institution may be sent the criminal insane from all parts of the state and from all state penal institutions. In addition to the above institutions of a public nature caring for the insane, there is the semi-state institution at Dixmont in Allegheny county. This existed down to July, 1907, as the insane department

144 *Laws of the General Assembly,* 1868, pp. 90 ff.; Fertig and Hunter, p. 123.

145 *Laws of the General Assembly,* 1873, pp. 333 ff.; Fertig and Hunter, pp. 124 ff.

146 *Laws of the General Assembly,* 1876, pp. 121 ff.; Fertig and Hunter, pp. 126-7.

147 *Laws of the General Assembly,* 1891, pp. 379 ff.; Fertig and Hunter, pp. 127-9.

148 *Laws of the General Assembly,* 1901, pp. 130 ff.; Fertig and Hunter, pp. 129-30.

149 *Laws of the General Assembly,* 1915, pp. 1055 ff.; Fertig and Hunter, pp. 132-3.

150 *Laws of the General Assembly,* 1905, pp. 400 ff.; Fertig and Hunter, pp. 132-3.

of the Western Pennsylvania Hospital of Pittsburgh, the partial state control dating from an act of March 19, 1856. By a judicial decree of July, 1907, it was made a distinct institution known as the Dixmont Hospital for the Insane.[151]

Nothing like as complete provision has been made for the care of the allied class of idiotic and feeble-minded, which is a much more numerous and, on the whole, a more dangerous class than the insane. The first step in this direction was taken by an act of April 7, 1853, which incorporated what is now known as the Pennsylvania Training School for Idiotic and Feeble-minded Children at Elwyn in Delaware county.[152] Like the Philadelphia House of Refuge, this originated and has remained a semi-private institution. The first state institution of this type created in Pennsylvania was the State Institution for the Feeble-minded of Western Pennsylvania at Polk in Venango county, established by an act of June 3, 1893, and opened April 21, 1897.[153] Two others have since been provided, the Eastern Pennsylvania State Institution for the Feeble-minded and Epileptic at Spring City in Chester county, established by an act of May 15, 1903, and still uncompleted, though it has been opened for the reception of patients;[154] and the Pennsylvania Village for Feeble-minded Women at Laurelton in Union county, established by an act of July 25, 1913, and scarcely more than in the initial stages of construction at present.[155]

In recent years the progress in abnormal psychology has definitely demonstrated that chronic inebriety is but a

151 *Laws of the General Assembly*, 1856, pp. 135 ff.; Fertig and Hunter, pp. 163 ff.

152 *Laws of the General Assembly*, 1853, pp. 341 ff. See on this subject H. H. Goddard, *The Criminal Imbecile*.

153 *Laws of the General Assembly*, 1893, pp. 289 ff.; Fertig and Hunter, op. cit., pp. 133 ff.

154 *Laws of the General Assembly*, 1903, pp. 446 ff.; Fertig and Hunter, pp. 136 ff.

155 *Laws of the General Assembly*, 1913, p. 1319; Fertig and Hunter, pp. 140 ff.

form of psychic instability and aberration rather than a special and obstinate form of voluntary perverseness. In accordance with the recognition of the significance of this undoubted fact, the legislature passed an act on July 25, 1913, authorizing the establishment of a state institution for inebriates, but, unfortunately, little has been done to carry out this laudable intention.[156]

While no one would deny enthusiastic support to the movement for a better and more thorough care of the more grossly abnormal mental types, such as the insane and the idiotic and epileptic, it is coming to be generally recognized that this is but the feeble beginning of the desirable application of medical psychology to the solution of the problems of penal administration. To remove from the prison the violently insane is but to prepare the way for the examination of the psychic characteristics of those who remain and may be suffering from less obvious mental and nervous disorders. Though it is impossible to deny a considerable weight to the economic and social factors in the causation of crime,[157] it has now come to be generally recognized that, to a hitherto wholly unsuspected degree, crime is the product of mental abnormality and instability. Even those convicts whose criminality seems traceable to adverse economic status or unfavorable social environment normally fall into those strata or circumstances which invite crime because of mental defects which prevent them from making a normal adjustment to the problems of existence. Dr. William A. White, one of the most eminent of living psychiatrists, has thus summarized the very significant prevalence of mental and nervous defects in the convict population:

A considerable proportion of the prison population are not normal in their developmental possibilities. Upwards of

156 *Laws of the General Assembly*, 1913, p. 1306; Fertig and Hunter, pp. 143-4.

157 Cf. W. A. Bonger, *Criminality and Economic Conditions*.

fifty per cent, as they are admitted, have demonstrable disease at the central nervous system level. That is, they are mentally defective, psychotic, or have gross central nervous system diseases such as arteriosclerosis or syphilis. This does not include bodily diseases other than those of the central nervous system.[158]

This estimate given by Dr. White is not only conservative, but is based on fairly concrete and scientific evidence which is continually being confirmed by every investigation in this field. Dr. William Healy, by his close personal study of delinquency in Chicago and Boston, particularly among juveniles, has found a close correlation between psychic aberration and criminal behavior.[159] Perhaps the most thorough and convincing study which has been made in this field has been carried on in the psychopathic clinic opened at Sing Sing Prison in New York state in August, 1916, under the direction of Dr. Bernard Glueck. A careful investigation of the psychic state of 608 convicts consecutively admitted revealed the significant fact that 359, or 59 per cent, were so obviously abnormal in mentality as to be readily detected, while there was reason to believe that a more extended analysis of the remaining 41 per cent would have demonstrated many of them to be mentally unstable.[160]

Another simultaneous investigation was carried on by Dr. A. L. Jacoby at the United States Naval Prison at Portsmouth, New Hampshire, following November 1, 1917. After a careful and exceedingly comprehensive examination of the court-martialed sailors sent to the prison, Dr. Jacoby arrived at the conclusion that 54 per cent were suffering from serious mental or nervous dis-

158 W. A. White, *The Principles of Mental Hygiene,* p. 143. See also Thomas W. Salmon, in *Mental Hygiene,* January, 1920; pp. 29-42, and bibliography appended.

159 William Healy, *The Individual Delinquent; Mental Conflicts and Misconduct;* and *Pathological Lying, Accusation and Swindling.*

160 Bernard Glueck, in *Mental Hygiene,* January, 1918, pp. 85-151; April, 1918, pp. 177-216; October, 1918, pp. 546-56.

orders which should have been detected at the time of enlistment, and that an additional 12 per cent had developed mental or nervous disease subsequent to their entry into the naval service. In other words, at least two-thirds of these naval prisoners were distinctly abnormal, mentally or nervously, and one-third of this abnormal group was of distinctly subnormal mentality. These statistics are of particular significance as being based upon the examination of a special class of prisoners drawn from what would be theoretically at least a select group from which the unhealthy or inferior individuals had been eliminated by severe tests at the time of enlistment.[161] Subsequent work has tended to confirm the findings in these pioneer studies by Glueck and Jacoby.

In the matter of providing for this more advanced and scientific entry of psychiatry into the solution of the problems of successfully dealing with the criminal class, Pennsylvania has not made any progress comparable to that achieved in the erection of hospitals for the insane and in making it possible to transfer the insane convicts to these institutions. In this respect, however, Pennsylvania is not different from most of the other commonwealths of the United States. There has been little or nothing done to make a psychiatric clinic a part of the administrative mechanism of the penal institutions of the country. Even that at Sing Sing was merely tolerated by the state of New York while being supported by a private foundation for scientific research.[162] Attempts to introduce this indispensable element into penological practice has normally done little more than to furnish the occasion for

[161] *Mental Hygiene,* January, 1919, pp. 137-141. Dr. Jacoby has continued his interesting investigation in connection with his work with the Recorder's Court of Detroit. For a summary of later studies, see J. L. Gillin, *Criminology and Penology,* pp. 106 ff.; and P. A. Parsons, *The Question of Crime,* Chaps. VII-VIII.

[162] As far as the writer's knowledge goes only the State of Illinois has created an office of state criminologist in order to make possible the systematic study of the mental traits of convicts. Massachusetts, by an act of 1924, ordered the psychiatric examination of prisoners.

coarse and ignorant banter and buffoonery by legislators wholly unacquainted with the essentials of the question at issue.[163] Though it will doubtless require many years to educate the public as to the vital significance of the careful psychological examination, differentiation and treatment of the inmates of all penal institutions, all the evidence at hand today justifies the assertion that until this innovation is accepted American penology can scarcely be held to have penetrated beyond the most superficial externals of a scientific curative or reformatory treatment of the delinquent class.

Of the six state or semi-state penal, reformatory and correctional institutions in Pennsylvania only one—the Girls' Department of the Glen Mills Schools—has made the slightest attempt to make use of the progress of modern psychology in the study and treatment of the inmates of these institutions. Here a psychologist has been added to the staff in order to study the mental conditions of the children committed and suggest the best method of dealing with the various types while at the institution and of fitting them for ultimate freedom.[164] It should be noted, however, that some of the more progressive officials of the other institutions have expressed their sympathy with the employment of psychiatry in penal administration and their willingness to make use of this valuable aid to their disciplinary and reformatory system when legislative sanction makes it possible for them to do so.[165] The gulf

163 A fair sample of the difficulty of obtaining adequate legislative support for this essential department of penological research and procedure was brought out in the bill introduced in the Massachusetts legislature in 1920 to provide for the psychiatric examination of the inmates of the state penal institutions. The discussion on the bill consisted in almost unrelieved buffoonery which culminated in the remark of Senator Cavanaugh that "a psychiatrist is a nut employed to chase another nut." It is needless to remark that the bill was rejected. The fact that in 1924 a bill was passed in Massachusetts providing for the mental examination of prisoners indicates that progress is possible even in the face of politicians.

164 *Annual Report of the Glen Mills Schools,* 1916, pp. 50-53.

165 This attitude was expressed to the writer by Warden Francies of the Western Penitentiary and Superintendent Penn of the Training School at Morganza.

which now separates the state penal institutions from an adequate appreciation and utilization of medical psychology is apparent from the statement in the report of the Eastern Penitentiary for 1917 that only 20 out of 572 convicts admitted during the year were mentally abnormal in any degree.[166] In other words, only a little over 3 per cent were designated as mentally unsound while the investigations of Drs. Glueck and Jacoby have demonstrated that from 50 to 66 per cent are in this condition.

SELECTED REFERENCES

Cass, E. R. *A Study of Parole Laws and Methods in the United States.*

Curti, M. W. "The Intelligence of Delinquents," in *Scientific Monthly,* February, 1926.

Flexner, B., and Oppenheimer, R. *The Legal Aspect of the Juvenile Court.*

Fosdick, R. *European Police Systems.*

Fosdick, R. *American Police Systems.*

Glueck, S. S. *Mental Disorder and the Criminal Law.*

Goddard, H. H. *Feeble-mindedness.*

Hoag and Williams. *Crime, Abnormal Minds and the Law.*

Murchison, C. "American White Criminal Intelligence," in *Journal of Criminal Law and Criminology,* 1924.

Pound, Roscoe. *Criminal Justice in America.*

Pound, Roscoe (Ed.). *Criminal Justice in Cleveland.*

Robinson, L. R. *Penology in the United States.*

Saleilles, R. *The Individualization of Punishment.*

Smith, R. H. *Justice and the Poor.*

Stephen, J. F. *A History of the Criminal Law of England.*

Sutherland, E. H. *Criminology.*

Train, A. *The Prisoner at the Bar.*

[166] *Annual Report of the Eastern Penitentiary,* 1917, p. 61.

CHAPTER VII

The Historical Development of Prison Industry

I. THE RELATION OF PRISON INDUSTRY TO THE PROGRESS OF PENOLOGY

While much has been written on the history of criminal jurisprudence and penal discipline and administration, little attention has been given to a very important aspect of prison history, namely, the genesis of prison industry and its relation to the evolution of economic processes, methods and institutions as they have developed in the world outside prison walls. In this chapter we shall deal with the economic history of penal institutions, with the aim in view of indicating its bearing upon the general problem of prison administration.

It is scarcely more than an obvious platitude to remark that the history of prison industry is inseparably connected with the history of criminology and penology as a whole. Every phase of it has been to a very considerable degree determined or conditioned by the attitude of society towards the criminal, and by the administrative systems and ideals in vogue in the penal institutions. The earliest institutions for incarcerating or detaining individuals were not prisons, in the modern sense of that term, nor were they places in which those detained were set at work. Down to about the middle of the eighteenth century those who were detained against their will in the prisons or jails were almost exclusively persons accused of criminal conduct, debtors and material witnesses, along with certain religious and political offenders and an occasional person held for ransom. The great majority of convicted criminals were fined or subjected to corporal punishment. A typical penalty of this period is that prescribed for burglary in the East Jersey Code of 1668, which was modelled after the New Haven Code of 1642 and the Hempstead Code of 1665:[1]

> If any person within this Province shall commit burglary, by breaking open any dwelling house, storehouse, warehouse, outhouse or barn, or any other house whatsoever, or shall rob any person in the field or highways, he or they so offending shall for the first offence be punished by being burnt in the hand with the letter T, and make full satisfaction of the goods stolen, or the damages that are done; and for the second time of offending in the like nature, besides the making of restitution, to be branded in the forehead with the letter R. And for the third offence to be put to death as incorrigible.

The wide difference in regard to the treatment of criminals, as between the practices of the early eighteenth century and our own day, is further admirably illustrated by the laws of 1732, 1736 and 1744 passed in New York State, which authorized magistrates to sentence to corporal punishment those accused of less serious offences who could not furnish bail within forty-eight hours after arrest. Jail delivery, then, was the chief ambition of the early criminologists and jurists.

Normally, there was no work prescribed or supplied for those who were thus being held in prison awaiting trial, or for debt or inability to pay imposed fines. In the latter part of the eighteenth century in England, when imprisonment was gradually being substituted for corporal punishment as the penalty for crime, it was not uncommon for those accused of crime to be thrown together with the

[1] H. E. Barnes, *History of the Penal, Reformatory and Correctional Institutions of New Jersey*, p. 344.

convicted. In some cases both were put to work at various forms of crude and simple industry or consigned to the tread-mill. Broadly speaking, however, it may be safely stated that prison industry, like the institution of the prison itself in any true sense, is a product of the penological developments of the last two centuries. As imprisonment came to be the classic procedure in treating convicts, and the prison population became more numerous and permanent, the problem arose of how best to occupy the time of the inmates of penal institutions in order to secure the most effective administration and discipline, and at the same time to make the institutions at least in part self-supporting. Throughout the history of prison industry these two major motives of discipline and maintenance have been intertwined and have operated with varying degrees of potency. Only in recent years has the third objective, vocational education, in order to fit the prisoner for a more successful existence in freedom, become a prominent consideration. Throughout the last century theories and systems of prison administration have exerted an important influence upon prison industry as an integral part of the problem of the conduct of penal institutions.

II. THE ORIGINS OF PRISON LABOR

The institution which furnished the significant suggestion as to the desirability of work in prison was the workhouse, which was in existence in Europe as early as the sixteenth century and was introduced into this country during the colonial period. This institution was not originally entrusted with the custody of prisoners convicted of crime, but rather was utilized in the relief and repression of paupers, vagrants and "other vain and loose idle folk." In some cases it was later employed as the place of detention of youthful offenders on whom the courts hesitated to impose the savage punishments which were well-nigh universal for adults at the time. The work-house system had reached a high state of development in the Netherlands by the middle of the seventeenth century, and it is believed that William Penn conceived of his novel juristic and penological ideas and practices in part from an inspection of these institutions.

It seems that, in all probability, the first instance of the imposition of the penalty of imprisonment at hard labor as a penalty for crime occurred in the criminal code of the Quaker colony of West Jersey, enacted in 1681 and embodying the notions of William Penn, one of the leading Proprietors. A year later the principle was adopted on an even wider scale in "The Great Law or Body of Laws" of the colony of Pennsylvania, where Penn's ideas had fuller freedom and scope. Here the majority of crimes other than murder were penalized by fine or imprisonment at hard labor. It is doubtful if the economic or educational motives played any prominent part in the theory underlying this important innovation. It is much more probable that the dominating desire on the part of the Quakers was to avoid the harshness and brutality of the various types of corporal punishment then practically universal, particularly the frequent application of the death penalty for what would today be regarded as minor offences. These Quaker colonial advances were, however, of more historical than practical significance because of the fact that before the close of the first quarter of the eighteenth century both West Jersey and Pennsylvania had given up the Quaker theories and practices and reverted to the usual English and Puritan brutality in treating convicts through ingenious methods of corporal punishment and fines. It was not until a century after Penn's period that imprisonment gradually established itself as the conventional penalty for crime, and in due time industry began to make its way into the prison economy and administration.

Between 1725 and 1800, largely due to the activities of the American Quakers and the reformers in the fields of jurisprudence and penology, such as Oglethorpe, Montesquieu, Beccaria, Howard, Romilly, Miss Fry, Buxton, Peel and Mackintosh, corporal punishment was gradually supplanted by imprisonment as the usual method of dealing with convicts. This revolutionary change in criminal jurisprudence and penal practice brought into existence the modern prison as a relatively permanent institution. Slowly, but very generally, there developed the notion that the large number of incarcerated convicts should be put to work to aid in meeting the maintenance cost of the prison. In some cases the deterrent, disciplinary and reformative aspects of prison labor were even more strongly emphasized. Mr. and Mrs. Webb, in their admirable monograph on *English Prisons Under Local Government,* have thus described the origins of prison labor in England: [2]

The prison workshop became, like the eighteenth-century "House of Industry," merely a device for profitably employing one class of paupers, and thus reducing the burden cast on the rates. . . . Thus, all sorts of handicrafts were carried on in the reformed gaols, some of these becoming regular factories, dominated by the hum and clatter of their scores of looms in constant work, and earning a profit which defrayed a large proportion of the cost of the prisoners' maintenance. This transformation of the prisons into "busy scenes of cheerful industry," the men in the weaving shed or tailor's workshop, the women in the sewing room or laundry, delighted the somewhat emotional philanthropists of the Society for the Improvement of Prison Discipline; and secured, right down to her death, the warm approval

[2] Op. cit., p. 83.

of Mrs. Fry. The new House of Correction, for instance, which the Lancashire Justices built at Preston in 1790, was highly commended as a model of what a prison should be. It was, from the first, run mainly as a cotton weaving factory, employing constantly a hundred and fifty men on the hand looms of the period, and keeping the rest at tailoring, shoemaking, cotton picking, etc.

These promising beginnings were, however, cut short by the deplorable intervention of the practical and "common-sense" penologists of that day, who then, as now, feared lest any innovation might result in the "coddling" of the prisoners and lead to the forgetting of the salutary principles of social revenge and deterrence, which were held by this group to be the chief, if not the sole, object of imprisonment. Their criticism and opposition were couched in the following terms:[3]

It was urged that profitable employment of prisoners tended to ignore what must always be one main object of the treatment of criminals, that of deterring from future crime by supplying every person with a strong motive for resisting the temptation to transgress the laws of the land. It was presently complained that, under the system of profitable employment, the prison became, for many a poor labourer or mechanic, rather a comfortable place. . . . It began to be alleged that the great increase of the numbers committed to prisons was due to their positive attractiveness. . . . "I would banish," wrote Sydney Smith in the widely read *Edinburgh Review* of 1822, "all the looms of Preston Gaol, and substitute nothing but the tread-wheel or the capstern, or some species of labour where the labourer could not see the results of his toil—where it is as monotonous, irksome and dull as possible—pulling and pushing, instead of reading and writing—no share in the profits—not a single shilling. There should be no tea and sugar, no assemblage of female felons round the washing-tub—nothing

[3] Ibid., pp. 87-8.

but beating hemp and pulling oakum and pounding bricks—no work but what was tedious, unusual and unfeminine."

This genial ideal presented by Mr. Smith triumphed over the program of the prison reformers, and there followed the orgy of the experiment with the treadwheel and crank, which will be described below. In this manner prison labor in England was set back for a half century by the meddling of those practical and sober souls who had God's ear on the matter of penal administration.

Prison industry in America received its initial impetus from the innovations in Pennsylvania. Once the province was freed from English control and oversight it reverted at once to the original Quaker penological principles, and the Constitution of 1776 provided that imprisonment at hard labor should be imposed as the penalty for other than capital crimes. This provision was not enacted into law until September 15, 1786, when it was decreed that convicts should be punished by "continued hard labor, publicly and disgracefully imposed." Specifically the prisoners were to be employed in caring for the jails and workhouses, in the repairing of the streets and highways, and in "such other hard and laborious work within the county" as the courts should prescribe. It is worthy of passing comment to note that this earliest of all American provisions for convict labor, excepting only the sporadic and temporary colonial precedents noted above, allowed extra-mural employment, something which was not concretely realized on any significant scale until the twentieth century. This experiment proved a failure, largely because of inadequate protection of the convicts, with the result of frequent street fights between the prisoners and the bystanders. Roberts Vaux thus describes the situation as it existed in 1787:[4]

[4] Roberts Vaux, *Notices*, pp. 21-2.

The law of 1786, although in many respects less sanguinary than the former enactments, contained some provisions, the execution of which led to the most injurious consequences. It directed that a certain description of convicts should be employed in cleaning the streets of the city and repairing the roads in the neighborhood; and authorized the keeper of the jail to shave the heads of the prisoners, and otherwise to distinguish them by an infamous dress. In this very objectionable manner they were brought before the public. The sport of the idle and the vicious, they often became incensed, and naturally took violent revenge upon the aggressors. To prevent them from retorting injuries still allowed to be inflicted, they were encumbered with iron collars and chains, to which bomb-shells were attached, to be dragged along while they performed their degrading service, under the eyes of keepers armed with swords, blunderbusses, and other weapons of destruction. These measures begot in the minds of the criminals and those who witnessed them disrespect for the laws executed with so much cruelty.

As a result of the failure of the act of 1786 to accomplish the desired end, the legislature passed an act on April 5, 1790, which controlled the prison industry situation until the act of 1829, designed to create the industrial system of the new state penitentiaries. This law of 1790 directed that the convicts "shall be kept, as far as may be consistent with their sex, age, health, and ability, to labor of the hardest and most servile kind in which the work is least liable to be spoiled by ignorance, neglect or obstinacy and where the materials are not easily embezzled or destroyed." For a brief time after 1790 a few simple industries were conducted at the Walnut street jail in Philadelphia with some little success, but the excessive overcrowding made a thriving industrial situation quite impossible, and general idleness became the rule. So greatly did the interest in prison industry decline that the law establishing the Western Penitentiary made no provision for prison labor, and the institution was erected according to an architectural plan which did not include shops or other space for industrial activities. In fact, it required active lobbying on the part of Philadelphia prison reformers to secure the enactment of the law of April 23, 1829, which created the industrial system of the state as it existed during the next half century. From 1776 to 1829 one finds in the comments of the time little evidence of an interest in the productive or educational aspects of prison industry. Rather it was looked upon as an agency whereby to execute society's revenge on offenders and deter them from further transgression. Only towards the close of the period mentioned does there appear any emphasis upon the value of teaching a useful trade.

The early enthusiasm of Pennsylvania for a reformation of the barbarous methods of treating convicts soon spread to New York State. Men like Ambrose Spencer, Philip Schuyler, Thomas Eddy, De Witt Clinton and John Jay became interested in the penological progress in the "City of Brotherly Love," investigated it in person, and secured the passage of an act in 1796 which introduced imprisonment as the approved method of punishing crime in New York. Down to about 1825 the industrial situation in the prison in New York City was much like that in the Walnut street jail, namely, overcrowding and idleness. Beginning with the second quarter of the last century, however, the industrial developments in the New York prisons were much more significant and rapid than those in the Pennsylvania prisons. New York departed at that time from the system of solitary cellular confinement, which Pennsylvania originated and continued, and created the famous Auburn system of separation at night and congregate work in shops by day. This was not so much of an advantage in the days of the handicraft economy, but, with the gradual introduction of machinery accompanying the Industrial Revolution, the shop system possessed great advantages over a cellular system of industry—a fact which Pennsylvania only grudgingly admitted as late as 1869, when congregate shops were first permitted in the Western Penitentiary. The exponents of the Auburn system always laid considerable stress upon the industrial advantages of their system, and it is not without significance that the first law providing for commutation of sentence passed in the United States was designed to stimulate the industrial activity of the prisoners. But in about the same way that the educational aspects of prison industry were overlooked in Pennsylvania, in the enthusiasm for discipline and reformation, so in New York they were ignored in the interest of productivity and income. Between 1800 and 1850 the great majority of the states then in existence adopted either the Pennsylvania or Auburn systems of prison administration, and with them the industrial methods adhering to them. In general, while the Pennsylvania system was at first very popular, it was soon abandoned in most states and the Auburn system was practically universal in the field in this country after 1845. In Europe the Pennsylvania system proved rather more popular than the Auburn.

III. THE DEVELOPMENT OF LEADING CONCEPTS AND PRACTICES IN AMERICAN PRISON INDUSTRY

In England, where the Pennsylvania cellular system was extensively adopted after 1835, there was a notable trend away from productive labor and an adoption of punitive labor. In many prisons the treadwheel was extensively used, with results so disastrous to the health of convicts that even hardened wardens condemned it. But even more popular, and better adapted to cellular prisons, was the "crank," a device of the following nature:[5]

> Crank labour consists in making 10,000 revolutions of a machine resembling in appearance a Kent's Patent Knife Cleaner, for it is a narrow iron drum placed on legs, with a long handle on one side, which when turned causes a series of cups or scoops in the interior to revolve. At the lower part of the interior of the machine is a thick layer of sand, which the cups, as they come round, scoop up, and carry to the top of the wheel, where they throw it out and empty themselves, after the principle of a dredging machine. A dial-plate, fixed in front of the iron drum, shows how many revolutions the machine has made. It is usual to shut up in a cell the man sent to crank labour, so that the exercise is rendered doubly disagreeable by the solitude. . . . As may easily be conceived, this labour is very distressing and severe. . . . A man can make, if he work with ordinary speed, about twenty revolutions a minute, and this, at 1,200 the hour, will make his task of 10,000 turns last eight hours and twenty minutes.

Though an act of 1865 prescribed the treadwheel or the crank for the earlier portion of the term of convicts sentenced to long periods of imprisonment, there was a gradual reversion to the industrial operations of the first third of the century. Some few local prisons and jails secured a large income from their manufacturing activities. At the present time the inmates of the government prisons are very generally employed at different forms of industry under the so-called "state-use" system. The chief industry is the making of mail-bags for the government. In spite of the fact that some American investigators have praised the industrial system of the English prisons, the recent Prison System Enquiry Committee thus condemns the existing situation:[6]

[5] Webb, op. cit., p. 146, note.
[6] Hobhouse and Brockway, *English Prisons Today*, p. 120.

The punitive conception degrades prison labour. The work is unnecessarily crude and monotonous and does not inculcate habits of industry. There is practically no up-to-date machinery.

There is scarcely any choice of labour.

The daily "task" is not proportioned to the capacity of the individual.

No wages are paid to prisoners.

The minute disciplinary supervision of the working parties is degrading and wasteful.

There is an absence of industrial training of prisoners sufficient to enable them to earn a living outside.

The trade instructors are usually themselves untrained.

The prison workshops are often ill-lit and unsuitable.

The number of prisoners employed in agriculture or open-air work is very small.

Even more influential than any English influence on American prison industry were the reports of the remarkable success in introducing productive prison labor which had been achieved by Montesinos in Spain and Obermaier in Bavaria between 1835 and 1850.

In the United States the attitude towards prison labor and the resulting practices have varied widely. While, as has already been made clear, labor was introduced into the newly organized penitentiaries in the quarter of a century following 1790, the innovation was viewed primarily from the aspect of its alleged deterrent and reformative virtues, and only secondarily as a means of defraying in part the cost of maintaining penal institutions. The inscription placed over the door of the first state prison of New Jersey, opened in 1799, is an eloquent testimonial to the interlacing of penological views on discipline and industry:

Labor, silence, penitence
The Penitentiary House
Erected by legislative
Authority
Richard Howell, Governor.
In the XXII year of
American Independence,
MDCCXCVIII
That those who are feared
For their crimes
May learn to fear the laws
And be useful.
Hic Labor, Hoc Opus.

The real beginning of the expansion and high prosperity of prison industry did not come until the period from 1825 to 1840. In the earlier days sales of prison-made products were difficult because there was no well-established connection between the prison shops and customers in the world outside. With the rise of the "merchant-capitalist" in America, in the period following 1825, this serious handicap of the earlier era was eliminated and an intermediary or agent was discovered who was only too glad to avail himself of this cheap labor supply, and to furnish raw materials and take the finished product at an agreed-upon rate. The merchant-capitalist usually employed the so-called "piece-price" system of contracting for the labor of the convicts, but in some cases the process was carried one step further and he leased the prisoners during the working day and assumed full control and direction of their labors. This development of enthusiasm and success in prison labor was, then, but a phase of the rise of the merchant capitalist, of which home labor and the sweat-shop were other aspects of his effort to obtain labor effort at a low cost.

This period of relatively prosperous contract labor continued for a generation, being particularly stimulated by the American Civil War, which produced an unprecedented demand for cheap clothing and boots and shoes. Then followed a conflict with labor organizations, which ended very generally in the abolition of contract labor and the substitution of public-account and state-use systems. It also resulted in a notable decline in the relative amount of prison industry, particularly in such states as Pennsylvania, which was slow to make the transition to a new system of applying and controlling convict labor.

From the very period of its origin convict labor has been opposed by free labor. As early as 1823, at the very time when the Auburn system was first coming into existence, the mechanics of New York City protested against the alleged menace of convict labor:[7]

> Your memorialists have seen the convicts imperfectly educated in various trades, hired out to individuals, in some instances at reduced compensation, and in others employed for the benefit of the state, and the products of their labour thrown into market and disposed of at a price very little above the cost of materials of which they were manufactured, to the ruin of free mechanics.

The opposition of free labor to convict labor did not abate, and the only reason that it was unable to effect any particular change in the methods of convict labor until the seventies and eighties was that labor organizations had not become powerful enough until that time to exert much pressure in either an economic or a political way.

With the rise of the *Knights of Labor,* following 1869, and of the *American Federation of Labor,* after 1885, the free laborers were provided with organizations of sufficient size and coherence to exert some adequate influence on economics and politics. From 1880 to the present time

[7] J. R. Commons, *A History of Labour in the United States,* Vol. I, p. 155.

a steady fight has been kept up by labor and its political agents and allies, until at the present time contract convict labor has been abolished in most of the states of the Union. The tendency has been to substitute for the contract system the public-account and the state-use systems. To some degree the success which labor has met in abolishing contract convict labor has been due to the political exploitation of the labor vote by politicians, who felt that they might readily concede this insignificant demand and thereby divert labor from vigorous demands for more vital liberal policies. The whole issue of convict labor has nowhere been more judiciously summarized than in the following citation from Carroll D. Wright:[8]

In the many investigations which have been made in relation to the prison labour question, few instances have been found where prices have been affected in the least, and rarely a case where wages have been lowered in consequence of the employment of convicts in productive industry. Nevertheless, the moral effect of the supposed competition, and of whatever real competition may have occurred, has been sufficient to create a demand in nearly all of the States of the Union for some regulation of the employment of convicts under which competition can be entirely or largely removed, and for the last twenty years or more political platforms have often contained a paradoxical plank demanding that convicts should be employed, not only as a matter of health, but as a source of revenue to the state, but in such a way as to relieve honest industry of competition. It is an absolute impossibility to prevent competition if convicts are to be employed in any way whatever. It must be admitted by all sane men that they should be employed and constantly employed upon intelligent labour. The problem, therefore, so far as the economics of the question is concerned, is either to reduce the competition to the lowest point or to manufacture goods in such a way and under such conditions that prices and wages can in no sense be affected. This is the

[8] *An Outline of Practical Sociology*, pp. 380-81.

whole of the economic side of the question from the productive point of view.

By a curious irony of fate, Pennsylvania, which was the pioneer in prison labor both in the world at large and in the United States, has had the most disastrous experience of any state in this violent reaction against convict labor and towards the enforced idleness of prisoners. It culminated in the notorious Muehlbronner Act of April 18, 1897, probably the most foolish and ill-conceived law in the history of legislation noted for opportunism and short-sightedness. This act ordered [9]

That, from and after the passage of this Act, no warden, superintendent, or other officer of any State prison, penitentiary, or State reformatory, having control of the employment of the inmates of said institution, shall employ more than five per cent of the whole number of inmates of said institution in the manufacture of brooms and brushes and hollow-ware, or ten per cent in the manufacture of any other kind of goods, wares, articles or things that are manufactured elsewhere in the State except mats and matting, in the manufacture of which twenty per cent of the whole number of inmates may be employed: Provided, That this Act shall not apply to goods manufactured for the use of inmates of such institutions.

That no machine operated by steam, electricity, hydraulic force, compressed air, or other power, except machines operated by hand or foot power, shall be used in any of the said institutions in the manufacture of any goods, wares, articles or things that are manufactured elsewhere in the State.

As if to make the effect of this law still more pernicious, the attorney-general of the state rendered an opinion that the law meant that either 5, 10, or 20 per cent might be employed, but never the maximum of 35

[9] *Laws of the General Assembly*, 1897, pp. 170-71.

per cent of the inmates. From that date until very recently prison labor has been a farce and a misnomer in Pennsylvania. According to the statistics gathered by an investigator in 1909, out of the 2,900 idle able-bodied prisoners in the entire United States, no less than 2,073 were listed as being in Pennsylvania. Yet penologists unite in agreeing that the chief evil of unemployment is not economic loss so much as disciplinary and personal deterioration. It is impossible to state in any quantitative way the volume and diversity of evils in prison administration and personal suffering which have flowed from this deplorable law. Thousands of men have been compelled to spend months and years at a time in complete idleness in their cells.

While most other states escaped so extreme a form of legislation as that which afflicted Pennsylvania, the period from 1885 to the opening of the present century was one characterized by a general slump in prison industry. In the last two decades, however, there has been a steady increase in the volume of prison industry, dominated very generally by the state-use and public-account systems. The making of supplies for state institutions, certain special types of profitable manufacturing, such as the making of binding-twine in Minnesota, the provision of prison farms, and the beginning of extra-mural labor on roads and public works have furnished the opportunity and occasion for this laudable industrial renaissance. The opposition of union labor has been to some degree diminished through the abolition of the direct competition with free labor which characterized the old contract system.

While the present industrial system is far from what one might wish, even in regard to pecuniary gain and steady employment for the incarcerated, perhaps its chief defect lies in the lack of any adequate training of the inmates in the learning of a trade which will enable them to lead an honest self-supporting life after release. The progress which has been made in regard to vocational education has taken place in the reformatories rather than the prisons. Even in a state like Minnesota, which has the most successful manufacturing system of any commonwealth in the Union, the experience in manufacturing binding-twine and agricultural implements can scarcely be regarded as adequate vocational training. And even less pertinent and practicable as industrial training is the farm labor and work on roads which has become so popular in recent years as an advanced way of handling prison labor. To be sure, a goodly number of convicts can never be adapted to anything beyond unskilled labor, but in the penal system of the future there will need to be a working compromise between productivity and vocational education. Indeed, as reformation rather than punishment becomes the objective of penal administration the teaching of some trade will probably be put ahead of mere monetary income as a desirable aim of penal authorities. And, as has already been discovered in our other set of more benign institutions for involuntary detention, the public school system, it will soon be seen impracticable and unscientific to attempt to deal with the prison population as an undifferentiated unity. From the standpoint of administration, education and industry the population of penal institutions will come to be dealt with by classes and types, based upon their relative ability and responsiveness to ameliorative and reformative treatment and to vocational education.

The chief obstacle to a more adequate type of prison industry and vocational training has been, and still remains, the wrong-headed notion of society as to the purpose of penal institutions. As long as social vengeance and deterrence are looked upon as the chief objects of imprisonment, any progressive innovation is viewed as a betrayal of social and moral obligation and a surrender of principle. Closely related to this general attitude of society is the whole orientation of the staff of administration in the average prison. From their point of view their function is that of the efficient jailer, and any new proposal as to prison labor which threatens the well-lubricated machine that preserves the deadly daily routine and insures the relatively safe and certain incarceration of the prison population is looked upon by them as something which threatens the whole scheme of the cosmos. This attitude has been well summarized by Tannenbaum:[10]

> The function of the prison is to keep the men confined. The function of the warden is to make sure that the purpose of the prison is fulfilled. He is primarily a jailer. That is *his* business. Reform, punishment, expiation for sin—these are social policies determined by social motives of which he, as jailer, becomes the agent. He is a jailer first; a reformer, a guardian, a disciplinarian, or anything else second. Any one who has been in prison, or who knows the prison régime, through personal contact, will corroborate this fact. The whole administrative organization of the prison is centered on keeping the men inside the walls. Men in prison are always counted. They are counted morning, noon and night. They are counted when they rise, when they eat, when they work, and when they sleep. Like a miser hovering over his jingling coins, the warden and keepers are constantly on edge about the safety of their charges—a safety of numbers first, of well-being afterwards.

Until reforming the reformable element within the prison becomes the main aspiration and source of solicitude of the prison authorities, this orientation of the jailer will stand in the way of any variegated and selective scheme of industries and vocational guidance and training. In other words, as was pointed out at the outset of this historical section, the problem of improving the industrial system of our prisons is an integral phase of the general

10 *Wall Shadows,* pp. 11-12.

task of devising a more rational method of dealing with those regarded by society as the class of dangerous delinquents.

IV. HISTORIC METHODS OF INDUSTRIAL ADMINISTRATION IN AMERICAN PRISONS

The types of industrial administration which have been tried out in American prisons are six in number. The following description of these types is adapted from the official analysis in *Senate Document* 494 of the Second Session of the Sixty-third Congress.

1. *The leasing of the person and labor of the convicts.*—Under this system the contractors assume entire control of the convicts, including their maintenance and discipline, subject, however, to the regulations fixed by statute. In general, the prisoners are removed from the prisons and are employed in outdoor labor, such as mining, agriculture, railroad construction, etc., though manufacturing is sometimes carried on. The nature and duration of the employment are, within the restrictions of the law, fixed by the lease.

2. *Leasing or contracting for the labor of the prisoners.*—The employment under this system is usually within the prison shops or yards, discipline and control remaining in the hands of the officers, only the labor of the convicts being let to and directed by the contractors for manufacturing purposes. The state usually furnishes shop room and sometimes also provides power and machinery.

3. *The piece-price form of the contract system.*—Not only the discipline of the convicts, but the direction of their labor as well, is retained by the state under this system, the contractors furnishing the material to be made up and receiving the finished product, an agreed price per piece being paid for the labor bestowed.

4. *The public-account system.*—There is no intervention of outside parties under this system, the employment of the convicts being in all respects directed by the state, and the products of their labor being sold for its benefit.

5. *The state-use system.*—This system is similar to the above, except that such articles are produced as will be of service to the state in supplying and maintaining its various institutions, and are appropriated to such use instead of being put on the general market.

6. *The public-works-and-ways system.*—Under this system convicts are employed in the construction and repair of public streets, highways, and other public works.

The first system has few or no defenders among penologists and sociologists, and is no longer (1925) found in any progressive state or penal institution. Its advantage was that it relieved the state of the burden of caring for the prisoners, but this was more than offset by the impossibility of safeguarding the treatment of the convicts and maintaining any program of reformation and education. Some of the most atrocious evils of prison labor have existed under this system in the chain gangs used for construction work and in the turpentine camps of the South. The second type, the most usual form of contract convict labor, freed the prison of industrial responsibility and possessed the advantage over the lease system of allowing the prison authorities to exert a more active supervision of the treatment of the convicts. The arguments against it were chiefly that emphasis was likely to be laid upon productive efficiency rather than reformation and industrial training, and that this convict labor constituted an unfair type of competition with free labor outside the prison. The piece-price system has been regarded as more desirable than the contract-lease system, because it permits complete control of the convicts by the prison authorities. The main objection advanced against it has been the competition which it produces with outside labor. The public-account system, likewise, has been criticized because prison-made products compete in the market with goods made outside. The state-use system has been devised to find a channel for the sale of prison-made products which will reduce to a minimum competition with outside goods, and will, at the same time, allow the state institutions to obtain commodities at a relatively low cost to the state. The public-works-and-ways system is but the application of the state-use principle to the extramural employments of convicts. While the state-use system has quite generally come to be regarded as the most satisfactory method of controlling prison labor, it has rarely been found successful unless the purchase of prison-made products, when available, has been made compulsory with state institutions, and it has been found to operate best in conjunction with the public-account system.

Historically speaking, the lease-system was never as important as the "piece-price" variety of the contract scheme. It was most utilized in the period around the time of the Civil War, and Alabama, the last state to retain it, abolished it on January 1, 1924. The piece-price system was ever the most popular form of contract convict labor, but has retired under the assaults of organized free labor until today less than ten states retain the practice. The public-account system is today probably the most popular form of industrial administration, some thirty states operating this system alone or in connection with the state-use plan. As to the state-use method, while ten years ago most progressive students of prison industry advocated this as preferable to all other forms of industrial administration, only six states, New York, Pennsylvania, Ohio, Virginia, New Jersey and Idaho, adhere to it exclusively. The best expedient seems to be the combination of a basic state-use system with the public account system as supplementary and for the sale of excess products. Extra-mural employment on public works and roads is now permitted in nearly every state.

V. HISTORIC TYPES OF INDUSTRIAL ENTERPRISES IN AMERICAN PRISONS

The specific character of the industrial operations carried on in American prisons has been determined chiefly by the general nature of the industrial evolution of the country and the artificial restrictions on prison industry due to prevailing penological theories or the legislative capitulation to the opposition of organized labor. In the early days, down to around 1835, the typical forms of prison industry were crude and simple, conforming well to the stipulation in the Pennsylvania law of 1790 that the work should be "of the hardest and most servile kind, least liable to be spoiled by ignorance, neglect, or obstinacy, and in which the materials are not easily embezzled or destroyed." They consisted chiefly of nail-making, sawing stone, and picking over oakum, wool and hair. There was also some weaving and shoemaking. With the coming of the contract system, paralleling the rise of the merchant-capitalist, the prison industries came to be like those which the merchant-capitalist promoted in his ordinary activities outside the prison, namely, chiefly weaving of woolen cloth and shoemaking, with some attention to the making of crude furniture and the cane-seating of chairs. Some prisoners were also employed at the simpler forms of industry which were carried along from the earlier period. During the Civil War there was a great stimulation of industry and a strong tendency to concentrate on shoemaking and the weaving of woolen and shoddy cloth. Practically all of this work was carried on by handicraft methods. In the Pennsylvania penitentiaries, and for a portion of the period in those of Rhode

Island and New Jersey, the work was done in separation in cells. In the majority of the prisons, which were administered according to the Auburn system, the work was executed in shops, but these contained few or no machines in the modern sense. From the period of the Civil War onward the industrial revolution outside the prisons forced the adoption of machinery in the prison shops, if there was to be any hope of competing with firms outside the prisons. From this time forward the cellular prisons were doomed to carry on industrial operations under a great handicap because of the impossibility of introducing mechanical devices. It was a recognition of this fact that led the Western Penitentiary of Pennsylvania to abandon cellular separation in 1869.

For a time after the Civil War there was no little development of prison industry, based upon shop and machine technique and devoted to manufacturing cloth, hosiery, shoes, chains and other heavy hardware, along with a large number of minor industries still carried on by handicraft methods, among them cigar-making. Then came the attack upon prison industries by organized labor from the middle of the "seventies" to the close of the century. One method of meeting their objections lay in shifting the industries of the prison to a type in which there would be a minimum of competition with free labor. Consequently, the manufacture of cocoa-mats, burlap bags, coarse brushes and brooms, and cheap hosiery and cotton cloth was popular in the last quarter of the century. Another method of meeting the situation lay in shifting to the state-use system and manufacturing furniture, clothing and other supplies for schools, asylums, hospitals and other state institutions. There has also been in the last two decades a marked trend towards extramural employment in the way of labor on roads, or the purchase of great prison farms on which many of the inmates may work and thus provide much of the food for the prisoners, together with some surplus to be sold in the open market.

Several states present conspicuous illustrations of these various types of industry. The most successful state in manufacturing for the open market is Minnesota, which specializes in the manufacturing of binding twine and agricultural implements, the net profits from which in the year 1920-21 are said to have been in excess of half a million dollars. The state is also progressive in its pecuniary attitude towards convicts, in that it pays them a decent wage, the average earnings of each man in that year being $538. California has a thriving jute bag industry. New York State has probably the most highly developed state-use system of industries, specializing on school and office desks, institutional furniture and supplies, and the manufacture of automobile registration plates. Not much can be said, however, for conditions of labor in the New York prison shops. In the matter of prison agricultural operations two southern states, Louisiana and Mississippi, take the lead, making their penal institutions self-supporting, the former through the operation of sugar plantations, and the latter by maintaining cotton plantations. Pennsylvania is also taking steps to develop extensive prison farming operations. Wisconsin and Illinois furnish examples of states which have thriving and prosperous prison industries combining all of these forms—state-use manufacturing, prison farms, and public-account manufacturing. Probably the worst situation as regards idleness and unemployment, for which the local prison authorities are in no sense responsible, exists in the Eastern Penitentiary of Pennsylvania.

SELECTED REFERENCES

Barnes, H. E. *History of the Penal, Reformatory and Correctional Institutions of New Jersey,* pp. 60 ff., 99 ff., 124 ff., 141 ff., 174 ff., 378 ff., 467 ff., 493 ff., 541 ff.

Barnes, H. E. "The Economics of American Penology as Illustrated by the Experience of the State of Pennsylvania," in *Journal of Political Economy,* October, 1921.

Commons, J. R., *et al.* *A History of Labour in the United States.*

Garrett, P. W. *A Handbook of American Prisons.*

Hobhouse, S., and Brockway, E. F. *English Prisons Today,* Chapter VII.

Klein, Philip. *Prison Methods in New York State,* Chapters VIII-IX.

Lewis, O. F. *The Development of American Prisons and Prison Customs, 1776-1845.*

Robinson, L. N. *Penology in the United States.*

Robinson, L. N. *Report of the Penal Commission on the Employment and Compensation of Prisoners,* Harrisburg, 1915.

Votaw, A. H. In *Prison Journal,* October, 1921, passim.

Votaw, A. H. In *Proceedings of the Annual Congress of the American Prison Association,* 1921, pp. 57-70.

Webb, S. and B. *English Prisons Under Local Government,* pp. 77-89, 144-57, 196-98.

Whitin, E. S., and Lichtenberger, J. P. *Prison Labor.*

Whitin, E. S. *Penal Servitude.*

CHAPTER VIII

How Prisons Punish the Human Mind

I. CRUEL AND VICIOUS NATURE OF CONTEMPORARY PRISONS

Imprisonment as it exists today is a worse crime than any of those committed by its victims; for no single criminal can be as powerful for evil, or as unrestrained in its exercise, as an organized nation. . . . We have to find some form of torment which can give no sensual satisfaction to the tormentor, and which is hidden from public view. That is how imprisonment, being just such a torment, became the normal penalty. The fact that it may be worse for the criminal is not taken into account. The public is seeking its own salvation, not that of the lawbreaker. It would be far better for him to suffer in the public eye; for among the crowd of sightseers there might be a Victor Hugo or a Dickens, able and willing to make the sightseers think of what they are doing and ashamed of it. The prisoner has no such chance. He envies the unfortunate animals in the Zoo, watched daily by thousands of disinterested observers who never try to convert a tiger into a Quaker by solitary confinement, and would set up a resounding agitation in the papers if even the most ferocious maneater were made to suffer what the most docile convict suffers. Not only has the convict no such protection: the secrecy of his prison makes it hard to convince the public that he is suffering at all.—George Bernard Shaw.

In this chapter we shall make no effort to present a technical analysis of the development of the prison psychoses, but rather to describe in a brief and general way the effect of contemporary imprisonment on the mind of the prisoner, the prison officials and the public at large. The key to the defects, abuses and cruelties of the present prison system is to be found in the fact that, whatever the pretense, the actual purpose of imprisonment is not reformation but punishment. If this were not so we would design our institutions and their administration so that they might more intelligently and directly promote the various methods and processes of reformation. Of course, the older attitude of conventional penology was that punishment itself necessarily produces reformation, but we now know that in most cases exactly the opposite result is brought about.

The modern prison system brings into play a large number of disastrous influences constituting a vicious circle. The present prison system would put the most severe strains upon even a thoroughly normal person, but its savagery actually operates in most cases upon those who are physically or mentally abnormal upon commitment. These emotionally unstable persons are upon entry into prison denied the assertion or enjoyment of the more important and basic human urges and impulses. Normal sociability is severely curtailed; self-assertion is practically denied; interesting work is rarely provided; play and recreation, if existent at all, are grotesquely inadequate. The desirable outlet for the sex instinct is totally denied in the average prison, though the sex urge is rendered abnormally active, due to the blocking of the other forms of emotional and intellectual expression which might otherwise drain off or sublimate sex desires. The effects of all these abnormalities and abuses are greatly intensified by the regimentation and cruelty inevitable in the conventional prison administration of today. Hence, it is but natural that prison life should result in various types of explosion such as psychoses, neuroses, sex perversions and general physical and moral disintegration. No understanding can be expected from the average warden, as his function is primarily that of a jailer who must keep a certain number of human beings safely herded within the prison walls. Nor can any sympathy be hoped for from the majority of those outside the walls, as the prison supplies the herd's machinery for collective vengeance through which the individual gets a vicarious satisfaction as well as experiencing a pleasant indirect and symbolic release of the cruel and sadistic impulses which most citizens could scarcely apply in personal contact with another individual. This perverse emotional motivation of the average citizen renders him unfavorably disposed toward any proposal for an improvement of the situation, thus making it very difficult to break into the vicious circle and bring about any significant and permanent advances and reforms.

II. THE PRISON AND THE CONVICT

We may now briefly consider the various disastrous effects of imprisonment upon the individual convict. First and foremost should be placed the denial of one of the most basic human motives and impulses, namely, normal human sociability. The fact that the association and communication of criminals are looked upon as mutually degrading, together with the greater supposed ease and simplicity of administration with the relative isolation of prisoners, leads the average prison warden markedly to curtail the opportunities for normal sociability between the inmates of his institution. We have now in most places abandoned the unmitigated savagery of the old Pennsylvania System of solitary confinement, but almost never is there any adequate provision for healthy social intercourse among the inmates of modern prisons. Along with the blocking of sociability goes the impossibility of normal self-assertion. The whole plan and psychology of prison administration are based chiefly upon the desire to repress and intimidate the prisoner, in order that he may in this way feel very directly and certainly the displeasure of society over his violation of its rules and his threat to its safety. Rarely is there any interesting work provided for the prisoner which might allow the development of some sense of craftsmanship and some absorption in a definite task. More and more, modern mental hygiene is coming to emphasize the fundamental integrating function of a definite job or task in which the individual is interested. This salutary and dynamic motive is obviously almost entirely absent in the case of the majority of the inhabitants of our present-day penal institutions. Then there is the notorious lack of adequate physical exercise which is accompanied by unfortunate results both physical and psychological.

The inferior food and the unattractive methods of serving it remove practically all of the desirable psychic exuberance which is supposed to accompany the most successful execution of the process of nutrition. There is little opportunity for any considerable degree of emotional outlet in recreation, games, contests, music or sex. Particularly serious, though almost uniformly overlooked, is the total denial of any sex life to all of the inmates of penal institutions, in spite of the fact that many prisoners are of a hyper-sexed type who have been leading an unusually free sex life before incarceration. This human animal, thus denied practically every phase of a normal expression of his personality, is still further rendered "safe and secure" through an elaborate scheme of regimentation and rules which are designed to simplify the task of a warden as a successful jailer. There is no attempt to understand or minister to the specific needs of a prisoner or to meet him on any ground of sympathetic human contacts. Rather, he is faced with a bewilderingly complete and rigid set of rules, any violation of which is punished either by physical pain or a decrease in his already slight body of privileges.

In the light of the above atrocious situation it is not surprising that many and diverse types of psychic abnormality are either intensified or generated by prison life. First, one must remember the general attitude of hopelessness and despair which dominates the majority of convicts when they reach these living tombs. The "Mark Twain Burglar" thus describes his feelings on arriving at the Wisconsin State Prison:[1]

> I shall never forget the bleak November day during which the train passed through the barren country on its way north. I sat handcuffed to the sheriff and absorbed in my own thoughts, watching through the window of the car for the prison walls which were to receive me and shut me away from the world for six years.
>
> At last it appeared in the distance, the tall water tower and smoke-stack, then the group of gray buildings with their parapets and the watch towers on the high walls. A sickening feeling took hold of me, and a lump rose in my throat. Any other place in the world, I thought, except that awful prison! The loud voice of the brakeman announcing our arrival at Waupun roused me from my reverie. The sheriff took me by the arm, and we dropped off the train to the platform. When we arrived at the prison and the numerous iron-barred gates closed behind me, I felt as though some great cavern had swallowed me up and I would never see the light of the free outside world again. Society had fed another individual into the great iron jaws of the prison hopper.

In addition to the general atmosphere of fear, isolation and hopelessness which is produced by the architecture and punitive psychology of the modern prison, there is

[1] *In the Clutch of Circumstance*, pp. 84-5.

the even worse situation generated by the usual method of handing over the practical control and operation of the prison to certain selected prisoners or "trusties" with the resulting cliques, favoritism, corruption and cruelty which this system produces. The results are bound to be evil in any event. If the prisoner "plays the game" and aligns himself with one of these inner gangs based on special favoritism and on "snitching" and "squealing" on his fellow prisoners he may get along fairly well while in prison, but instead of being trained to become a decent citizen he is getting the most effective education in fundamentally anti-social, and contemptible—even criminal—conduct, not matched by employment in the Prohibition enforcement service. On the other hand, if he remains a decent and honest gentleman and refuses to co-operate with the scheme of prison politics he is hopeless, unprotected, and the legitimate prey of any who desire to secure special favors by passing on false stories about him to the prison authorities, who are usually themselves involved in the system of intrigue and conspiracy which honeycombs the whole institution. The decent convict is thus without friends inside the walls, and unable to communicate with those outside except through letters read and censored by the selected representatives of this same group of official-convict intriguers from whose persecution and machinations the individual is seeking relief. There is thus generated in the mind of the convict a feeling of utter hopelessness and helplessness which not only promotes mental and personal disintegration, but also in many cases physical disease. The disciplinary system of the average prison, then, far from promoting efforts at reformation and personal rehabilitation, results either in most efficient training in crookedness, corruption and intrigue or in the gradual but certain breakdown of the body and mind of the convict.

If sufficient space were afforded we could describe in detail the numerous and varied psychoses and neuroses which modern psychiatrists have demonstrated to be the result of the abnormal modes of life forced upon inmates by the contemporary prison system. Suffice it to say that an extremely broad range of psycho-neuroses are thus induced. Particularly should there be emphasized the inevitable development of the greatest variety of sex perversions, the pathogenesis of which has been so well described by Alexander Berkman. The sex situation in prisons is even worse than in abnormal modes of existence outside, for, in addition to the blocking of normal sexual manifestations, there is no opportunity whatever for sublimation through professional, cultural or recreational outlets. Hence, the sex urge necessarily finds expression in all sorts of pathological conduct. If one were to plan an institution designed to promote sexual degeneracy he would arrive at the modern prison. The wide prevalence of masturbation and homosexuality among men prisoners is a commonplacc to all prison administrators and investigators, but Mrs. O'Hare thus describes an almost unbelievable condition existing in the women's department of one of the leading contemporary state penitentiaries:[2]

Whether or not we agree fully with Dr. Sigmund Freud and the psychoanalytic school that sex is the dominating force of human life, we must admit that it is a powerful factor. Prison life, by denying the normal expression of sex, breeds and fosters sex perversions and all the degenerating vices that these perversions include. . . . It is a stark ugly fact that homosexuality exists in every prison and must ever be one of the sinister facts of our penal system. In the Missouri State Penitentiary it is, next to the "task," the dominating feature of prison life and a regular source of revenue to favored stool pigeons. . . . In fact, homosexuality was not only permitted, but indulgence was actively fos-

[2] K. D O'Hare. *In Prison*, pp. 112, 159-60.

tered, and in the cases of young, helpless, and unprotected women actually demanded and enforced.

The vile and degrading conditions which are thus brought about are, after all, the least serious aspect of this abnormal situation. The most deplorable result is the fact that these sex perversions are normally correlated with the parallel or consequent pathogenesis of many types of psychic abnormality and emotional instability, many of which emerge in definite criminal compulsions. Thus the sexual results of prison life, which have been practically ignored by both conventional criminologists and reformers, would by themselves alone suffice to train up a veritable crop of degenerates and potential criminals. Not only is the sex situation in the modern prison one of the most challenging of the social, psychological and administrative problems existing in penal institutions; it is also one of those most impossible to deal with in a direct or efficient fashion. With society still medieval in its attitude towards the sexual problem in the general social world outside the prison, there is little hope that it will be able to handle the sexual problem within prisons in an intelligent or expeditious manner. This constitutes an additional argument for the abolition of the prison.

Along with these various emotional defects and disorders, emerging chiefly on an unconscious level, should be mentioned the conscious resentment of the prisoners at the general complex of cruelty and dissatisfaction in which they find themselves, with the resulting unfortunate desire not to reform but to devise better and more efficient methods of avenging themselves upon society. Thus, the net result of modern imprisonment upon the average criminal is not only to produce an emotional situation which bears with it the high probability of generating subconscious criminal compulsions, but also to create a conscious desire to commit crime in order to get even with society for its cruelties to the individual convict. We are not, of course, contending that society can afford to ignore criminal conduct, but are rather endeavoring to make it clear that it is a strangely ineffective method of dealing with criminal conduct which inevitably and uniformly results in the creation of a more serious and determined potential criminal as the chief product of the expensive machinery of the modern prison system.

Properly planned and administered a prison might be a good thing, but it would not be the institution which has passed under the name of prison up to the present time. Hospitals are extremely humane and therapeutic institutions as at present conducted, but they would scarcely be so regarded if they followed the practice of throwing a recently received patient suffering from double pneumonia into an ice-cold bath and then leaving him half-clothed on an exposed balcony in zero weather. The administrative and disciplinary system of the modern prison acts in a wholly comparable fashion upon the inmates of penal institutions. They inevitably render more unfit for civilized existence those unfortunates committed to their custody ostensibly for reformation and rehabilitation.

III. THE PRISON PSYCHOSIS AND PRISON OFFICIALS

In describing the psychological effects of the contemporary prison system upon prison officials it is necessary, in the first place, to recognize the relatively low types of individuals who are normally chosen for positions in prison administration, particularly for those posts beneath the office of warden. Such appointments normally fall to a rather inferior grade of human being, usually as a part of the spoils system, and the salaries paid are not sufficient to act as an incentive to any competent person to seek the appointment. Mrs. O'Hare has thus admirably described these important, if regrettable, facts: [3]

[3] K. D. O'Hare, *In Prison*, p. 161.

Because public opinion concerns itself less with prisons than with any other sort of public institution except, perhaps, almshouses, prison management has for the most part fallen into the hands of the most ignorant and corrupt type of politicians, and prison jobs have become the dumping ground for the inefficient and unfit relatives and political hangers-on of the professional politicians. These human misfits and failures are thrust into prison jobs because, as a rule, they are too worthless for other employment. So far as I have been able to study them, I have found court bailiffs, jail turnkeys, prison guards, and prison matrons industrially unfit and generally illiterate human scrubs, mentally defective, morally perverted, and very often of much lower type than the prisoners whom they handle.

Starting with an inefficient and ignorant type of *homo sapiens* as the basis of the personnel of prison administration, we have to add to this the inevitably degrading and brutalizing aspects of the details of contemporary prison administration. The primary function of the prison warden is to act as an efficient jailer. It is not usually regarded as a part of his duty to bring about the reformation of the convict, except in so far as it is believed that this may be produced by the miseries inflicted through imprisonment. He is supposed, above all, to keep his subjects safely incarcerated during the period of their sentence, and his success as warden is measured very largely by the degree to which he is able to insure the minimum number of escapes and the least possible volume of friction and scandal. To achieve this he naturally turns to the most rudimentary conceptions of discipline and regimentation. He relies almost entirely upon rules and coercive administrative procedure. This prevents practically all possibility of sympathetic human contact with the inmates of the prison, and the system thus generates a purely mechanical spirit which brutalizes both the prison officials and the prisoners, and creates a fatal antipathy between these two groups. This severe prison regimentation, being widely different from the life of freedom to which the prisoner will ultimately be restored, constitutes the worst type of training, if indeed it can be called any training at all, for the responsibilities of citizenship. Frank Tannenbaum, in his interesting book, *Wall Shadows,* has well summarized the effect of this mechanical attitude, inseparable from the conception of a warden as a jailer, upon the development of prison cruelty as well as the unfortunate results of the system upon the prison population:[4]

The function of the prison is to keep the men confined. The function of the warden is to make sure that the purpose of the prison is fulfilled. He is primarily a jailer. That is *his* business. Reform, punishment, expiation for sin—these are social policies determined by social motives of which he, as jailer, becomes the agent. He is a jailer first; a reformer, a guardian, a disciplinarian, or anything else, second. Any one who has been in prison, or who knows the prison régime, through personal contact, will corrobate this fact. The whole administrative organization of the jail is centered on keeping the men inside the walls. Men in prison are always counted. They are counted morning, noon, and night. They are counted when they rise, when they eat, when they work, and when they sleep. Like a miser hovering over his jingling coins, the warden and the keepers are constantly on edge about the safety of their charges—a safety of numbers first, of well-being afterwards.

This leads to some very important consequences. It is the core of the development of prison brutality. It is the feeding basis upon which a number of other important elements tending in the direction of brutality depend. The warden is human. Being human, he is strongly inclined to follow the path of least resistance. And the path of least resistance, in the light of the ordinary understanding of a prison warden, is to make jail-breaking hard by making the individual prisoner helpless. . . .

[4] Op. cit., pp. 11-21.

Punishment takes the form of a greater isolation, of more suppression, and for the prisoner has the result of greater discontent, more bitterness, and the greater need for friendship, for communication, and the very pleasures of attempted association, in spite of opposition. This simply means that the more rules there are, the more violations there are bound to be; and the greater the number of violations, the more numerous the rules. The greater the number of violations, the more brutal the punishments; for variety of the punishments and their intensification become, in the mind of the warden, the sole means of achieving the intimidation of the prisoner by which he rules.

Brutality leads to brutality. It hardens official and inmate alike, and makes it the ordinary and habitual method of dealing with the criminal. It adds hatred to the prisoner's reaction against the individual official, and makes the individual official more fearful, more suspicious, more constantly alert, and develops in him a reaction of hatred against the prisoner, making the need for brutality greater and its use more natural. This general consequence holds true for the whole prison. The punishment of the individual prisoner develops within the whole prison a feeling of discontent and hatred because of the natural sympathy which the prisoners feel for one whom they know to be no more guilty than themselves; and particularly because solidarity of feeling is in proportion to individual physical helplessness. This adds to the tensity of the situation in the prison, adds fuel to the discontent, and makes the need for isolation in the light of the warden's disciplinary measures more justified, brutality more normal, hatred on the part of the prison group more constant, and irritation more general. . . .

The harshness, silence, twilight, discipline, hold true, not only for the prisoner, but also for the keeper. The keeper, too, is a prisoner. He is all day long in this atmosphere of tense emotional suppression and military discipline, and, in addition, he is generally there at least two nights a week when on special duty. He is a prisoner. For him there is little beyond the exercise of power. This exercise is a means of escape and outlet, but it is not a sufficient means. It does not make the keeper a happy person. It makes him a harsh and brutal one.

The brutality and grossness of male prison guards have long been recognized, but we have frequently supposed that matrons in the women's wards are of an altogether different type characterized by kindliness, sympathy, and insight. The following comments by Mrs. O'Hare on the nature of the matrons of the Missouri State Penitentiary are very illuminating on this point.[5]

The matrons were required to live in the prison and were never, except on rare leaves of absence, out of the sights and sounds and smells of prison. They were prisoners to almost the same degree that we were, and they all staggered under a load of responsibility far too great for their limited intelligence and untrained powers. They handled human beings at their worst, and under the worst possible conditions, and saw nothing day or night but sordid, ugly things ungilded by the glow of hope or love.

These women who were our keepers had missed love and wifehood; they had nothing to look back upon or forward to. There is a sort of stigma attached to their work that makes the possibilities of love and mating for them very limited indeed. The ordinary social relations of normal life were impossible for them, and they lived in a very inferno of loneliness and isolation. . . .

The conditions under which these prison matrons lived and did their work would have made harpies and shrews out of the finest types of women—and these certainly had never been fine types. For the conditions that place women of their attainments and character in such positions, the public is incontrovertibly responsible.

IV. PUNISHMENT AND THE PUBLIC MIND

Though it is usually overlooked in discussions of the psychological effects of prison administration, it is prob-

[5] Op. cit., pp. 162-3.

able that the most serious and disastrous aspects of modern prison cruelty are not those which affect the prisoners or the prison officials but rather the results of this system upon the public mind. In the first place, imprisonment supplies the present method of carrying out the revengeful spirit of outraged society, which thus secures satisfaction for the wrongs, real or alleged, that are brought upon it by the convict. In an earlier period of criminal justice culprits were punished by mob vengeance, and imprisonment is the present substitute for this more primitive technique. Along with this element of social protection expressed in a crude psychological form, there must be taken into consideration the fundamental sadistic and cruel tendencies of human groups, well analyzed by S. Sighele, E. D. Martin and others. The savagery of contemporary imprisonment offers a vicarious release of these sadistic traits under respectable and approved circumstances, whereas relatively few individuals would personally and individually find themselves able to carry out, or to admit themselves subject to, such obviously sadistic impulses. These points have been very well summarized by Bernard Shaw:[6]

It is said, and it is in a certain degree true, that if the Government does not lawfully organize and regulate popular vengeance, the populace will rise up and execute this vengeance lawlessly for itself. The standard defense of the Inquisition is that without it no heretic's life would have been safe. In Texas to-day the people are not satisfied with the prospect of knowing that a murderer and ravisher will be electrocuted inside a jail if a jury can resist the defense put up by his lawyer. They tear him from the hands of the sheriff, pour lamp oil over him, and burn him alive. Now the burning of human beings is not only an expression of outraged public morality: it is also a sport for which a taste can be acquired much more easily and rapidly than

[6] Preface to Webb, *English Prisons Under Local Government*, pp. xxiv-xxv.

a taste for coursing hares, just as a taste for drink can be acquired from brandy and cocktails more easily and rapidly than from beer or sauterne. Lynching mobs begin with Negro ravishers and murderers; but they presently go on to any sort of delinquent, provided he is black. Later on, as a white man will burn as amusingly as a black one, and a white woman react to tarring and feathering as thrillingly as a Negress, the color line is effaced by what professes to be a rising wave or virtuous indignation, but is in fact an epidemic of Sadism. The defenders of our penal system take advantage of it to assure us that if they did not torment and ruin a boy guilty of sleeping in the open air, the British public would rise and tear that boy limb from limb.

Along with the function of imprisonment as a means of manifesting social revenge and securing social protection, and as an "elegant" method of expressing collective sadism, there should be added the powerful factor of social catharsis which rests upon the age-old notion and symbol of the scapegoat. Our individual sense of guilt is drained off, and we inevitably feel a certain vicarious release and satisfaction at the conviction and imprisonment of an alleged culprit, who symbolically bears to the prison the sins of his social group. The insistence of those who wreck corporations, banks, and railroads, leaving a train of poverty-stricken widows and orphans, upon the necessity of solemn severity in the punishment of a man who has stolen a few dollars' worth of bread or cloth or failed to pay his debts admirably illustrates the operation of this mechanism.

Beyond all of these aspects of the function and effect of imprisonment upon the public mind must be mentioned the fact that at the present time crime and punishment have in them a high degree of publicity appeal, curiosity, and exhibitionism which arouse the more sordid emotions of the public and prevent it from having any intelligent insight into the basic questions and problems involved.

Then, our system of justice is not free from being exploited in the interests of the political and personal careers of those in charge of it. These factors have been admirably summarized by Mr. Mencken:[7]

If the criminal's art is irrational, then society's instinctive reaction to it is equally irrational. This fact blew up the work of the old-time criminologists. They accepted the current scheme of punishments, but tried to purge it of revenge. They found very quickly that revenge was an essential part of it—that no criminal would ever be brought to justice if there were not somebody in the background, full of strong feeling against him. When the crime that is proceeded against is one that seems to offer a menace to the general security—that is, when every citizen feels that he is himself in danger unless something is done about it—then that feeling is generally dispensed, and we have a spectacle such as was witnessed during the Leopold-Loeb trial, with a District Attorney applying all the art of forensics to the undoing of the accused, the press full of inflammatory stuff about them, and even the ambassadors of Christ snorting and bawling from the pulpit against them. It is idle to say that such a process is rational. It is as full of pure emotion as a necking match. Its aim is to discharge emotions, to achieve a communal orgasm, not to establish and enforce a scientific fact.

There is even more to it than this. Criminal trials, if they are gory and obscene enough, make capital shows—perhaps the best shows that the average human being can imagine. They offer hunting in the grand manner; the quarry is man. They thus take on something of the character of war, and are just as powerful in their emotional appeal. To convert them into scientific investigations, entirely calm and impersonal, would be as grave an offense against the public happiness as to enforce Prohibition. Thus, even when *mòbile vulgus* is not enraged against the criminal, and hence eager to see him barbarously used, it is delighted by the battle that goes on over him. Such battles make heroes. The

[7] *American Mercury,* January, 1925, pp. 122-3.

District Attorney, if he wins, is sure to be elected to higher office; some of our most eminent statesmen got their starts that way: the names of Hughes, Folk and Brandeis come to mind at once. And if the District Attorney loses, then the counsel for the defense is the hero.

V. THE SOLUTION

These psychological characteristics of society's attitude toward crime and punishment thus quite apparently create attitudes which obstruct, if they do not entirely prevent, any true appreciation of the real problems involved in the detection, conviction, and treatment of the criminal. The psychological attitudes which prevail are in their core identical with the reactions of primitive man to those who violated the taboos and mores of tribal society. Society's reactions are almost entirely emotional and scarcely at all intellectual. Joined to this is the fact that the cruelties of present-day imprisonment are for the most part screened from the concrete and specific knowledge of the public. The individual can endure, can even get satisfaction out of, contemplating punishment in the abstract, but he tends to recoil in the face of concrete and specific pain and suffering, except when a member of a mob or when in personal danger. It is for this reason that we have outbursts of public indignation against prison officials following every sporadic revelation of unusual cruelty in a particular penal institution. As Shaw well suggests, much of the hideous nature of present-day penal institutions is due, not so much to our specific intent as to the fact that they have grown up unconsciously without our full knowledge:[8]

We must, however, be on our guard against ascribing all the villainy of our system to our cruelty and selfish terrors. That would be inconsistent with the fact that, as I have

[8] Loc. cit., p. lviii.

pointed out, the operation of the criminal law is made very uncertain, and therefore loses the deterrence it aims at, by the reluctance of the sympathetic people to hand over offenders to the police. Vindictive and frivolous as we are, we are not downright fiends, as we should be if our modern prison system had been deliberately invented and constructed by us all in one piece. It has grown upon us, and grown evilly, having evil roots; but its worst developments have been well meant; for the road to hell is paved with good intentions, not with bad ones.

This being the case, it is quite obvious that one of the most direct methods of assaulting and alleviating the cruelties of the present system of prison administration will be found in making more frequent and more specific and concrete the revelations of contemporary abuses. It is here that books like Tannenbaum's *Wall Shadows,* Mrs. O'Hare's *In Prison,* and Fishman's *Crucibles of Crime* perform a useful educational function.

SELECTED REFERENCES

Anonymous. *In the Clutch of Circumstance.*

Berkman, A. *Prison Memoirs of an Anarchist.*

Briggs, L. O. *Reformatory Reform.*

Fishman, J. F. *Crucibles of Crime.*

Gordon, M. *Prison Discipline.*

Hobhouse, S., and Brockway, A. F. *English Prisons Today.*

Nitsche, P., and Willmanns, K. *History of the Prison Psychoses.*

O'Hare, K. D. *In Prison.*

Osborne, T. M. *Within Prison Walls.*

Shaw, B. Preface to Webb, *English Prisons Under Local Government.*

Tannenbaum, F. *Wall Shadows.*

Whitlock, B. *The Turn of the Balance.*

CHAPTER IX

Trial by Jury

MR. CROWE: That [Dr. W. A. White's record as a psychiatrist] is objected to as incompetent, irrelevant, and immaterial. The only purpose of it will be to lay a foundation for him to testify as an expert on the question of the sanity or insanity of the defendants. On a plea of guilty, your honor has no right to go into that question. As soon as it appears in the trial it is your honor's duty to call a jury. . . . I insist that the question of sanity or insanity is a matter under the law for a jury. . . . From the moment you hear evidence on insanity everything you do becomes of no effect under the law, and this becomes a mock trial.—*Chicago Tribune,* July 31, 1924.

I. ORIGIN OF JURIES

Consciously or unconsciously, the learned attorney for the State, if he had exhausted a day in formal argument and exposition, could not have more thoroughly evinced the utter bankruptcy of his scientific knowledge and the totally archeological nature of his juristic concepts and orientation. . . .

Walter Bagehot is said to have remarked that the chief cure for admiration for the English House of Lords was to go and give it an ocular inspection. It is equally true that in most cases we can be cured of our reverence for contemporary social institutions by a casual investigation of their history. What has been viewed hitherto as a gigantic example of divine solicitude, condescension and revelation appears upon research to be but a clumsy and awkward product of centuries of historic evolution, embodying, like the great rock formations, a vast number of fossil and vestigial remains, many of them quite as anachronistic today as the theory of the four humors or medieval astrology. Of no other institution is this more true than of the jury as an instrument for the ascertainment of the guilt or innocence of men accused of crime.

We have not space here for a thorough review of the history of the jury, such as might be founded upon the illuminating researches of Brunner, Pollock, Maitland, Thayer and Haskins, but we may point out briefly the salient facts in the matter. In the first place, more than ninety-nine per cent of human history was passed without any such institution as the jury having a place in criminal procedure. It had, indeed, a very recent origin. Even the highly developed Roman jurisprudence knew it not. Its beginnings in late medieval times in Western Europe were due as much to accident as to design. During the greater part of the Middle Ages the ordeal, trial by battle and compurgation were the most widely used devices for ascertaining the guilt of the accused. But early in the period the political, rather than the juristic, conditions of the times were evolving machinery which, though far removed in its origin from court procedure, was destined ultimately to beget the modern jury.

Its remote origins are to be found in the nature of the *fiscus,* which was related to the royal revenue jurisdiction in imperial Rome. This power was carried over by the Franks, to whom the royal lands were known as fiscal lands. Among the more important administrative business of the Frankish Empire was the inquiry into royal rights, and particularly into disputes over royal lands. In order to establish his rights the King would frequently direct an *inquisitio,* or inquiry into the actual state of affairs. The matter was usually settled after conversations and adjustments between the royal representatives and private citizens. In due time the *inquisitio* was extended still further. The King's representatives would summon a group of leading citizens and extract from them an opinion or statement as to the taxable wealth of their community, the state of the public order, and the prevalence of offenses against the King and his laws. This group of citizens or neighbors was known as a *jurata* and its report to the King or his representatives was called a *veredictum.* Here we have in embryo both the terminology and the procedure of the modern jury.

This first stage of its development, as primarily an administrative rather than a juristic instrument, was most perfectly realized by the Normans, who took the practice to England in 1066. There the royal inquisition soon came to be known as an assize. Exactly a century after the landing of William the Conqueror, namely, at the famous Assize of Claredon in 1166, the grand jury took definite form. A varying number of country gentlemen and burghers were summoned before the royal representatives and compelled to tell whether they knew of anyone accused of crime in the neighborhood. At least twelve of those summoned had to agree as to the accuracy of the report in order to secure royal action. That so large a number was summoned was due to the fact that in the case of powerful violators of the King's peace a single individual feared to make accusation. This jury of accusation, which appeared shortly after the middle of the twelfth century, was, of course, the grand jury rather than the trial or petit jury of today. Those accused of crime by it were commonly subjected to the ordeal or duel in order to ascertain their guilt, though as early as 1166, in certain civil cases, Henry II is said to have allowed the accused to decline trial by battle and resort to a crude form of jury trial. The development of the trial jury, as we know it, however, was delayed for half a century or more.

The thing which did more than anything else to establish it was Innocent III's condemnation of the ordeal in 1215. This strong pronouncement of the Church against the prevalent method of ascertaining guilt led to the gradual substitution of the jury trial, which made its appearance in England by the close of the first quarter of the thirteenth century. At first, it was rather common for the grand jury also to act as a trial jury, but in due time the two bodies came to be definitely separated in composition and function. For a century or so a person who preferred to do so might decline a jury trial and resort to trial by battle or accept torture. The incentive in these cases was the fact that conviction by a jury led to the seizure of the property of the accused and the possible destitution of his relatives. Trial by battle was gradually outlawed, but torture remained legal to the close of the eighteenth century. In the early juries there had been no definite uniformity as to numbers, with the exception that usually twelve of those chosen were compelled to agree before a decision could be made, but in the course of time the English jury came to consist definitely of twelve "good men and true." The choice of the number twelve unquestionably was based upon Scriptural precedent, and the primordial jury was clearly related to the earlier device of compurgation, by which, in the absence of direct evidence, twelve friends of the accused could swear to their belief in the veracity of the defendant when he was protesting his innocence. The Holy Spirit was assumed to hover in close proximity to the compurgators, and when the jury developed it was believed that It watched with equal solicitude over the decisions of jurymen. The Holy Ghost was supposed to be particularly favorable to the number twelve because of the fact that there had been twelve tribes of Israel and Twelve Apostles. It is probably only an accident that the sacred Hebrew number seven was not chosen instead of twelve. A definite deterrent advantage might certainly have arisen had the choice fallen on the number thirteen! The following quotation from *Duncomb's Trials* (1665) gives a good idea of the mystical and theological attitude towards the number twelve as applied to the jury system:

> As to the sanctity and foreordained character of the number twelve, and first as to their (the jury's) number twelve; and this number is no less esteemed by our law than by Holy Writ. If the Twelve Apostles on their twelve thrones must try us in our eternal state, good reason hath the law to appoint the number twelve to try our temporal. The tribes of Israel were twelve; the Patriarchs were twelve, and Solomon's officers were twelve (1 Kings IV, 7). Therefore, not only matters of fact were tried by twelve, but in ancient times twelve judges were to try matters in law. In the Exchequer Chambers there were twelve counsellors of state for matters of state and he that appealed to the law must have eleven others with him who believe he says true and the law is so precise in their number of twelve that if the trial be by more or less than twelve it is a mistrial.

At the outset the trial jury performed the functions of the present jury plus that of the witnesses. The jurymen were usually men who had knowledge of the facts in question and they based their verdict upon their own information or judgment. By the opening of the fifteenth century in England, however, the jury was gradually transformed into a body which founded its decisions mainly upon evidence supplied by witnesses. For a considerable period the only witnesses summoned were those for the prosecution, and the defendant was at a distinct disadvantage. Gradually, however, he was given the right, under progressively lessened handicaps, to call upon witnesses to testify in his behalf. Along with this went the development of rules of evidence, of the right to challenge jurymen, and of improved methods of impanelling the jury. The rules of evidence and the court-room procedure which prevail today are a curious mosaic, embodying elements which originated as early as the fourteenth century in juxtaposition to such highly novel devices as the summoning of trained psychiatrists to aid judges and juries in their decisions. The modern rules of evidence and procedure, in other words, present a recapitulation of the entire history of trial by jury.

It should be quite evident from even this brief and casual sketch that the jury is far from the divinely created and sanctioned bulwark of human liberty which right-thinking men now suppose it to be. It took its origin in a non-juridical field and was clumsily adapted to its present purpose simply because nothing better was at hand. Far from being a rampart of human freedom or safeguard of democracy, it was in its origins one of the most potent and highly prized instruments of royal absolutism and monarchial oppression. Compared to other institutions of the time, trial by jury probably made a fairly respectable showing in the sixteenth century, when there were relatively few highly trained lawyers, and the men summoned for jury service represented the intelligent and cultured upper class. But the progress of medical knowledge, sociology and jurisprudence, and democracy since that time has made it as preposterous and out of date as the sun dial of James I or the coach of Charles II. Moreover, the average jury is today chosen from an altogether less intelligent class than that which furnished jurymen in the sixteenth century.

II. INCOMPETENCE OF JURIES

The complete futility and inadequacy of the trial by jury can be best indicated by a brief analysis of the actual procedure from the impanelling of the jury to the rendering of the verdict. The selection of the panel is determined by lot, the names of a definite number of citizens being drawn at random from a collection of slips or cards bearing the names of all the qualified citizens of the county. At best, any such panel can only at rare intervals include a better than average group of citizens. It cannot be limited to those possessing unusual intelligence or special knowledge of criminal matters. In the usual case, the panel is made up of an average collection of farmers, shoemakers, barbers, plumbers, clerks, drummers, hodcarriers, and day laborers, with a few professional or business men sprinkled among them. In many cases, of course, the theory of a choice by lot has become a legal fiction, and accommodating commissioners of juries are willing, for a reasonable consideration, to draw the names of the men desired by district-attorneys or lawyers for the defense. Such selected panels are by no means rare, and when one of them supplies a jury the outcome of the trial is assured before a single witness has been summoned. Even when a panel is honestly selected it fulfils exactly the democratic doctrine that special training is in no way essential to competence in the handling of public affairs. It is drawn from precisely the classes from which a mob might be raised by the Ku Klux Klan.

In the choice of the actual jury from the panel we observe the operation of a process that may be called counter-selection. The obviously more intelligent and abler members, drawn from the business and professional classes, are for the most part automatically excused from service, leaving only the farmers, cobblers, barbers, clerks, hodcarriers and day-laborers. These men are questioned forthwith as to whether they have read about or formed any opinion concerning the case. Those who answer in the affirmative are likewise automatically disqualified. It is quite apparent that in regard to any significant case any honest man possessing a modicum of literacy is compelled to give an affirmative answer to this interrogation.

Hence, the actual choice of jurymen is limited for the most part to the illiterates and the liars.

Naturally, the attorneys on the two sides desire to obtain a jury which will be *a priori* as favorable as possible to their sides. Therefore, they challenge all jurymen who, because of party affiliation, religious belief, class membership or nationality may possibly be against them. If the defendant is a prominent Democrat, the district attorney will naturally desire a Republican jury, and a Catholic defendant suggests immediately the desirability of having a heavy representation of Methodists and Baptists. If a so-called Red is on trial the district attorney endeavors to get a jury of bank-clerks and stock-brokers, while the counsel for the defense labors to secure veniremen who admire W. Z. Foster. The liberal legal arrangements for challenging without cause, and the practically unlimited right of challenging *for* cause, make this manœuvring easy. Only an exactly equal balancing of knowledge and wits on the part of the approving barristers can prevent it. The jury chosen is thus often either "fixed," "hand-picked" or composed of the most colorless and feeble-minded of the illiterates and liars.

The jury, after a few days of bewilderment in the new and strange atmosphere, settles down into a state of mental paralysis which makes it practically impossible for the majority of its members to concentrate intelligently and alertly upon the testimony and the rulings of the court. At best, it is in a state of distraction and absent-mindedness. The farmer wonders whether his hens are being fed or his horses properly bedded down, and the drummer bemoans his lost sales and "dates." Awakened from time to time from this stupor and these fantasies by the unusual beauty, volubility, resonance or obscenity of the witnesses and testimony, the jurymen suddenly pounce upon some more or less irrelevant bit of testimony and forget or overlook the most significant facts divulged by the witnesses. Thus we have, in a typical jury trial, the testimony of the witnesses and the rulings of the judge presented to a group of colorless men drawn from the least intelligent elements in the population at a time when they have lapsed into a mental state which practically paralyzes the operation of their normally feeble intellects.

The situation as regards the testimony itself is scarcely more satisfactory. Psychologists, following the pioneer work of Münsterberg, have proved time and again that the most honest and intelligent eye-witnesses, having observed an act in question leisurely and directly, are unable to testify about it with any degree of exactitude or unanimity. The testimony normally produced in a courtroom is incomparably inferior to that brought forth in carefully controlled psychological tests. There is usually a paucity of eye-witnesses, and those that actually exist are rarely persons of intelligence. Quite as likely as not they are among the "undesirable citizens" of the place, who would not be believed under oath if they were disgorging from any other vantage point than the witness-chair. But even these inferior persons with their inadequate information are rarely allowed to testify in a straightforward fashion. The technical rules of evidence often prevent their being permitted to tell the most pertinent things they know. On the other hand, counsel may seduce them into making all sorts of vague insinuations about things of which they know practically nothing.

But even this is not the worst of it. As everyone who is not absolutely innocent of court procedure knows, witnesses are usually as carefully coached by counsel as prize speakers in a rhetorical contest. Very frequently the "best" type of witness is one who knows absolutely nothing about the case and so may be coached from the beginning to tell a coherent story. Convictions or confessions of perjury in all sorts of cases, from the celebrated

Mooney case to the recent case of Sacco and Vanzetti have demonstrated the frequency of this building up of "impressive" testimony by counsel and witness without the slightest factual basis. It is one of the marvels and injustices of our criminal procedure that in the case of a conviction of perjury the witness alone, instead of the witness and counsel together, is compelled to suffer the penalty of the law. But even if we had the most accurate testimony by witnesses of the highest intelligence and undisputed veracity, its value and significance would be practically lost upon the illiterate, inattentive and distracted jury. Hence, the outcome is essentially this: a body of individuals of average or less than average ability who could not tell the truth if they wanted to, who usually have little of the truth to tell, who are not allowed to tell even all of that, and who are frequently instructed to fabricate voluminously and unblushingly, present this largely worthless, wholly worthless, or worse than worthless information to twelve men who are for the most part unconscious of what is being divulged to them, and would be incapable of an intelligent interpretation of the information if they heard it.

In case there is intelligent, pertinent and damaging testimony and a few competent and alert jurymen have slipped by the lawyers during the period of challenging the jury, an attempt is made by the lawyer whose side seems likely to lose by this testimony to obscure its significance and divert the attention of the jurymen from it. Every form of inflammatory oratorical appeal is permitted by the rules and every type of effort to stir the prejudices of the jurymen. The jury may even be covertly threatened with mob reprisal if it does not render a certain type of verdict. Particularly in closing appeals is this rhetorical gaudiness utilized. If the evidence is strongly unfavorable to one party, the lawyer representing it is likely to ignore the testimony altogether and to appeal solely to the emotions of the jury. And it need not be said that to the average jury an emotional appeal is far more potent than a factual demonstration. Mr. Wellman thus describes the contribution to juridical objectivity and scientific criminological accuracy by one J. J. Parker, a venerable and learned barrister of Mobile, Alabama:

Once, while he was defending a case in the criminal court in Mobile and during the argument of the prosecuting attorney, who was a rather prosy man, Parker moved his chair around so as to be under the judge's desk and behind the speaker, so that neither could see him. But he was in full sight of the jury. After a short time he began to nod his head as though very drowsy, and to tilt his chair back until it looked as if he would fall backwards. He would then make a little start and right his chair, and then pretend to go to sleep again, much to the amusement of the jury. The prosecutor realized that something was going on to distract the attention of the jury, because their faces were covered with broad grins in spite of his solemn argument. Finally Parker lost his balance and fell over backwards, making a good deal of commotion. The bystanders, who had been enjoying the scene as much as the jurors, broke into uncontrollable laughter, which was joined in by the jury, and the prosecutor's argument was completely destroyed.

Perhaps the most instructive thing about the modern jury trial is that neither the district-attorney nor the counsel for the defense is vitally interested about the hard facts. The district-attorney commonly desires to convict whether the defendant is innocent or not, and the counsel for defense desires an acquittal whether his client is guilty or not. Moreover, it is the jury which invites the lavish use of money in hiring expensive counsel to obscure facts and create fiction—that transition which Hobhouse describes as the substitution of battle by purse for the ancient battle by person. Before a group of trained experts the vaporings of high-priced counsel of the variety of Martin Littleton would have about as much standing as the pulpit gymnastics of Billy Sunday.

The technical rulings of law are as ineffective before the jury as is the testimony. The average juryman is abjectly ignorant of even the most elementary law, and almost invariably misses the significance of the judge's interpretations of it. Even in those cases where the rulings are simple, explicit and direct, the jury often brazenly and defiantly ignores them. A writer cites an interesting case where a judge instructed the jury to bring in a verdict in a certain manner unless they felt that they knew more about the law than he did. Astonished when they disregarded his advice, he reminded them of his charge. Whereupon the foreman responded; "Well, jedge, I reckon we considered that point, too." Especially futile are the rulings with respect to the rejection of evidence that has been actually presented. If a juryman has been impressed with testimony, in not one case out of ten will he be influenced by a subsequent ruling of the judge that it is irrelevant and must be excluded from consideration.

The burlesque upon science and justice which trial by jury thus presents is carried from the court-room to the room where the jury deliberates. Here it is free to, and frequently does, ignore absolutely all the instructions of the judge and all the testimony presented, and comes to its decision upon the basis of the prejudices of the members. In a recent notorious murder trial in New Jersey the jury frankly disregarded all the testimony, knelt in prayer, and then found a unanimous verdict for the defendant. The case was unique only in regard to the frankness of the jury's confession of the method it pursued and the publicity which that confession received in the press. Even in cases where a jury is reasonably alert in following the testimony, the desirable results of such an unusual phenomenon are likely to be destroyed by the presence upon the panel of a powerful and impressive personality or an unusually stubborn moron. There are innumerable cases of a miscarriage of justice due to the conversion of the jury to the point of view of a prejudiced but convincing orator or to the presence of a juror who through bias, bribery or stupidity has held out against the judgment of his eleven colleagues. And even the most elementary psychology makes it clear that though we had twelve able men on the jury they could rarely come to a concise, definite and well-reasoned agreement upon the basis of a study of the same body of facts.

We have thus the spectacle of a "fixed" or "selected" jury, or one of colorless liars and illiterates deciding the matter of the corporeal existence, public reputation, property rights or personal freedom of a fellow-man upon the basis of prayer, lottery, rhetoric, debate, stubbornness or intimidation, in ignorance or defiance of legal rulings which they do not understand and of testimony, perhaps dishonest, which they have only imperfectly followed, and from an intelligent comprehension of which they have been diverted by the fervid emotional appeals of counsel. If one were to protest against the accuracy of this picture by the counter-allegation that most verdicts are nevertheless sound and that such a result could scarcely be expected from so grotesque a procedure as we have described, the first answer suggested would be the query as to how one knows a particular verdict is a correct one. The majority of our convicted murderers go to the chair bawling protestations of innocence, while many obviously guilty ones are freed. There being under our system an opportunity only for a verdict of guilty or not guilty, by the mathematical laws of chance verdicts should be right in fifty per cent of all cases, taking a sufficiently large number of cases and extending them over an adequate period of time. Surely there is no person of reasonable *IQ,* sanity and literacy who would contend that more than half of our jury verdicts are accurate, or that the majority of those which are sound are such for any other reason than pure chance. An equally satisfactory result might be obtained far less expensively and in a more expeditious and dignified manner by resort to dice or the roulette wheel. I should be quite willing to defend the thesis that, in so far as certainty and accuracy are concerned, the modern jury trial is not a whit superior to the ordeal or trial by battle.

That the juridical joke perpetrated by the jury often follows them out of the court room is borne out by a not unusual episode, the accuracy of which can be vouched for by the writer. A jury in a leading eastern state about a decade ago decided the fate of a woman accused of murder, of which she was found guilty. The jury proved an unusually congenial group who regretted greatly the fact that they ultimately had to disband and return to their ordinary drab daily pursuits. But they decided to commemorate properly their emotional affinity and cordiality, and to renew the memory of their cheerful and convivial association. Hence, they formed the Mrs. X— Jury Picnic Association, and have since met once each year for a rollicking and vociferous outing at a lakeside amusement park and emporium, the joy of which is not a whit abated by the fact that less than three miles away the recipient and beneficiary of their juristic acumen and sagacity withers under the stony stare of "Copper John," as the symbolic figure surmounting the top of the state prison structure is conventionally christened.

When, through accident or the grace of God, the jury happens to return an accurate and sound verdict the chances are about even that it will be set aside by the court on the ground of some hair-splitting technicality. Mr. Mark O. Prentiss in a recent interesting article in the New York Times *Current History Magazine* for October 1925, gives an interesting collection of the sacrifice of justice in the interest of "pin-head jurisprudence":

A defendant was convicted under an indictment charging the theft of $100, "lawful money." The conviction was set aside because the indictment did not say "lawful money of the United States." The court gave as the reason for granting the defendant a new trial that the victim might have been carrying around Mexican money.

A defendant was convicted of stealing a pistol under an indictment which described the pistol as a "Smith & Weston" revolver. A new trial was granted because the proof showed that the defendant stole a "Smith & Wesson" revolver.

In Chicago, a notorious criminal known as "Eddie the Immune" was convicted of stealing $59. There was never the shadow of a doubt as to his guilt. The verdict was set aside on appeal because the jury did not find the amount stolen.

In Georgia a defendant was convicted under an indictment which charged that he stole a hog that had a slit out of its right ear and a clip out of the left. The appellate court granted the defendant a new trial because, while it was proved that the defendant stole the hog, the evidence disclosed that it was a hog with a slit out of its left ear and a clip out of its right ear.

In another case where a defendant was convicted of a serious crime the conviction was set aside by the higher court because the word "the" was left out of the concluding phrase of the indictment, "against the peace and dignity of the State."

In another case a defendant was convicted of stealing a pair of boots. The judgment of the trial court was set aside by the higher court, because it appeared that while the defendant had stolen two boots, he had stolen two rights.

In yet another case a conviction for larceny was set aside because the indictment averred that it occurred in a "storehouse" when it should have used the word "storeroom."

In a Montana case a verdict of guilty of larceny was set aside on appeal because the trial judge instructed the jury that it must find intent to steal instead of a criminal intent.

Under another absurd ruling a conviction for stealing was set aside because there was no proof that 800 pounds of cotton was a thing of value.

In yet another case involving some offense along a public road the conviction was set aside because, while the proof showed that the road had been used for thirty years as a public road, it did not show that the road had ever been formally dedicated to the public.

There are a few examples of the absurdly technical holdings of the courts which have delayed the punishment of crime, in many cases absolutely defeated it, and have brought contempt upon the administration of justice.

There is an Alabama case which held that the omission of the letter "I" from the word "malice" in an indictment for assault with intent to murder rendered the indictment bad, and the conviction of a defendant under that indictment was set aside.

In another Alabama case it was held that an indictment charging that murder had been committed "with malice aforethou" did not allege "malice aforethought," and that the indictment was legally insufficient. The court noted in that case: "Great precision should be observed in matters which vitally affect the life and liberty of the citizen." In England the judge would simply have corrected the indictment with his pen and gone on with the case.

In another Alabama case a defendant was charged in the indictment with stealing a cow. The evidence proved him guilty of stealing a bull. In either event the defendant was guilty of grand larceny. The higher court, however, set aside the judgment of conviction.

In another case the defendant was charged with stealing eleven cow hides. The higher court said: "There was a total absence of evidence that the hides stolen were cow hides. Non constat, they were horse hides, or hides of some other animal than that of the cow kind." The sentence of the lower court in that case was set aside, although the evidence showed that the defendant in that case was guilty of grand larceny.

III. CRIMINOLOGY BECOMES SCIENTIFIC

The amusing but tragic travesty which almost invariably accompanies a jury trial is due, chiefly, of course, to our democratic hallucination as to the intellectual acumen, information, and judgment of the average specimen of *Homo sapiens,* and to our entirely wrong-headed and antiquated concepts in regard to society's proper attitude toward the criminal. Hitherto, our criminal justice has been concerned almost entirely with the crime and its commission and not with the criminal and his personality. Modern criminal science repudiates this mode of approach. It is the criminal and not the crime which must be primarily considered, whether we emphasize the reformation of the criminal or the protection of society. The nature of the criminal personality is the point of attack for the rational criminologist, and there is no greater scientific fallacy extant today than that which was urged so tenaciously by Mr. Crowe and his associates in the recent Chicago trial, namely, that the penalty should be made to fit the crime. Only in a very limited degree is the crime any real criterion of the potential danger of the criminal to society or of the possibility of his reformation. The California Bluebeard, J. P. Watson, who was discovered some four years ago to have killed at least nine wives, was potentially less dangerous to society than a low-grade feebleminded boy whose chief offense to date has been the pilfering of marbles and candy. Mr. Watson, under proper therapeutic treatment, could probably have been cured of his compulsion neurosis in a couple of years and restored as a safe member of society, but every criminally inclined imbecile is an incurable potential murderer as long as he lives, even though he may never commit any crime during his entire career.

Accepting, then, as basic the notion that we should deal with the personality of the criminal and not with his alleged act, it immediately becomes apparent that criminology is a highly complex technical subject. To be successfully pursued it requires the collaboration of biologists, psychologists, psychiatrists and social workers. Obviously, its problems are not to be entrusted to lawyers or to the sort of men who serve on juries. The jury-room is no more a place for the functioning of the common man than the operating-room of a hospital, the designing-room of the American Bridge Company or the research laboratory of the General Electric Company. Least of all can we rationally entrust the decision in a case of alleged insanity to the average man. Imagine, for example, a group of plumbers, barbers and the like being assembled before a class of medical students to diagnose a case of inflammation of the pancreas, or gallstones, or tumor of the uterus. Such a grotesque absurdity would be exactly comparable to the burlesque of calling a jury to decide upon the insanity of a defendant in a criminal case were it not that the determination of insanity is often a much more difficult and subtle task than the diagnosis of a physical disease. If Mr. Crowe desired to have himself laughed out of the society of rational men, he could have furnished no better ground than his plea for a jury to determine the mental state of Loeb and Leopold.

The following account from the Boston *Post* of the expeditious trial of Dr. Thiery in Boston in the spring of 1925 indicates what can be done through the coöperation of an honest judge, district attorney and counsel for the defense, even when all three are still formally handicapped by the presence of a jury. The contrast between this procedure and the long days of legal bluster and subterfuge which characterized the trial of Loeb and Leopold is a fair example of what it costs us in terms of both money and scientific accuracy to maintain the archaic legal and rhetorical duel which is basic in modern criminal jurisprudence and procedure. And it also proves that it is the lawyers as much as the jury that need curbing, as the Thiery case was conducted with a jury formally present while Loeb and Leopold were tried without a jury before an intelligent and open-minded judge:

> Dr. Raymond D. Thiery of Somerville, confessed slayer of his brother-in-law, David M. Noble, because "God directed him and everybody wished it," last night was under guard at the Bridgewater State Hospital for the Insane, where he was committed for life by Judge James M. Sisk of the Middlesex Superior Criminal Court yesterday.
>
> A constant vigil is to be kept over Thiery because of fears that he will attempt to take his own life.
>
> The trial of the confessed slayer lasted less than two hours yesterday, and the jury, at the instruction of Judge Sisk, returned a verdict of "not guilty by reason of insanity." Assistant District Attorney Robert M. Bushnell, who conducted the State's case, declared the government was not opposed to such a verdict. He stated that the government at no time has been able to find a motive for the slaying.
>
> Judge Sisk's instructions to the jury followed immediately after the remarkable confession of Dr. Thiery regarding the crime was disclosed in the court room. In his confession, which was made to alienists, the doctor showed no remorse for his act, it was stated, but believed his act a righteous one and one that Noble, could he speak, would be thankful for.
>
> Three alienists testified that Dr. Thiery was a "constitutional psychopathic inferior." A letter from Dr. L. Vernon Briggs, noted specialist on mental diseases, in which he stated it as his belief that Dr. Thiery was insane at the time of the slaying and still is insane, was read.

Modern criminal science, indeed, makes it clear that a lawyer is a wholly improper person to have any dealings whatever with criminals. He is as much out of place in the criminal court-room as he would be in the hospital or the chemical laboratory. Of course, we shall probably need legal forms and prescriptions for the conduct of the new criminology, in the same way that we now have legal regulation of medical practice and hospital organization, but the lawyer is not today thought to have any proper function in the bacteriological institute, the psychiatric clinic or the observation ward of a hospital. We can, perhaps, tolerate the presence of a judge, but we can safely assume that all the legal guidance necessary may be supplied by this judge without the assistance of prosecuting attorneys or lawyers for the defense. The legal profession, of course, will not welcome any proposal, however scientific and logical, which will forthwith remove a considerable portion of its professional income. But this obstacle, in due time, will be worn down, as it has been in the past in connection with the progress of scientific knowledge in other fields. We have taken the practice of medicine from shamans, and surgery from barbers, and in time we shall take criminology from the legal profession. No unprejudiced and informed person can deny the need for this reform, for it is probably true that the average contemporary barber is better equipped to perform a major surgical operation than the average lawyer is to deal scientifically and efficiently with criminals.

The new criminology will delegate the study and treatment of the criminal to a permanent group of experts under the leadership of trained and enlightened psychiatrists. Such a group will not be concerned primarily with the mere legal guilt of the person accused. Guilt of criminal action will be regarded only as a symptom of initial significance. Accusation and guilt will be viewed chiefly as means of bringing a criminal personality into the custody of scientists. The important question will be the menace of the individual to society and the possibility of so treating him as to eliminate that menace. If it is found that his personality is such as to make it permanent and serious, he will be segregated for life, whether he has committed a multiple murder or stolen a bag of peanuts. On the other hand, many a person who has committed a murder will be committed to a sanitarium for treatment, with the expectancy of his ultimate release to a life of freedom if his motivating compulsive disorder is of the type which promises recovery under treatment.

Those who allege that the new criminology will not offer adequate social protection argue badly and in a circle. Surely no person would contend that our present criminal jurisprudence in the United States offers adequate protection against, say, crimes of violence. A careful statistical study by the Metropolitan Life Insurance Company has recently shown that there is only one execution to every one hundred and forty-six homicides in this country and that our homicide rate is seventeen times as high as that of England. There is now being launched an hysterical campaign against lawlessness and crime. The new criminology will prescribe a technique and procedure which will be much more effective than even the English procedure. For the first time in the history of criminal jurisprudence there will be a group of individuals actually interested in the real facts about crime and capable of making use of them in an intelligent manner. It will no longer be a matter of gubernatorial ambitions on the part of the district-attorney or fees and reputation for the counsel for the defense. The new system will go beyond Chief Vollmer in urging improvements in our police, so as to make the discovery of crime and the subsequent retribution swift and sure. It will advocate devices to discover in advance of criminal action the existence of personalities likely to become menaces to society. In the case of a young person suffering from incipient dementia-præcox we do not insist upon waiting until he has assassinated his grandmother with a bread-knife before we commit him to an institution. Likewise, it is not invariably necessary to wait until a potential murderer has committed his crime before he is detected and segregated. Many will allege that it will be very difficult to discover such potential criminals in advance, but it may be retorted that it is equally difficult to discover persons who are spreading contagious diseases. Yet it is only as we succeed in this last that we are capable of giving any reality and value to preventive medicine. In all probability, arrest by ever more scientifically trained police will remain a major method of bringing the criminal to the attention of psychiatrists, but a greater and greater percentage of anticipations will be realized through mental hygienic clinics, compulsory mental testing, and the extension of psychiatry into the work of the public-schools.

Even more, the scientific criminology will emphasize the necessity of sterilizing and segregating that class which produces many of our potential criminals, namely, the feeble-minded. There will be no more time sentences; the period of segregation will depend entirely upon the progress made toward the cure of the disorder which motivates and precipitates criminal conduct. The same criteria will guide our procedure that governs it today with respect to the release of patients from hospitals for the insane.

How far we actually are from any prospect of a practical realization of the goal of the abolition of the jury nuisance is to be seen in the following eulogy of the jury by so distinguished and experienced a jurist as the late Joseph H. Choate. It is probable that nothing short of a veritable avalanche of crime and unrepressed criminals will suffice to overcome the inertia of legal tradition and the vested interests of the criminal lawyers:

The truth is that the jury system is so fixed as an essential part of our political institutions; it has proved itself to be such an invaluable security for the enjoyment of liberty and property for so many centuries; it is so justly appreciated as the best and perhaps the only known means of admitting the people to a share in maintaining their wholesome interest in the administration of justice; it is such an indispensable factor in educating them in their personal and civil rights; it affords such a school and education in the law to the profession itself, and is so embedded in our constitutions, which declare that it shall remain forever inviolate, requiring an amendment to alter it,—that there may be no substantial ground for fear that any of us will live to see the people consent to give it up. I cherish, as a result of a life's work now nearing its end, that the old-fashioned trial by jury of twelve honest and intellectual citizens remains today, all suggested innovations and amendments to the contrary, the best and safest practical manner for the determination of facts as the basis of judgment of courts, and that all attempts to tinker or tamper with it should be discouraged as disastrous to the public welfare.

SELECTED REFERENCES

Brunner, H. *Die Entstehung der Schwurgerichte.*

Clemens, S. L., and Warner, C. D. *The Gilded Age,* Chaps. LIV-LVIII.

Dreiser, T. *An American Tragedy,* Book III.

Haskins, C. H. *Studies in Norman Institutions.*

Hobhouse, L. T. *Morals in Evolution,* Chap. III.

Parmelee, M. *Anthropology and Sociology in Their Relation to Criminal Procedure.*

Pollock and Maitland. *A History of English Law.*

Smith, Eugene. *Criminal Law in the United States.*

Smith, R. H. *Justice and the Poor.*

Thayer, J. B. *The History of Trial by Jury.*

Wellman, F. L. *Gentlemen of the Jury.*

Williams, E. H. *The Expert in Court.*

CHAPTER X

Recent Literature on Crime and Prisons

I

Prisons of one type or another have existed since Joseph was incarcerated for having resisted the amorous advances of Potiphar's wife, indeed, since the days of primitive cannibalism, but only during the last century have they been used as the essential basis of the punishment of those convicted of crime. From the days of John Howard and Jeremy Bentham the prison problem has received the thoughtful attention of some of the best minds which have been devoted to social betterment. The list of Americans who have contributed to the science and practice of penology, such as Louis Dwight, Richard Vaux, Francis Lieber, E. C. Wines, T. W. Dwight, F. B. Sanborn, S. J. Barrows, C. R. Henderson, G. W. Kirchwey, T. M. Osborne and others, is one of which we may well be proud. During the last year (1923) we have had two very notable additions to the literature of American penology which, fortunately, admirably supplement each other. Dr. Louis N. Robinson, of the Philadelphia Municipal Court, in his *Penology in the United States,* has produced an excellent systematic survey of the development and present state of penal science and administration in this country. Mr. Tannenbaum's book,[1] while in no sense a comprehensive factual survey of American penology, is an invaluable interpretation of the spirit and methods in the actual operation of American prisons, and brings out the somber fact that the real progress of the

[1] *Wall Shadows: A Study in American Prisons.* By Frank Tannenbaum. New York: G. P. Putnam's Sons.

new penology is far less in practice than the volume of legislative achievement, as given in Dr. Robinson's work, would seem to indicate.

We have long needed just such a work as Mr. Tannenbaum has produced—one which reveals the sinister spirit of the old repressive penal administration and presents convincing evidence that this system still dominates the majority of American prisons, in spite of the popular presentiment that we are entering an era characterized by the "coddling of prisoners." Alexander Berkman's *Prison Memoirs of an Anarchist* was a valuable contribution to this indispensable interpretative literature of actual penology, but the limitations of the author were real and his generalizations were based chiefly upon experiences in one prison—the Western Penitentiary of Pennsylvania. Mr. Osborne's works, valuable as they are, were the product of an advocate, albeit an enlightened advocate, of a particular phase of penal reform. Mr. Tannenbaum's volume is sufficiently objective, and founded upon wide enough observation to make it both comprehensive and reliable.

Mr. Tannenbaum writes as a disciple of Mr. Osborne, who contributes an appreciative introduction to the book. The author first discusses the psychology of prison cruelty, indicating that it is a result of the mediocre type of human being who becomes the conventional prison guard, of the ignorance on the part of most wardens and guards of even the elementary principles of social and penal science, of the fact that the prison administrators under the existing system must inevitably regard themselves as primarily jailers and disciplinary officials, and of the tendency of the officers, like the prisoners, to succumb to the vicious system of isolation and repression and to lose whatever sentiments of humanity and kindliness they may originally have possessed. Next comes an excellent discussion of the nature, implications and achieved results of prison democracy, as realized through Mr. Osborne's system of inmate self-government. The progressive student of penology will dissent chiefly, if at all, from Mr. Tannenbaum's apparent opinion that the "professional criminal" is usually sound physically and mentally, is the victim solely of an unfortunate social environment, and may almost invariably be reclaimed by a system of social re-education. An interesting chapter is contributed on the old repressive system of prison administration, as it is in operation today in most American prisons. The facts were gathered on a recent transcontinental tour of investigation, and will constitute an illuminating and salutary disillusionment to those who had believed that considerable practical progress had been made in introducing the more scientific and humane methods of the newer penology. The chapter should also constitute a quietus on the lawyers and judges who frequently burst into print with the charge that wardens are "coddling" prisoners. In his closing chapter Mr. Tannenbaum outlines the desirable changes in the old system. He presents nothing new, but does set forth most of the conventional program of the progressive penologists—the development of a trained profession of prison administrators, the abandonment of the idea of punishment and repression and of the old type of prison plant, the substitution of prison farms, industrial prisons and extra-mural employment, the provision of adequate machinery for academic, industrial and social education, and a wider use of the indeterminate sentence and parole. Singularly enough, nothing is said about the sex problem in penology, and students will continue to have to rely for their information on this subject upon the somewhat morbid analysis in Berkman's work and Mrs. O'Hare's more recent book.

Few informed persons will quarrel with Mr. Tannenbaum's proposals, but they will not be sanguine as to the rapidity with which they will be realized, in the face of public ignorance, stupidity and perversity. Only education and enlightened propaganda can achieve much in hastening the process, and a wide circulation of *Wall Shadows* should contribute much to this desirable end. Mr. Tannenbaum's book is admirably supplemented by J. F. Fishman's *Crucibles of Crime,* which gives much more detail on the atrocious conditions existing in contemporary jails and county prisons.

II

A number of events and documents, such as riots at the Joliet Prison in Illinois and the Western Penitentiary of Pennsylvania, the investigations of state penal systems in New Jersey, Pennsylvania and New York, the revelation of atrocious methods in our federal prisons, and the writings of men like Lewis, Osborne and Tannenbaum have recently served to remind thoughtful and informed Americans that all is not well with *our* prison system. We have, however, generally shared the belief that the English penal organization and administration—the product of the cumulative efforts of Howard, Bentham, Romilly, Buxton, Miss Fry, Whatley, Crawford, Maconochie, Crofton, the Hills, DuCane and Ruggles-Brise—is an admirably conceived, smoothly operating and conspicuously efficient system for the detention and reformation of those guilty of anti-social action. Now we are shocked out of this amiable illusion by two comprehensive and authoritative volumes which constitute a most thorough-going indictment of the whole English prison system on the basis of its historical development, of an elaborate cross-section of the methods of today, and of a penetrating analysis of the whole foundation of the prevailing English theory and practice of criminology and penology. Not that these volumes prove the English system worse than those of most other Western countries. It is unquestionably one of the best of the contemporary examples of penal agencies. What is achieved is an incontrovertible arraignment of the anachronistic, wrong-headed and utterly unscientific nature of our whole body of conventional concepts and practices concerning the nature of the criminal and the desirable modes of treating him. These works [2] should constitute a landmark in the literature of English penology comparable to that of the writings of Howard, Blackstone, Bentham and Romilly, which sounded the requiem of the old pre-prison system of torture, mutilation and transportation.

Probably the most striking section in these significant volumes is the brilliant Preface of seventy-three pages by Bernard Shaw, in which he generously devotes the great resources of his intellectual courage, analytical acumen and trenchant phraseology to the cause of the reconstruction of our notions concerning crime, the criminal and prison methods. Mr. Shaw was a member of the Prison Enquiry Committee, the results of whose labors are gathered in coherent form in the volume edited by Hobhouse and Brockway, and, with characteristic energy, he seems to have acquainted himself with both the concrete facts and the significant auxiliary scientific literature necessary to equip himself for the task. Consequently, it contains little nonsense, and is unquestionably the most brilliant impeachment of the conventional views and the most lucid and compelling summary of the newer attitudes which has yet appeared in any language. He indicts the brutal terroristic methods, riddles the arguments for the three basic conventional aims of imprisonment, and proves the utter futility of modern prisons in securing reformation and their deadly effectiveness in producing the complete degradation and demoralization of the pris-

[2] *English Prisons Under Local Government.* By Sidney and Beatrice Webb, with a preface by Bernard Shaw. London: Longmans, Green and Company. *English Prisons To-day: Report of the Prison System Enquiry Committee.* Edited by Stephen Hobhouse and A. Fenner Brockway. London: Longmans, Green and Company.

oners. He argues that the root of the evil is "the belief that virtue is something which can be imposed upon us from without, like the tricks taught a performing animal, by the whip." The chief vice of the penal system which grows out of this attitude is "the anti-Christian vice of vengeance, or the intentional duplication of malicious injuries in compliance with the expiatory superstition that two blacks make a white." We must completely abandon the whole notion of punishment, segregate or exterminate the abnormal habitual criminals, educate those that must be temporarily restrained to the life of the law-abiding citizen through the enjoyment of normal liberties, and fine rather than imprison those whose incarceration is not rendered necessary in the interest of public safety. Above all, we must be relentlessly logical and inclusive in applying the test of anti-social action as the criterion for establishing the existence of criminality. The most brilliant passages in Mr. Shaw's Preface are those in which he compares the gentleman and the criminal, with results disastrous to the reputation of the former.

We may take it, then, that the thief who is in prison is not necessarily more dishonest than his fellows at large, but mostly one who, through ignorance or stupidity, steals in a way that is not customary. He snatches a loaf from the baker's counter and is promptly run into gaol. Another man snatches bread from the tables of hundreds of widows and orphans and simple credulous souls who do not know the ways of company promoters; and, as likely as not, he is run into Parliament. . . . We have whole classes of persons who waste, squander, and luxuriate in the hard earned income of the nation without even a pretense of social service or contribution of any kind; and instead of sternly calling on them to justify their existence or go to the scrap heap, we encourage and honor them, and indeed conduct the whole business of the country as if its object were to produce and pamper them. How can a prison chaplain appeal with any effect to the conscience of the professional criminal who knows quite well that his illegal and impecunious modes of preying on society are no worse morally, and enormously less mischievous materially, than the self-legalized plutocratic modes practised by the chaplain's most honored friends with the chaplain's full approval? . . . How is the divine judgment, by which all mankind must finally stand or fall, to distinguish between the victims of these two bragging predatory insects, the criminal and the gentleman? The most obvious reply is "By their number." For the depredations of the criminal are negligibly small compared to the military holocausts and ravaged areas, the civic slums, the hospitals, the cemeteries crowded with prematurely dead, the labor markets in which men and women are exposed for sale for all purposes, honorable and dishonorable, which are the products of criminal ideals imposed on the whole population. . . . The gentleman really believes that he is an instrument of national honor, a defender of the faith, a pillar of society; and with this conviction to strengthen him he is utterly unscrupulous in his misplaced pride and honor, and plays the wholesaler in evil to the criminal's petty retail enterprises.

The historical monograph by the Webbs and the voluminous descriptive report of the Prison Enquiry Committee will be of less interest to the general reader than to the technical student of social and administrative history and to the penologist. It will be sufficient to state that the history is fully up to the standard set by Mr. and Mrs. Webb in their earlier monographs, which have won for them the undisputed place as the leading contributors to institutional economics and sociology among writers in the English language. It treats of the history of English prisons from the vague anticipations of a prison system in the sixteenth century to the application of the important Prisons Act of 1877, which transferred the control from local government agencies to the central authorities.

Particularly important are the first eight chapters, which describe the transition from corporal punishment to incarceration in England. For the first time the significant facts of this important revolution in the treatment of crime have been authoritatively summarized. This monograph finds its logical sequel in the extensive treatise on *English Prisons To-day.*

The cross-section of actual English penology as it exists today, which has been edited by Hobhouse and Brockway, is a voluminous work of some 728 pages. With the possible exception of the Report of the New Jersey Prison Inquiry Commission, executed under the direction of Mr. Dwight W. Morrow a few years ago, it is doubtful if another collection of concrete material concerning contemporary prisons of equal scope and content has appeared. Not only does it present with candid thoroughness every aspect of the existing methods and administration in the English prison system, but it also includes references to advanced experiments made elsewhere in the newer penology, particularly in the United States. It would appear that some of the members of the Committee may have cherished the opinion that the United States has a civilized prison system. That the Committee has no illusions concerning their own is apparent from the concluding words of the Chairman:

> In our prisons we put away men for our own convenience, and, for the sake of financial economy, control them by mechanical methods which not only deteriorate their own characters and dissipate their inheritance in humanity, but in a majority of cases ensure that if we release them we shall have to put them away again, and continue the process of their destruction till nothing but animal life can be said to remain to them.

If pertinent information can achieve anything for human betterment, then the end of the repressive prison system in England should verily be in sight. But facts, unfortunately, in spite of the hopes of enlightened philosophers from Bacon to Lester F. Ward, have rarely proved efficacious in the way of inducing desirable social reforms until they have been integrated in public opinion through a persistent campaign of social education. A reprinting of Mr. Shaw's Preface and its wide circulation as an educational pamphlet should do much to awaken the English conscience to the pressing need for a thorough reconstruction of the existing theory and practice of penal "science."

III

The whole progress of criminal law and prison administration is traversed in the three books[3] under review. Phillipson's work is an exhaustive and valuable study of the three pioneers in the history of the reform of the criminal law and the proposal for a new method of treating criminals through imprisonment rather than corporal punishment. Beccaria, taking his cue from the notable section on the criminal law in Montesquieu's *Persian Letters* and *Spirit of Laws,* called for an elimination of the barbarous methods of trial and torture, the reduction of the number of capital crimes, the closer adjustment of the crime and punishment, and the reduction of all classes to equality before the law. But to this most advanced reformer of the age the ideals were an exact apportioning of the punishment to the crime and the provision of swift and sure justice as a deterrent to crime. His viewpoint was that of the enlightened eighteenth-century student of jurisprudence, not that of the modern

[3] *Three Criminal Law Reformers: Beccaria, Bentham, Romilly.* By C. Phillipson. London: Dent, 1923, 344 pp. *Penal Discipline.* By Mary Gordon. New York: E. P. Dutton and Company, 1922, xii, 238 pp. *Crime, Abnormal Minds and the Law.* By E. B. Hoag and E. H. Williams. With an Introduction by H. H. Goddard and Special Chapters by R. H. Gault and Miriam Van Waters. Indianapolis: The Bobbs-Merrill Company, 1923, xxiv, 405 pp.

psychiatrist or sociologist. His most modern notion was his emphasis on the prevention of crime. Bentham was the most versatile of the trio. In his voluminous *Panopticon* with its many appendices, and his *Principles of Penal Law,* he touched upon or suggested most of the proposals for juristic and penal reform actually achieved down through the period of the Elmira Reformatory. He was most influential practically in arousing an interest in Beccaria's doctrines in England and advancing the cause of the reform of the barbarous English criminal law. The actual leadership in this movement was taken by Romilly, who never lived to see the fruition of his efforts, which were brought to a conclusion by Mackintosh and Peel. Bentham's famous "panopticon" scheme for a prison was never adopted by the British government, though a structure on this general model constituted the first Western Penitentiary at Pittsburgh and has been adopted for the present state prison of Illinois. It was Romilly's efforts in 1816 which led to the erection of the first modern English prison, the expensive medieval fortress known as the Millbank prison. Present-day laborers in the cause of prison reform can get encouragement from a study of Phillipson's work, which reveals the existence of a much more depressing degree of primitive superstition and general indifference than that which faces the present reformer. It also furnishes an enlightening and encouraging contrast of the most advanced ideals of a century and a half ago with those of Mr. Osborne or Drs. Glueck and Healy.

Dr. Gordon's book constitutes a valuable supplement to the recent voluminous report of the Hobhouse-Brockway Committee on the state of contemporary English prisons. The work of an intelligent English inspector of prisons, it deals more thoroughly with the human problems of prison administration and the tragic and hopeless products of the present system of penal discipline.

Further, her book is concerned entirely with the female prisoner, being one of the few important treatises on that subject in English. She has special chapters on the prostitute as a type of female criminal, and an interesting one on the "tattooed woman" as a prison type frequently met with. There is an important chapter on the attempt to treat venereal disease during the imprisonment of the prostitute, in which the author quite rightly concludes that little can be done unless the prisoner remains in detention long enough to effect a cure, if it is possible at all, and unless she can be prevented from reëntering the profession after discharge. The weakest part of the chapter is the failure to lay stress upon the desirability of a general dissemination of knowledge of venereal prophylaxis to protect both the prostitute and her customers, until the barbarous institution shall have passed through a lack of demand or necessity.

The book contains an admirable exposition, realistic but constructive in its criticism, of the well-known facts of mental and physical deterioration during the prison sentence, which is rendered more than usually original and valuable because of the illustration of how the savagery or stupidity, as the case may be, of our present system operates to produce the disintegration of the *female* personality. Probably the chief impression which her analysis of the effect of the English prison system upon women prisoners will leave upon the reader is more the futility than the overt cruelty of the contemporary penal system. Her suggestions as to the desirable method of dealing with offenders in the hoped-for rational system of the future are sane and convincing, if not especially novel. They consist in a careful differentiation of offenders through a psychological and sociological study, and a determination of the treatment according to a scientific diagnosis of this sort, rather than on the basis of a system of arbitrary sentences adjusted to a particular category of crimes and punishment. The feeble-minded and psychopathic criminals ought to be separated from the others and handled in appropriate special institutions. Petty offenders should be dealt with chiefly through probation and the suspended sentence. The residual element can then be treated with some intelligence, and discrimination, leading to reformation or permanent segregation according to the needs of the individual case. Her own conclusions, the product of a lifetime of observation of modern prison methods, and of a good knowledge of psychiatric science, are of the highest significance and pertinence:

During my service I found nothing in the prison system to interest me, except as a gigantic irrelevance—a social curiosity. If the system had a good effect on any prisoners, I failed to mark it. I have no shadow of doubt of its power to demoralize, or of its cruelty. It appears to me not to belong to this time or civilization at all.

My main argument here is that we not only do not deter, but that we do actually make-over our criminal to crime. The fallacy of applying force to a being who is inherently insusceptible of being managed by force, lies in the fact that the proceeding ends, not in the alteration of the prisoner's point of view, but in his spiritually triumphing over us, and bringing the strong arm of the law to naught. We merely ill-treat a man or woman who still ignores and escapes us.

The time is ripe for us to convince ourselves of this. We should turn a fresh leaf in our treatment of the offender, fortified not by precedent, or by age-long prejudice, but by the findings of science which is, at last, in the act of discovering the mechanism of the whole man. We know enough already about how he "works" to be able to consider when, under stress, he falls, what to be at in the matter of restoring him. We should act on what we know. When we have abandoned penal discipline we must not let ourselves be dismayed by the size of our scrap-heap, or the cost of our new road, but take up the problem anew, and get on with solving it. . . .

I believe if we had, in conjunction with a scheme of control, a scientific clearing and sorting house for convicted persons, with proper places of treatment provided in connection with it, that the doctor's work would soon become all-important, and the gaoler, as we know him, be out of work. If the thousands of petty offenders, on whom we now throw away time and money, proved largely and sufficiently controllable by other means, our places of detention might not be complicated or costly.

The deferred sentence appears to me to be one of the best methods by which petty offenders could be controlled. Under such a method the prisoner would understand, when it is the case, that he is convicted, and that therefore whenever the community chooses it can take away his liberty. He should understand that he owes the community something which it intends to get from him, but that, if he pays something on account his bill will be allowed to run. In short, he should be convicted but not deprived of his liberty unless it is found absolutely necessary. The sentence should continue to be valid all his life or for a number of years, and meantime, whether it is executed or not, he should have to do something as a guarantee of good behavior for a certain period.

In all serious crimes, especially those of an impulsive or deeply perverted nature, the prisoner should come to his trial bringing his *dossier* with him, so that he can be dealt with according to the findings of the skilled psychiatrists who have taken his measure, and understood the treatment of his neurosis. These experts should be made entirely responsible for the disposal of the criminal, or insane, or inebriate group, whose liberty may be forfeit, and should keep all records, and make all examinations that may be necessary for the due care and treatment of the prisoner.

When the young have been sent to schools, gymnasia, or other places of education, or to places of work, when the genuinely feeble-minded, the poor old men and women, and the large class of psychotic individuals have all been duly allocated to their right places, the treatment of the worst, and most needy criminal cases will have some chance of success.

To approach the problem by such a route would be reasonable, humane, and scientific, and much more hopeful for the cure of many. We are always trying to approach the problem in this way, and often speak as if, and perhaps believe, we are doing it. We fail for want of thought, courage, and organization, and because, let our dreams for improving our present scheme be what they may, we fall headlong over penal discipline at every step.

The general suggestions in Dr. Gordon's book are developed in much greater detail in the interesting work by Drs. Hoag, Williams et al. This is one of the most significant and useful semi-technical contributions to the new or psychiatric approach to criminal jurisprudence, criminology and penology yet published in this country. It is particularly significant that it is the product of the labors of psychiatrists and psychologists of the city of Los Angeles (with the exception of the excellent chapters by Professor R. H. Gault of Northwestern University), which will serve to dispel the illusion still prevailing in certain eastern urban centers of advanced criminology and penology that in all cities west of the Rocky Mountains convicts are handed over for tomahawking to Indians, who stroll freely and unimpeded into the courthouse yards. The progressive and intelligent ideals of the authors are epitomized in the following passage:

Viewed from the attitude of society towards crime, we should realize that any individual who seriously violates our present social customs or mores, and continues to do so is abnormal. Yet this rather obvious fact has been, and still is, almost totally ignored and the criminal who trespasses upon the most fixed of social usages is still usually regarded as a responsible individual who deliberately plans to injure his fellow men, with full knowledge of the possible consequences. . . . It is easy enough to define crime and fix penalties but far less easy to determine personal responsibility. What we should at present be most concerned about is, therefore, the character of the perpetrator of the crimes or the criminal himself. We need to recognize not only the fact of the commission of a crime but to know so far as possible the causes of the act. And this leads us to a study of all that enters into the make-up of individual character as manifested in behavior. . . . The old school of criminology makes the punishment fit the crime as measured by the injury done society; the new criminology would make the treatment fit the criminal, as measured by his mental, physical and social responsibility. We are well provided today with tribunals to dispense "justice" and with penal institutions to apply the sentence. What we need most are research laboratories for the study of the criminal before he is sentenced and the sentence should be in the nature of a legal prescription for his reformation or control, or if that is impossible, for his permanent segregation. . . . When this idea becomes at last well rooted in the legal mind, the prison will become a school and hospital for the re-education, treatment, cure, or control of those unfortunate members of society whose distorted lives tend towards abnormal behavior, and the long cherished false notions of revengeful, retributive punishment as a deterrent to crime will finally be discarded.

The work is devoted primarily to inculcating the information essential to a criminologist, penologist, social worker or lawyer who hopes to attack the problems of crime and its elimination or control from this promising standpoint. There are excellent chapters on the general nature of the psychiatric approach to crime, the psycho-social aspects of crime (really an epitome of progressive modern penology), a helpful and somewhat original classification of criminals on the basis of mental defect and pathological mental states (actually an outline of the symptomology of the major psychoses and neuroses), the drug addict as a problem for the criminologist, the problems of the juvenile court when conducted according to psychiatric concepts and methods, the procedure in diagnosing criminal cases from a psychological and psychiatric point of view, and the scheme of diversified institutions which would be required to carry out the new methods of rehabilitation and segregation. The appendix occupies just half of the book, and is given over mainly to a consideration of the interrelation of psychiatry and jurisprudence in criminal cases, a further elaboration of the chief psychotic types in their relation to crime, and some very interesting case histories of typical criminals. There is a good selected bibliography on all phases of mental hygiene, criminology and penology.

Perhaps the most interesting thing in the book is the case of J. P. Watson, "The Modern Bluebeard" (pp. 313-28). The reviewer has never read a more convincing demonstration of the futility and inadequacy of our present system of dealing with the crime and not the criminal. Watson, a man of high intelligence, was found, more or less accidentally, to have murdered at least nine of his successive wives. From the standpoint of criminal jurisprudence he would have required the traditional feline resurrective powers to have had the death penalty inflicted as frequently as legal justice would have indicated, but, from the standpoint of psychiatry, his case was a rather simple one—a compulsion neurosis, due to perverted overcompensation for an inferiority complex arising from an abnormal genital condition, which may have been intensified by a traumatic neurosis. His case was one which would probably have yielded rather promptly to psychiatric treatment, and he could have been restored to society with little danger of his becoming a subsequent menace. At least nine times a murderer, he might have been rendered by adequate treatment potentially less dangerous than a criminally inclined moron whose worst crime to date was breaking and entering a bakery.

It is to be regretted that a book so thoroughly up-to-date in its attitude towards criminology and penology should be anachronistic in its concepts of psychiatry. It assures the reader that it rejects the Freudian concept of the unconscious (p. xxiv), and the chapter on the Epileptic type is almost Hippocratic in its antiquity, when compared with the recent work on epilepsy done by Drs. L. Pierce Clark and John T. MacCurdy. The majority of the types of mental disorders which may emerge in criminal conduct, particularly the compulsion neurosis, yield readily only to psychoanalytic treatment, and to recommend the psychiatric approach to the study of the criminal and then reject the basic technique of modern scientific psychotherapy is like unto urging the wider utilization of modern surgery and then rejecting X-ray diagnosis and antiseptic methods. Fortunately the book is an outline of the problems to be attacked by psychiatry rather than a guide to psychiatric methods, and, hence, is not greatly injured by its somewhat archaic and static psychiatric concepts. One extremely important point is driven home by the book, and that is that criminology, from the psychiatric point of view, is more a consideration of the problems of psychopathic mental states than of feeble-mindedness, important as the latter may be. We are now past the stage where we can dismiss all cases of criminality and prostitution with a gesture as attributable to mental subnormality. When we are able to combine the psychiatric approach with a discriminating utilization of Mr. Osborne's scheme of social reëducation of prisoners we shall be started on the path toward efficient control and rehabilitation of the criminal population.

IV

Of the group of books here under review [4] by far the most important is that by Professor Sutherland. It is by all odds the best one-volume manual which has yet been prepared on the joint and related subjects of criminology and penology. It is more comprehensive than any other work of its kind, and contains more factual information than any other single volume on the subject, excepting only Parmelee's *Criminology*.[5] It has the advantage over the latter of being much more readable, and more up-to-date in point of view and information. The arrangement is admirable with respect to both logic and sequence. The general range of subjects and topics covered is the following: an introduction to the modern conceptions of crime and correction; the facts in the crime situation as revealed by criminal statistics; the real nature of the actual criminal population, in so far as it has been apprehended and isolated; the biological, psychological, social and economic causes of crime; the methods and machinery for the apprehension and conviction of the accused, including police methods, jails and detention insti-

[4] *Criminology.* By E. H. Sutherland. Philadelphia: J. B. Lippincott Company, 1924, 643 pp. *The Criminal as a Human Being.* By George S. Dougherty. New York: D. Appleton and Company, 1924, 290 pp. *Keys to Crookdom.* By George C. Henderson. New York: D. Appleton Company, 1924, xix, 429 pp. *In the Clutch of Circumstance.* By the Mark Twain Burglar. New York: D. Appleton Company, 1922, 272 pp. *Reformatory Reform.* By Isaac G. Briggs. New York: Longmans, Green and Company, 1924, xvi, 227 pp. *In Prison.* By Kate Richards O'Hare. New York: Alfred A. Knopf, 1924, 211 pp. *Prisons and Common Sense.* By Thomas Mott Osborne. Philadelphia: J. B. Lippincott and Company, 1924, 105 pp. *Prison Reform at Home and Abroad.* By Sir Evelyn Ruggles-Brise. New York: The Macmillan Company, 1925, v, 200 pp. *Man's Judgment of Death.* By Lewis E. Lawes. New York: G. P. Putnam's Sons, 1924, vi, 146 pp. *Murder and Its Motives.* By F. Tennyson Jesse. New York: Alfred A. Knopf Company, 1924, vii, 258 pp. *The Police Woman: Her Service and Ideals.* By Mary E. Hamilton. New York: Frederick A. Stokes Company, 1924, xiii, 200 pp. *Gentlemen of the Jury: Reminiscences of Thirty Years at the Bar.* By Francis L. Wellman. New York: The Macmillan Company, 1924, xv, 298 pp.

[5] This review was written before the appearance of J. L. Gillin's *Criminology and Penology.* See below, pp. 367-8.

tutions, and court procedure; the contrast between the anachronisms and savagery of the criminal court and the dawn of science and common sense in the juvenile court procedure; the theory, origins, evolution, ethics, economics and general wrong-headedness and futility of punishment; the evolution of the prison system; prison industry and education; methods of release, probation and parole; and general observations on the primary significance and potency of prevention and reformation in correctional theories, policies and methods.

The book is thoroughly modern with respect to both factual content and orientation towards the crime problem. The author's bibliographic mastery is remarkable. The reviewer does not recall having read another book by a sociologist on any phase of contemporary social problems which exhibited a superior acquaintance with the relevant literature on the subject. The ample footnotes are supplemented by an extensive and discriminating list of suggested readings following each chapter or section of the book. Professor Sutherland is candid and courageous in criticizing the anachronisms and abuses of our modern criminal procedure and prison administration without lapsing into cynicism or being disheartened. He clearly indicates that the clue to the crime problem and its solution is a careful study of the causes of crime and the methods of their elimination. Prevention and reformation are the only positive fields of action which can enlist the interest or secure the respect of the enlightened student of criminology. His critical comparisons of the American police systems, courts and court procedure with similar institutions and methods abroad should constitute doubly pertinent and salutary reading for our Hundred Percenters. Particularly satisfactory and convincing is his contention that the older views of personal responsibility for criminal action, with the resulting desirability of punishment, can in no way whatever be harmonized or combined with the modern viewpoint of determinism and treatment. "It is necessary either to keep the punishment attitude and abandon the effort to understand the situation, or else abandon the punishment attitude and continue the effort to understand the situation. The two attitudes are not in harmony and cannot be combined."

It is probable that ultimately distinct works on criminology and penology will be abandoned, and the subject will become a subdivision of psychiatry, mental hygiene and social work—a development of which the recent work by Hoag and Williams was a harbinger. Until that time comes, it is difficult to see how we can well expect a more adequate and satisfactory treatment in any manual than that executed by Professor Sutherland. It may, however, be possible to produce a somewhat clearer and more vitally interesting survey, and the promised revision of P. A. Parsons' *Responsibility for Crime,* in his *The Question of Crime,* may possibly constitute this very achievement.

The work by Mr. Dougherty is a book of a distinctly different sort from the systematic manual of Professor Sutherland. It is the highly interesting and illuminating, if rather miscellaneous, collection of the observations and reminiscences of the former deputy police commissioner and chief of detectives of the New York Police Department. Mr. Dougherty is an interesting "border-line case." He has passed his life in the police and detective service, which, particularly in the United States, is peculiarly destructive of a scientific interest in the real nature of crime and the criminal, though, as Chief Vollmer has so clearly proved, it may well serve as the vantage point for the acquisition of a unique body of reliable information on these very subjects. But he is apparently a humane person of much poise and good sense, and he seems to have been touched in one manner or another by the concepts of modern criminology. Hence his book constitutes a curious mixture of modern insight into the nature of crime and the criminal with the orientation and jargon of the police detective. The best chapter is the first, where Mr. Dougherty actually views the criminal as a "human being" in such passages as the following:

> With all his shortcomings, the criminal may be more human than the law-abiding citizen sunk in his rut of respectability—more human in his emotions, his resourcefulness, his sympathies.
>
> It is through understanding of his humanness that he is most often inspired to effect a genuine reform, either by his own initiative or the help of others.
>
> And I have always felt that, taking into account the many obstacles to be overcome, within himself as well as outside, the wrongdoer who has succeeded in gaining a place for himself among honest men is perhaps just a little more human than most of the rest of us. . . .
>
> The effort a criminal will make to go straight himself is much greater than reformers suppose, and if they left off cuddling and sentimentalizing over him, and simply found him the right kind of a chance, there would be many more lasting reforms.

The remainder of the book is of little value as a contribution to the technical psychiatric analysis of the criminal, but it does contain a large amount of cogent and interesting descriptive material relative to the various types of criminals, their characteristics and methods, and the procedure of the police and detectives in apprehending them and securing their conviction. The methods of criminals are presented through a description of the stage management of spectacular crimes, blackmailers, the dinner thief and the pickpocket, and the "stick-up" and the house-prowler. The procedure of detectives is described through an account of the art of "shadowing and roping," a description of the more modern and humane administration of the "third degree," and an analysis of the methods of the city detective. One gains from reading the book a respect for the uncanny powers of the trained and competent detective. It is not necessary to assume special egotism or prevarication as the basis of such passages as: "I have examined many prisoners charged with all kinds of murder, and could satisfy myself where there was no direct evidence as to the innocence or guilt of the suspect by a careful study of the eye. . . . Take six honest persons, six dishonest persons who have never been convicted of crime, and six criminals who have served prison terms. Let them all be of the same general build and type. Without experience, few people could distinguish the three different groups, but the detective frequently sorts them, and as correctly as a mailhandler slipping so many letters into the right boxes. . . . While in the police department in New York City as Deputy Commissioner and Chief of Detectives, I could, when a prisoner was arraigned before me, without any previous information on the subject, tell for what crime he was arrested." Mr. Dougherty includes an interesting chapter proving how the savagery of the conventional "third degree," is actually much less effective than the adroit and subtle methods now used by the best police detectives. He contends that "the cruel third degree is a thing of yesterday," but this is literally true only in the better types of police departments in a few leading American cities.

Important and informing as is Mr. Dougherty's work with respect to the concrete facts of criminal methods, Mr. Henderson's contains much more specific information and deals with a wider variety of criminals. His preface indicates that he also knows whereof he speaks, as he has studied the criminal at first hand under the most diverse conditions, in prison and out, and was aided by Police Chief August Vollmer in the critical editing of his book. He has separate chapters on thieves, pickpockets, burglars, safe-crackers, robbers, bandits, swindlers, forgers, counterfeiters, criminal promoters, mail-order crooks, the "con" man, fraudulent mediums and criminal spiritualism, bunko artists, gamblers, bucket shop operators and bookmakers, arsonists, bootleggers, drug venders, grafters and murderers. There are three concluding chapters on modern police technology, prisons, and methods of eliminating crime.

The book is not only of high value for criminologists in search of descriptive and illustrative material, but also to the general reader, who will here acquire much astonishing and protective information. After his elaborate study of the criminal types he comes essentially to the view of Bernard Shaw, as expressed in the latter's introduction to the Webbs' *History of English Prisons Under Local Government,* namely, that the gentleman is more of a menace to society than the criminal, because of the fact that his depredations are much more extensive and far-reaching. "I soon became convinced that the biggest scoundrels were outside the (prison) walls, and I began an investigation of profiteers, swindlers, criminal promoters, bucket shop operators and mail order crooks." The only serious departure of the author from science and sense is in chapter xxvii, where he attempts to scare prospective criminals out of such a career by painting the generally unsatisfactory nature of the criminal's life. While this might be effective in a few cases, it is, broadly speaking, as absurd as to believe that the general perusal of medical works by the citizenry would eliminate most physical diseases. It is interesting to note that Mr. Henderson, in contrast to Mr. Dougherty, not only admits the existence of the brutal methods of the police in the third degree and elsewhere but defends such procedure. One of the best things about this useful work is the introduction by Chief Vollmer, who thus indicates his thorough grasp upon the essentials of the civilized attitude towards crime and criminals:

The offender today is coming in for more genuine attention and scientific study than ever before in the annals of the world.

The time has passed when law violators were thrown into dungeons like beasts to rot there until the pleasure of some official secured their release. The time is coming when every criminal case will be handled with the same individuality that a good physician shows in caring for a patient, because after all the outlaw is a sick man, morally sick, perhaps mentally and physically ill.

The psychology, pathology, anthropology, physiology, sociology and other sciences that have been brought to bear upon criminal matters have convinced the thinker of one thing—there is no single cause for crime.

Crime is a social disease and it is produced by an accumulation of inequalities. Inequality in wealth, in physical vigor, in mentality and in environmental opportunity plays a tremendous part in the fertilizing of the ova of social degeneracy—crime. . . .

It is especially desirable that the student in criminology and the voter who runs the government should understand crime causes. Mental abnormalities, vicious environment, the wicked home, poverty, sinister heredity, physical defects, alcoholism, drug addiction, child labor, profiteering, the unequal distribution of wealth and lack of character training are decidedly causative agents. In considering causation the only factor in this connection of any importance is the antidote, the remedy. Little good can result from enumerating the reasons for criminality unless it is with the idea of eliminating them.

Punitory and penal institutions in the United States have been undergoing some drastic changes in the last few years. The theory that a criminal must be punished is giving way to the definite idea that he must be trained and reformed so that he may become an asset rather than a liability to the community.

In the Clutch of Circumstance is the autobiography of the famous "Mark Twain Burglar" who robbed Mark

Twain's Connecticut home at Stormfield on September 17, 1908. It is a human document which makes a far more serious case against society and American "justice" than against the culprit whose life story is contained herein. While one could scarcely be dogmatic in the situation without having available the *IQ* and the report of a psychiatric investigation of the personality of the author, the present case would seem to be notably one in which adverse circumstances, including our gross perversion of elementary justice in this country, were fundamentally responsible for a criminal career. It is also an excellent illustration of how decent human contacts and an opportunity will operate to induce reformation. It is another admirable book to recommend to Hundred Percenters and "right thinking" people. It should serve equally well as a first book designed to arouse an intelligent and reflective interest in the problems of crime. Incidentally, it adds to our already disheartening collection of concrete information regarding the brutality and corruption in our jail and prison systems. The case against the Wethersfield Prison in Connecticut is particularly damaging. The reviewer does not remember having read another book which brings out more clearly the practical helplessness of a friendless and uninformed person before the law in the United States, even when guiltless; in contrast with the practical helplessness of the law against wealthy and powerful offenders able to secure clever and competent counsel.

Mr. Briggs' book is somewhat similar in scope and nature to that of the "Mark Twain Burglar." It is the account of an Englishman who was thrown into a House of Correction when a child for a petty offense, but who was able to make good when released in spite of his "Reformatory" sentence and service. The author is, however, a better educated person than the "Mark Twain Burglar" and has more technical acquaintance with the newer penal methods. The closest American analogue to his work is that by Frank Tannenbaum. In addition to an enlightening account of the conventional and usual brutalities and stupidities of reformatory administration, there is included a sensible discussion of preventive and reformative measures, such as the children's court, better educational and administrative machinery and attitudes in reformatories, probation, the individualization of treatment, and a program of prevention based upon an adequate system of education. He comes to the sane conclusion of every competent student that the only constructive approach to the problem of crime is an analysis of causes, with the aim in mind of eliminating them. The book may be recommended to American readers as an example of the confirmation of the penal reformer's position on the basis of English data, and as an excellent concrete description of administrative methods in English institutions. English criminal justice is far more rapid, efficient and economical in its operation than American, but, as the Hobhouse and Brockway Report and the present work indicate, the administrative systems in the penal and reformatory institutions are by no means as much more advanced than our own.

Of all the books written in this country in the last ten years revealing the actual operation of the paleolithic system of savagery, ignorance and vice which we dignify by the term "our prison system" it is probable that Mrs. O'Hare's account of her experiences in the Missouri State Penitentiary at Jefferson City is the most striking and convincing indictment of one of our chief contemporary disgraces. Nothing except Fishman's *Crucibles of Crime* and the chapters of Tannenbaum's *Darker Phases of the South* dealing with southern prisons can compare with it in the revelation of hideous and gruesome details. This is not because the Missouri Penitentiary is worse than most other American prisons, but because Mrs.

O'Hare is an unusually intelligent woman who consciously utilized her prison experience for the purpose of gathering information concerning modern prison methods with the aim of influencing public opinion against its more flagrant abuses. Mrs. O'Hare's whole prison experience, as well as many of her prison cases, admirably illustrates once more Bernard Shaw's thesis of the gentleman versus the criminal. She was sacrificed to the profiteers during the late World War in that campaign against free speech and common decency, which, be it said to their lasting and eternal disgrace, was so ably aided and abetted by many prominent American sociologists. Yet few, if any, profiteers ever got behind prison bars, and the feeble effort to secure restitution from them was quickly squelched by now Vice-President Dawes. This Shavian observation is further exemplified in many cases cited by Mrs. O'Hare, of which that of Marie Montemann is representative. She was serving a sentence as a prostitute, a career into which she had been forced because both arms had been amputated at the shoulders by illegal machinery used in the shops of the Fulton Bag Company, against whom no conviction had ever been achieved or seriously attempted.

It would be futile to dwell at length upon the details of the filth, degradation and cruelties of prison life revealed by Mrs. O'Hare, for they are distressingly familiar to every student of the subject, but we may profitably mention some points which she emphasizes more fully than most other writers. She recognizes and resolutely calls attention to the importance of the sex problem in prison. "Prison life by denying the normal expression of sex, breeds and fosters sex perversions and all the degenerating vices that these perversions include." After dealing with the subject in general, she calls attention to the almost unbelievable situation in the women's ward in the Missouri Penitentiary. Here the ward was from six in the evening to six in the morning in charge of a vicious convicted negro murderess who actively forwarded homosexual practices. Perverts plied their trade for fifty cents per visit and the negress received one dollar for leaving the cell door open so that such practices could go on. In order to increase her "rake off" she not only permitted but forced, when it was necessary, indulgence in such perversions. "Because this stool pigeon had sole charge of the cell house and of the lives of the women at night; because her word was always and unquestionably accepted without investigation by the matrons; because she, in fact, held the power of life and death over us, by being able to secure endless punishments in the blind cell, she could and did compel indulgence in this vice in order that its profits might be secured."

Even more repulsive was the condition with respect to the prevalence and non-treatment of venereal disease. Mrs. O'Hare thus describes the condition of the syphilitic Indian woman whom she was compelled to follow into an undisinfected bath-tub under threats of the dungeon and beating. "As Alice stepped out of the bath-room she was one of the most terrible creatures I have ever seen. From her throat to her feet she was one mass of open sores dripping pus. I have seen her with her clothes so stiff with dried pus that they rattled when she walked, and I have seen live maggots working out of the filthy bandages about her neck." She had been in prison for eleven years and had never received any treatment whatever for her disease until Emma Goldman, while a prisoner at Jefferson City, risked her life to arouse sufficient disturbance about the case to secure treatment long after it was too late. When Mrs. O'Hare remonstrated that to follow Alice without disinfecting the bath-tub would mean probable infection with a possibly fatal disease the matron responded: "I don't know a thing about that, and care a damn sight less. You are a convict; this is what there is here for you to use. Now get ter hell outa here and take your bath." These abuses were not only in evidence in the bath-room; they were prevalent in the dining-room. "The women who were too ill to work in the shop were used in the dining-room. I think all of them were tubercular and syphilitic. I have seen the food which the women were forced to eat handled by women with pus oozing from open sores on their arms and dripping into the dishes, and it was a common sight to see our food sprayed with tuberculosis germs from the lips of coughing convicts."

In spite of the fact that the head matron and the chief stool pigeon in the women's ward seem to have been unusually low and contemptible types, even for the human race, Mrs. O'Hare gives evidence of no personal animosity. She recognizes that they are the product of a system which vests prison and jail administration in about the most vile and incompetent type of public agents and officials.

Mrs. O'Hare's suggestions as to ways out of this barbarism are those now common to reformers in general, except that, as would be expected, she lays somewhat more than the usual degree of stress on the economic causes and cures for crime, and suggests that better and more thorough labor organization would eliminate much of our present delinquency:

Common sense would seem to dictate that we try some new methods. It might be wise for us to try the industrial organizer, the educator, the psychologist and the physician. I realize that it sounds very unorthodox to suggest that the industrial organizer might help in solving the problems of crime, but he has helped and is helping now. It cannot be disproved that, wherever the workers are well organized and well disciplined and have a certain security of employment and living wages, crime is reduced to a minimum.

The Amalgamated Clothing Workers, the industrial union

of the immigrant garment makers, has done more to Americanize, to raise the standards of living, to safeguard and create mental, moral and physical health among the great mass of this potentially dangerous group, than all our courts and laws have done. The obscure, unknown organizers of the Amalgamated have taken from our fetid slums the poverty-cursed, disease-ridden sweatshop workers of yesterday, and made them the most self-reliant, self-respecting, forward-looking group of the American labor movement today. The Industrial Workers of the World, the industrial union of the itinerant and seasonal worker of the country, has cleaned up the industrial pestholes in the lumber camps, canneries, fruit-packing industries, harvest fields, and construction camps. It has made possible law-abiding lives for hundreds of thousands of our most oppressed but socially useful workers. The lowly and despised "wobbly" has done more to reduce crime and build men among the homeless laborers of this country than all the "bulls" and "bull pens" we have. The farmers' coöperatives and the Non-Partisan League have done more to lift the boys and girls of the farms above the danger of crime than all the repressive laws that were ever placed on statute books. The discoveries of the part that hookworm, malaria, pellagra, tuberculosis and venereal diseases play in producing the industrial unfitness that is such an important factor in delinquency, and the splendid efforts made by the medical profession to combat these evils, have done more for real progress in sane criminology in the last ten years than the lawyers have done in a century. The work of the newer school of psychiatry, based on the theories of Freud and his co-workers, has shed more light on causative factors in crime than all the musty law books ever compiled.

Mr. Osborne's little book contains nothing that has not been embodied in his earlier and larger works describing his prison experiences, his administrative labors, the Mutual Welfare League and his theories of crime and reformation. But it has the advantage of presenting in a hundred small pages a clear and convincing statement of his whole penal philosophy. In his preface he summarizes what he believes to be the fundamental dictates of both common sense and scientific knowledge in dealing with prisoners:

(1) Prisoners are human beings; for the most part remarkably like the rest of us.

(2) They can be clubbed into submission—with occasional outbreaks; but they cannot be reformed by that process.

(3) Neither can they be reformed by bribery in the shape of privileges—special favors or tolerant treatment.

(4) They will not respond to sentimentality; they do not like gush.

(5) They appreciate a "square deal"—when they get one.

(6) There are not many of them mental defectives; on the contrary, the majority are embarrassingly clever.

(7) All these facts must be taken into consideration if we want prisons which will protect society. Unless they are taken into consideration, our correctional institutions will continue to be what they have been in the past—costly schools of crime—monuments of wasted effort, of misguided service.

Few informed students of the problem would dissent from Mr. Osborne's summary, with the possible exception of point number (6). While we no longer look upon the majority of criminals as "feeble-minded," many are such, and many that possess an average *IQ* are emotionally disordered, which may be quite as serious and may make them even more non-responsive to merely administrative improvements in prisons. Mr. Henderson's *Keys to Crookdom* supplements Mr. Osborne on this point and shows that the "cleverness" of many criminals is of a superficial and limited type that proves no intellectual distinction. In the words of Vollmer "the individual crook is revealed as a deluded mountebank and the little box of tricks that appeared so wonderful is disclosed as a cheap and pitiful sham." But if Mr. Osborne is slightly in error in his theory of the criminal personality, he is far more than fifty per cent right even here, and his errors in this field scarcely affect his theories of penology, where he has done his real work. It is the opinion of the reviewer that his contributions to penal administration rank in importance second only to the findings of modern psychiatry in the development of contemporary criminology and penology, and that ultimately he will be placed with John Howard and Elizabeth Fry in the history of penal reform. The best that modern thought can now offer is a combination of the psychiatric work of Healy, Glueck, White, Adler, Jacoby, Hickson and others with Osborne's administrative innovations.

Perhaps the most interesting and significant thing about this small volume is Mr. Osborne's evident effort to prove that the Mutual Welfare League plan is not the product of gush and sentimentality, but a hard-headed scheme based upon long and varied experimentation, and capable of much further empirical modification. And he proves his point quite successfully. It is a melancholy fact that the League has now all but disappeared from penal practice. "At Auburn, politics and official stupidity have almost completely smothered it; at Sing Sing, politics of the foulest kind drove one warden from office, and it was a seriously curtailed League which the present warden inherited; but, crippled as it is, it has won his confidence and support. At Portsmouth, the League is gone; as soon as the present Naval administration came into power it hastened to undo what a former administration had created. So it is unfortunately true that a fully developed Mutual Welfare League can be seen nowhere at the present time." Yet Mr. Osborne has not lost heart. He contends that "the Mutual Welfare League is not dead and can never die; the principle on which it rests is eternal." We believe he is right.

Sir Ruggles-Brise was the Royal Commissioner of Prisons from 1895 to 1921, and it is an interesting reflection on the progress of criminology and penology in England that the man who was originally looked upon as a daring innovator was recently pretty thoroughly discredited by the Hobhouse and Brockway Report and other allied investigations. The book is a history of the more formal aspects of prison administration since 1872, with main emphasis placed upon the international prison congresses and the international aspects of prison reform. It is in many ways a very convenient and authoritative summary, but it gives little evidence of accord with or a grasp upon recent developments.

The work of Warden Lawes of Sing Sing is perhaps the most thorough study of the alleged deterrent effect of the death penalty. He has gathered elaborate statistics comparing the homicides in states which have abolished the death penalty and those which have retained it, and also the homicide rate in the same state before and after the abolition of the death penalty. In spite of the mass of concrete evidence collected, the exploitation of the statistical data is not highly scientific. He apparently knows little of such simple statistical concepts as weighted averages, ratios, standard of deviation, correlations and probable error. In many ways his book would furnish Professor Chaddock with admirable illustrative material as to the dangers in a popular utilization of statistical information. The great number of factors other than penalties affecting the homicide rate are largely ignored when assembling and interpreting the statistical data, though Mr. Lawes in various parts of his book recognizes their existence. Further, there is no adequate psychiatric classification of the different types of homicidal motivation, with a consideration of how far any penalty would obstruct murder in each case. Nevertheless, it must be held that he has made a definitive and authoritative case against those who contend that the death penalty alone will notably reduce homicides. He has rather effectively destroyed the stock argument that it is of undoubtedly great deterrent potency. With the following general conclusions of the book we may also heartily agree:

> Life imprisonment with a long unavoidable minimum provides a form of punishment that is more certain of application than the death penalty can ever be made; it is more scientific in application because with its long but variable minimum it presents a possibility for individualization and differentiation of treatment; by reason of these qualities its universal adoption will provide a more effective deterrent. . . .
>
> My own opinion, which is borne out by statistics, is that the comparatively small number of homicides in Canada and England and in France is due to the accuracy, the certainty and the celerity of justice as administered in those countries rather than to the form of severity of the punishment.

And it is satisfactory and pleasing to discover a prominent prison administrator able to use and approve of much of the nomenclature of scientific criminology. In the opinion of the reviewer it is now scientifically absurd even to talk of "capital punishment," for the very reason that it is as absurd to talk about "punishment" at all for criminals as it is to discuss "punishing" tubercular patients or paretics. Yet it seems to me that in the future, when we begin to "treat" criminals, it may well be that the method of "treating" by painless extermination may be greatly extended beyond the scope of the present death penalty. Low grade non-reformable criminals might well be brought within the range of the operation of this principle, along with idiots, imbeciles, paretics and thoroughly demented dementia-præcox types. The arguments for this procedure were long ago assembled by Dr. McKim, and contested by Dr. Parsons in his chapter on the death penalty.

Miss Jesse's work is an attempt to analyze and classify the motives for murder. This task is one which has been awaiting execution, as it is without scientific value to talk of murder as an act of uniform and universal nature and motivation. Miss Jesse finds that the motives of murder are desire for some resulting pecuniary advantage, blocked ambitions, jealousy, revenge, political rivalry and conviction, and mere desire for killing. That this classification may have some merit and validity may be admitted, much as the older classifications of criminals as criminals by passion, accidental criminals, and born criminals were of some preliminary significance, but it is probable that any substantial study of the nature and motivation of murder will have to be done by the psychiatrist, who can analyze the traits of the criminal imbecile, the genesis and nature of the unconscious compulsions, such as moved Loeb and Leopold, and the nature of the part played by pure passion. We are all subject in differing degrees to jealousy, revengeful spirit, ambition, and lust for wealth and position, but most of us endeavor to advance our aspirations through other means than the automatic pistol and the butcher-knife. The layman is no more likely to render definitive service in the classification of murder than in the description of the pathogenesis of epilepsy or the psychoses.

Mrs. Hamilton has given us an excellent brief account of the development of the policewoman as an important phase of the police administration of the modern metropolitan department. Her analysis is comprehensive, covering such things as standards, organization, education, duties on patrol, detective service, location of runaways, location of missing persons, dealing with women and children in crime, the prevention of crime, and possible dangers and improvements in the activities of women in the police service. The book is fairly free from either gush or special pride, and is a straightforward and sensible description of the problems and achievements of the work with which she is concerned. She proves that in many fields a woman can execute the function of both detection and prevention far better than the average male, and we may look for an even greater extension of this type of professional activity for women. It is quite evident, however, that there is nothing inherent in woman which makes her a born criminologist, and the real service of the policewoman will depend pretty much upon the degree to which she becomes acquainted with the modern scientific concepts of crime, its nature, causes and prevention. As an amateur criminologist woman possesses the special danger of becoming "snoopy" and petty, having already cheated many a "poor working girl" out of a good dinner by efforts to apprehend and discourage "mashers."

Of all the books on criminology under review here, that by Mr. Wellman is the most imposing in weight and dimensions and by far the least significant and important in content. It is also quite obviously paradoxically christened, there rarely being any gentlemen on juries. It is an extremely garrulous and anecdotal collection of observation by an eminent court lawyer on the history of trial by jury, and of experiences with witnesses, lawyers and judges. The chapter on the history of trial by jury misses nearly all the important points established by recent scholarship, and gives little hint at those weaknesses and anachronisms of the jury system today which are inseparable from the mode of its origin and development.

And the degree to which he has been able to profit by his experience as a court lawyer is indicated by his reverent quotation (pp. 25-6) of Joseph H. Choate's fervid defense of the jury system, and by his own estimate:

A very large part of my professional life has been spent before juries, and I have learned to regard them with the utmost respect. Physicians spend their lives among their patients and become sincerely attached to them during their efforts to heal them. A lawyer feels much the same way after he has spent a lifetime in trying to persuade jurors to see the light and decide cases in his favor; and while a lawyer sometimes meets with incurable cases, just as a physician does, yet the vast majority of jurors seem to me to try to do the right thing and come nearer the mark than any other tribunal yet devised.

It is significant that Mr. Wellman, probably unconsciously, suggests that from the lawyer's viewpoint the "sick man" in our modern criminal procedure is the juror rather than the criminal! But Mr. Wellman offers in the course of his book much concrete evidence as to the burlesque and futility of jury service and jury verdicts, one representative example being the destruction of a district-attorney's argument by the performance of vaudeville stunts by the attorney for the defense during the concluding argument of the prosecutor (p. 153). Incidentally, he shows that the travesty of criminal justice in the American courts is due quite as much to lawyers and judges as to jurors, citing one interesting case (p. 298) in which the "learned judge" had been asleep during the concluding speeches by both the district-attorney and the lawyer for the defense. We are, however, inclined to be tolerant and sympathetic with the justice. He was apparently a man of long service before lawyers and juries! Mr. Wellman's work contains a large number of interesting side-lights on court methods and famous lawyers and judges, but the material embodied will be most useful only when exploited and reinterpreted by one who has veritably "seen the light."

The sensations and observations of any even halfway informed scientific student of criminology to the data assembled in these books must of necessity be much like those of a learned surgeon or physician reading clinical notes describing over ninety per cent of his colleagues in the profession carrying on their work according to the concepts and practices of Hippocrates and Galen, and indicating that the barbers are still monopolizing the profession of surgery and the mid-wives that of obstetrics; or like those of a modern astronomer compelled to read elaborate descriptions of the late solar eclipse interpreted solely in terms of astrology. Indeed, the modern criminologist is actually in about the position of the most advanced physicians and surgeons of 1800, who were observing the painfully slow transition of their subject and profession from magic, superstition, folk-lore and tradition to scientific observation and inductive methods. We may hope that the progress in the general adoption of scientific criminological concepts and practices will not be less slow in the century before us than was the triumph of scientific medicine between 1800 and 1900.

While we should welcome the efforts of all reformers in penal administration like Mr. Osborne, it seems to the reviewer that the two most effective lines of assault upon barbarism in the treatment of criminals will be in the way of an even better development of the scientific study of the criminal personality through psychiatry and allied sciences, and the parallel attack upon our juristic system, including most notably the jury system. It is the whole system of contemporary court procedure, and the antiquated theories underlying it, which not only make possible the atrocious prison system, but effectively prevent science from entering seriously upon the task of treating and preventing crime. Along with these improvements should go a third, namely, more honest and efficient methods of detecting crime and apprehending its perpetrators. Here modern science is making advances quite as startling and revolutionary as anything done in the last generation in psychiatry and eugenics. All we need to do is to supplant the conventional police chiefs by men of the stamp of Vollmer and Woods. Which is likely, in the light of modern democratic and partisan political practices, to be "some job!"

V

In the four books in this group[6] we have contributions to the science of criminology of the first order, though far different in scope and subject-matter, and written from widely different points of view. The study by Dr. Thomas is one of the most important advances in methodology which has thus far been executed, as it is a pioneer attempt to combine thoroughly up-to-date concepts in sociology, social psychology and psychiatry in an approach to the study of delinquency. Dr. Thomas bases his methodology upon the leading concepts in his socio-psychological interpretation of human behavior, namely, the four fundamental human wishes: (1) the desire for new experience; (2) the desire for security; (3) the desire for response; and (4) the desire for recognition.[7] In this way he links up criminology with the dynamics of human behavior and provides an excellent key to the study of social attitudes. The first two chapters of the book constitute the best brief statement of Dr. Thomas's very important system of social psychology, well illustrated by cogent case material. They are devoted to an analysis of the nature of these major wishes and of the social methods whereby they are controlled and regulated.

6 *The Unadjusted Girl,* by William I. Thomas, Boston, Little, Brown and Company, 1923, xvii, 261 pp., $3; *Mental Disorder and the Criminal Law,* by S. Sheldon Glueck, Boston, Little, Brown and Company, 1925, xxi, 693 pp., $7; *Criminology and Penology,* by John Lewis Gillin, New York, Century Company, 1926, xiii, 873 pp., $4.50. *The Psychology of the Criminal,* by M. Hamblin Smith, New York, McBride, 1923, vi, 182 pp., $2.

7 There is an admirable extended review of this book by one of the most competent and appreciative of Dr. Thomas's former students, Professor Kimball Young, in the *Journal of Social Forces,* September, 1924, pp. 747-9.

Dr. Thomas contends, quite correctly, that the tendencies of the present age in the way of industrialization, urbanization, greater human mobility, educational progress, and the disintegration of past customs and institutions, definitely make for the individualization of conduct in this generation. By this he means that, more and more, human beings are compelled to meet the vital issues of life on the basis of their own personality traits, individual resources and experiences, rather than through a total dependence on the stereotyped institutions, traditions and customs which were transmitted and enforced through the family, local community and other primary groups. This has led to no little confusion and demoralization of youthful females in our society, and they have been ill-prepared through training and information to meet the vital problems of personal life and the complex adjustments of contemporary civilization.

Dr. Thomas examines the nature of the social agencies that endeavor to assist girls who have been led into serious difficulties by inability to secure adjustment to normal social situations. He finds much inadequacy here also, largely because they do not adopt a modern and scientific point of view on social and sexual problems, but cling to the same set of outworn traditions which were the cause of the inability of most of the victims to work out their problems unaided. Of all social agencies the school system is, perhaps, the most deficient in this respect. As the remedy for the situation Dr. Thomas suggests a careful preliminary study of the influences exerted upon the human personality by the various social groups and institutions. From such a knowledge of human behavior and its conditioning we may be able ultimately to fashion a rational scheme of behavior and an adequate institutional basis for its guidance and control. Nothing could better illustrate the gulf between criminal science and traditional procedure than to compare this work by

Professor Thomas with a typical treatise on criminal jurisprudence.

Dr. Glueck's voluminous work is by all odds the most important treatise in the English language on the relation of psychiatry and criminal law. It is not primarily a study of the psychological factors involved in criminal behavior and the criminal personality, but is rather a thorough study, by a master of both law and psychiatry, in the effort to indicate the status of the problem of introducing scientific tests and procedure into the practice of the courts in dealing with insanity and the mental state of the accused. The core of the book is a very careful analysis of the nature of existing statutory prescriptions, legal practice and judicial decisions with respect to the matter of irresponsibility in criminal cases because of alleged insanity. Dr. Glueck reveals at great length the complete confusion and the utterly unscientific nature of the practice and decisions which now exist. Pages 274-390 contain a clear presentation of the major types of mental defect and psychopathologies, and indicate the slight amount of legal progress which has been made in distinguishing between these various types of mental disease and the degree of irresponsibility involved in each type. Nothing could make more obvious the grotesque nature of the legal view of insanity as a single, unified disease or type of personal behavior. In his suggestions for the reform of procedure Dr. Glueck is unusually sane, as he recognizes the almost unparalleled slowness of fundamental changes in legal procedure, and for the most part limits himself to proposals which are possible of immediate adoption in some degree. The book is an indispensable handbook for intelligent criminal lawyers, judges and social workers devoting their attention to problems of crime and the criminal class.

Professor Gillin's present work is an even more voluminous and impressive compilation of orderly arranged information than was contained in his very useful compendium on *Poverty and Dependency*. It will prove the most comprehensive textbook in the field, and will have wide use as a monumental book of reference. The book is logically divided into five parts: (1) the problem of crime and criminals; (2) the factors involved in the making of the criminal; (3) the history of the methods of punishment; (4) the nature and diversity of modern penal institutions; and (5) the machinery of justice, including the police, courts, probation agencies and a program for the prevention of crime. The book is not easy or sprightly reading, but it contains a vast amount of information on nearly every subject related to criminology and penology, and there is a digest of much of the recent work done by earlier writers and investigators. There is little space devoted to the more advanced aspects of the psychiatric study of criminal compulsions, or to such vital matters as the sexual problem in prisons, but on the whole the book is open-minded and forward-looking. It will scarcely fire the reformer with zeal, but it will furnish the over-zealous reformer with a salutary ballast of relevant information in the premises. Not for another decade shall we need another book on this plan and scale.

The brief but compact and meaty volume by Dr. Smith is the only work known by the present writer which satisfactorily links up in a non-technical and readable form the fundamentals of modern psychiatry and the scientific view of the criminal and his treatment. It is an improvement over the book by Hoag and Williams in that the psychiatric concepts of Dr. Smith are thoroughly up to date.

CHAPTER XI

Summary and Conclusions

I. INTRODUCTORY

We may now bring together what appear to the author to be the general conclusions of the historical material in the present work, as well as the chief generalizations to be drawn from the literature just surveyed, with respect to the solution of the crime problem.

It is the fundamental thesis of this book that any significant plan for the reduction of law-breaking must be of that comprehensive type which will achieve permanent results, and at the same time have certain elements which can be put into immediate operation. One could completely eliminate law-breaking by arresting the entire population and putting it into temporary custody, but no such scheme would be any guaranty that the crime rate would be lower a decade hence. Such an inclusive scheme as we have in mind here falls under three main headings: (1) preventive measures; (2) more adequate provisions for the apprehension and conviction of the criminal; and (3) improved measures for effecting the reformation of the convicted criminal.

II. PREVENTIVE MEASURES

The first important phase of any scheme for the prevention of crime must be found in the provision for a thorough and accurate collection of criminal statistics. There can be no intelligent attack upon the crime problem which is not founded upon a complete knowledge of the relevant facts about the number, types, and frequency of the crimes committed, as well as of such accessory facts as the number of convictions and recommitments.

Next in order we would place those biological or eugenic provisions which would introduce all practicable measures to insure that future generations shall be, as far as possible, well born. There must be provided adequate means for the prevention of the marriage of those congenitally defective, or else some equally effective plan suggested for the sterilization of defectives. While modern psychological science is establishing the fact that mental disease rather than mental defect is a chief cause of criminal conduct, there is no doubt of the existence of a large body of defective criminals who are a potential menace to the community, and will remain such until an effective scheme of negative eugenics can be actually put into operation.

The first stage in preventing criminality is to see that the human individual is well born. The next requirement is to make provision for adequate education. We are not here interested in revolutionizing the school system of the United States, but any educational system which is to render effective service in preventing criminality must provide: (1) intelligent instruction in the ideals of American citizenship; (2) an inculcation of the necessity for obedience to law in any orderly society; (3) sufficient manual or vocational education to provide every able-bodied citizen with the means of making a livelihood; and (4) efficient methods of aiding backward children who might otherwise become easy victims of idleness and criminal suggestion.

Fourth in order we should put adequate provision for personal hygiene and proper housing and recreation. There should be compulsory examination of children to discover, and if possible to remove, various physical lesions or defects likely to produce unhealthy and inefficient modes of life, with the resulting increase of susceptibility to criminal temptation. Such clinics should not only provide for aid in regard to the removal of physical defects; they should also furnish adequate psychiatric treatment for "problem children" whose eccentricities constitute all too often the breeding-ground or initial stages of criminal behavior. Ever greater reliance should be placed on the juvenile court, which should be intimately associated with the school system and coordinated with psychiatric clinics.

Demoralizing living conditions in the slum areas should be remedied as rapidly as possible. Pending this achievement large reliance should be placed upon municipal recreational facilities designed to remove the inhabitants of such areas from their degrading homes and to inculcate in them through healthy sports the fundamental principles of both co-operation and competitive enterprise. Above all, an effort should be made to divert the youth of the slum areas from their life in street gangs into these recreational centers. In other words, we should supplement formal education as far as possible by social education, and do everything which we can to give the individual a stimulating and healthy social environment.

Next, while Socialists err in contending that poverty is the chief cause of crime, there can be no doubt that economic factors exert a large influence in producing criminal conduct. One of the best methods of preventing anti-social modes of making a livelihood is to train each individual to maintain a self-supporting existence through some trade or profession. Not only must the individual be prepared to work efficiently; he must have an opportunity to do so. Here appears the field of service for employment agencies and other instrumentalities for putting the potential worker in touch with the sources of demand for his services. The principles of economic co-operation and good-will should be inculcated to the highest possible degree in order to reduce the prevalence and duration of strikes and other causes of unemployment and industrial unrest. Unemployment insurance should be widely introduced to prevent overt temptation to criminal action during periods of economic depression, and the fundamental principles of thrift should be introduced both through education and savings institutions.

Again, normal and law-abiding social behavior being essentially a matter of adequate adjustment to the social environment, every step should be taken to reduce these difficulties of individual and cultural adjustment. The problem of the repression of crime very directly involves the question of immigration. Without in any way committing ourselves to a theory of the superiority of any particular race, it will be evident that it is desirable to limit immigration to that minimum which can be efficiently assimilated to the American population. In addition to numerical limitation, provision should be made for a rigorous selection on a physical and intellectual basis, which would insure our getting the very highest types from foreign countries.

Finally, recognizing the enormous psychological power of imitation and suggestion, we would recommend as the final phase of preventive measures the curbing of the exhibition of crimes in the moving pictures, as well as the publishing of lurid and attractive accounts of crimes in the newspapers. In distributing space devoted to crimes in the press more attention should be given to the arrest, conviction and sentencing of criminals and less to portraying the details of the crime itself. Everything consistent with the truth should be utilized in the way of making crime as described in the public press as unattractive and hazardous as possible.

III. APPREHENSION AND CONVICTION FOR CRIME

Whether one looks upon the criminal law chiefly from the standpoint of deterrence or of reformation, there can be no doubt that certainty of apprehension and conviction for criminal behavior is the first and most indispensable item in securing the immediate reduction in the volume and variety of crime.

In the matter of the efficient apprehension of criminals the first essential is the provision of an honest and expert police system. The police system must be taken as far as possible out of politics and made an expert profession based upon adequate specialized training. The police of American cities should develop as rapidly as possible that professional attitude and efficiency characteristic of such types of officials as the Canadian Mounted Police. In their war upon crime the police should be provided with the most up-to-date scientific equipment, thoroughly on a par with any of the resources of modern science and technology which are exploited by the criminals themselves. Promotion in the police system should depend entirely upon demonstrated efficiency and achievement in the repression of crime.

The energies of the police should be reserved as far as possible for the discovery and apprehension of the more serious types of criminals. The police should not be encouraged to concentrate upon the prevention of petty and trivial misdemeanors, but should rather bestow their energy upon the prevention of serious crimes, and the apprehension of their perpetrators. Too often at the present time the police are devoting their attention to the suppression of crap games and "petting-parties," while a safe is being blown or a murder committed in the same locality. This objective would in part be realized by doing away with a great many foolish and useless laws creating a large number of petty offences, the infraction of which more or less inevitably absorbs the energies of the police. The police department must, of course, have every scientific device available for the adequate recording of criminals, and it must include within its organization the best possible detective system which exploits every known potentiality of science, technology and psychology.

Certainty of apprehension and arrest must be paralleled by relative certainty of the conviction of the guilty. It does little good to fill our detention jails with arrested suspects, if the majority of these are to be turned loose, whether guilty or innocent, through defects in our court system. The most important modification of criminal jurisprudence now immediately demanded is a sweeping reconstruction of the jury system. The untrained lay jury should be at once eliminated, and in its place we should have permanent boards of paid experts specially trained in various branches of criminal science, and giving all of their time to such jury service. As a first step we should at once cease referring the question of insanity to the decision of a jury. There should be far-reaching changes in court procedure relating to the technical rules of evidence, so that the relevant facts as to guilt or innocence may be freely and intelligently presented, and miscarriages of justice through petty legal technicalities reduced to the lowest possible degree. Expert biological, psychological and social advice should be available to the sentencing judge, so that the sentence may be made to fit the criminal rather than the crime. This would prevent potentially highly dangerous offenders, who had on this particular occasion committed only a petty offence, from being turned loose upon the community after serving a short sentence. The judge, with this intelligent advice, should be enabled to make use of the indeterminate sentence in order to keep in custody dangerous criminal types until their reformation is assured, or, if this is not possible, until their demise. Without intelligent and adequate segregation and treatment of offenders, the results of efficient apprehension and conviction of criminals will be largely wasted.

IV. THE REFORMATION OF CRIMINALS

Unless we are willing to hold in segregation until their death all convicted criminals irrespective of the offence which they have committed, we must either see to it that the convicted criminal is upon his release less inclined toward crime than when committed, or we must admit the entire system of criminal repression to be in a high degree a failure. Our present institutions obviously fail to achieve this result of reforming the criminal. Instead of reforming criminals, they are in reality institutions for the training of more efficient and determined criminals. The hierarchy of penal institutions greatly resembles the hierarchy in our school system. The typical criminal gets his elementary schooling in crime in a juvenile reform school, takes his collegiate degree in a reformatory, and perfects his post-graduate work in a state prison under the direction and in the seminars of the most efficient and experienced teachers.

We would suggest the following reforms in our correctional and penal institutions. In the first place, these correctional institutions should be regarded as primarily places for such treatment of the criminal types as will return them to society both determined and equipped to lead a law-abiding existence. The jails should be entirely places of detention and in no sense institutions for the reception of convicted criminals. There should be no promiscuous association of accused first offenders and veteran convicts. Those convicted of petty offences should, as far as possible, be kept out of penal institutions and handled through fines, probation, psychiatric clinics and social guidance. This rule would apply to all except those potentially dangerous individuals, such as the mentally defective and abnormal, or hardened criminals, who happen to be apprehended for petty offences. Such types must, of course, be segregated and treated until cured or until death. Those convicted of more serious crimes should be sent to institutions where they will be properly examined, classified and subjected to appropriate treatment. The object sought should be the complete reformation of the reformable types, and the permanent segregation of the non-reformable, irrespective of the crime committed. This would prevent turning back into the city each month scores of hardened and skillful criminals whose prison sentence has only served to make them more determined to commit crime and more capable in the act. Provision should be made for a normal sex life on the part of inmates of penal institutions who are detained for a period of more than thirty days.

It is obvious that an institution designed to achieve reformation must be manned by non-political and trained experts, comparable to the staff of physicians and nurses in the best hospitals. Inasmuch as many, if not most, criminals are the victims of inadequate social training, there should be sufficient provision for social re-education in the fundamental principles of social responsibility, as taught by the system of rewards and punishments. Such an end may be achieved either by inmate self-government or some better method if it can be devised. As an important aspect of social re-education and administrative reform the practice should be adopted of finding the form of employment in prison best adapted to the qualifications and enthusiasm of the individual prisoner. For such labor wages should be paid on a scale fully equal to that paid outside the prison walls for comparable labor and skill, and from this the cost of maintenance should be deducted. The proceeds should be utilized to indemnify the party injured by the prisoner through his crime, as well as to support the dependents of the prisoner.

It should be recognized, however, that physical and mental health and a determination to lead a law-abiding existence will be of little consequence unless the individual is able to maintain himself through honest labor. Hence, those prisoners not possessing a trade or profession should be adequately trained before being given their freedom. The unusual difficulties associated with securing employment which confront the released prisoner should be overcome by the provision of public and private agencies whose business it shall be to secure steady employment for the released prisoner. The problems of readjustment after release, together with desirable social protection against premature release, should be cared for by the development of a really efficient parole system, manned by well-trained and socially-minded experts, and controlling its activities between those extremes of carelessness and indifference, which characterize the present parole system, and that inquisitorial supervision which would paralyze the efforts of the individual in his determination upon reformation. If we can make penal and correctional institutions ever more efficient instruments of reformation or permanent segregation, we shall cut off one of the most important sources of the production of criminals, and render socially effective any improved type of criminal jurisprudence and criminal procedure.

SELECTED REFERENCES

Briggs, L. G. *Reformatory Reform.*

Eliot, T. D. "The Juvenile Court and the Educational System," in *Journal of Criminal Law and Criminology,* May, 1923.

Osborne, T. M. *Prisons and Common Sense.*

Smith, M. H. *The Psychology of the Criminal.*

Stutsman, J. O. *Curing the Criminal.*

Tannenbaum, F. *Wall Shadows.*

Van Waters, M. *Youth in Conflict.*

INDEX

Patterson Smith Reprint Series in Criminology, Law Enforcement, and Social Problems

1. Lewis: *The Development of American Prisons and Prison Customs, 1776-1845*
2. Carpenter: *Reformatory Prison Discipline*
3. Brace: *The Dangerous Classes of New York*
4. Dix: *Remarks on Prisons and Prison Discipline in the United States*
5. Bruce *et al: The Workings of the Indeterminate-Sentence Law and the Parole System in Illinois*
6. Wickersham Commission: *Complete Reports, Including the Mooney-Billings Report.* 14 Vols.
7. Livingston: *Complete Works on Criminal Jurisprudence.* 2 Vols.
8. Cleveland Foundation: *Criminal Justice in Cleveland*
9. Illinois Association for Criminal Justice: *The Illinois Crime Survey*
10. Missouri Association for Criminal Justice: *The Missouri Crime Survey*
11. Aschaffenburg: *Crime and Its Repression*
12. Garofalo: *Criminology*
13. Gross: *Criminal Psychology*
14. Lombroso: *Crime, Its Causes and Remedies*
15. Saleilles: *The Individualization of Punishment*
16. Tarde: *Penal Philosophy*
17. McKelvey: *American Prisons*
18. Sanders: *Negro Child Welfare in North Carolina*
19. Pike: *A History of Crime in England.* 2 Vols.
20. Herring: *Welfare Work in Mill Villages*
21. Barnes: *The Evolution of Penology in Pennsylvania*
22. Puckett: *Folk Beliefs of the Southern Negro*
23. Fernald *et al: A Study of Women Delinquents in New York State*
24. Wines: *The State of the Prisons and of Child-Saving Institutions*
25. Raper: *The Tragedy of Lynching*
26. Thomas: *The Unadjusted Girl*
27. Jorns: *The Quakers as Pioneers in Social Work*
28. Owings: *Women Police*
29. Woolston: *Prostitution in the United States*
30. Flexner: *Prostitution in Europe*
31. Kelso: *The History of Public Poor Relief in Massachusetts: 1820-1920*
32. Spivak: *Georgia Nigger*
33. Earle: *Curious Punishments of Bygone Days*
34. Bonger: *Race and Crime*
35. Fishman: *Crucibles of Crime*
36. Brearley: *Homicide in the United States*
37. Graper: *American Police Administration*
38. Hichborn: *"The System"*
39. Steiner & Brown: *The North Carolina Chain Gang*
40. Cherrington: *The Evolution of Prohibition in the United States of America*
41. Colquhoun: *A Treatise on the Commerce and Police of the River Thames*
42. Colquhoun: *A Treatise on the Police of the Metropolis*
43. Abrahamsen: *Crime and the Human Mind*
44. Schneider: *The History of Public Welfare in New York State: 1609-1866*
45. Schneider & Deutsch: *The History of Public Welfare in New York State: 1867-1940*
46. Crapsey: *The Nether Side of New York*
47. Young: *Social Treatment in Probation and Delinquency*
48. Quinn: *Gambling and Gambling Devices*
49. McCord & McCord: *Origins of Crime*
50. Worthington & Topping: *Specialized Courts Dealing with Sex Delinquency*

Patterson Smith Reprint Series in
Criminology, Law Enforcement, and Social Problems

51. Asbury: *Sucker's Progress*
52. Kneeland: *Commercialized Prostitution in New York City*
53. Fosdick: *American Police Systems*
54. Fosdick: *European Police Systems*
55. Shay: *Judge Lynch: His First Hundred Years*
56. Barnes: *The Repression of Crime*
57. Cable: *The Silent South*
58. Kammerer: *The Unmarried Mother*
59. Doshay: *The Boy Sex Offender and His Later Career*
60. Spaulding: *An Experimental Study of Psychopathic Delinquent Women*
61. Brockway: *Fifty Years of Prison Service*
62. Lawes: *Man's Judgment of Death*
63. Healy & Healy: *Pathological Lying, Accusation, and Swindling*
64. Smith: *The State Police*
65. Adams: *Interracial Marriage in Hawaii*
66. Halpern: *A Decade of Probation*
67. Tappan: *Delinquent Girls in Court*
68. Alexander & Healy: *Roots of Crime*
69. Healy & Bronner: *Delinquents and Criminals*
70. Cutler: *Lynch-Law*
71. Gillin: *Taming the Criminal*
72. Osborne: *Within Prison Walls*
73. Ashton: *The History of Gambling in England*
74. Whitlock: *On the Enforcement of Law in Cities*
75. Goldberg: *Child Offenders*
76. Cressey: *The Taxi-Dance Hall*
77. Riis: *The Battle with the Slum*
78. Larson *et al: Lying and Its Detection*
79. Comstock: *Frauds Exposed*
80. Carpenter: *Our Convicts.* 2 Vols. in 1
81. Horn: *Invisible Empire: The Story of the Ku Klux Klan, 1866-1871*
82. Faris *et al: Intelligent Philanthropy*
83. Robinson: *History and Organization of Criminal Statistics in the United States*
84. Reckless: *Vice in Chicago*
85. Healy: *The Individual Delinquent*
86. Bogen: *Jewish Philanthropy*
87. Clinard: *The Black Market: A Study of White Collar Crime*
88. Healy: *Mental Conflicts and Misconduct*
89. Citizens' Police Committee: *Chicago Police Problems*
90. Clay: *The Prison Chaplain*
91. Peirce: *A Half Century with Juvenile Delinquents*
92. Richmond: *Friendly Visiting Among the Poor*
93. Brasol: *Elements of Crime*
94. Strong: *Public Welfare Administration in Canada*
95. Beard: *Juvenile Probation*
96. Steinmetz: *The Gaming Table.* 2 Vols.
97. Crawford: *Report on the Pentitentiaries of the United States*
98. Kuhlman: *A Guide to Material on Crime and Criminal Justice*
99. Culver: *Bibliography of Crime and Criminal Justice: 1927-1931*
100. Culver: *Bibliography of Crime and Criminal Justice: 1932-1937*